—STAY—

–STAY–

SARAH LEAMY

LAKE DALLAS, TEXAS

Requests for permission to reprint or reuse material
from this work should be sent to:

Permissions
Madville Publishing
PO Box 358
Lake Dallas, TX 75065

All photos and drawings by Sarah Leamy

ISBN: 978-1-956440-43-0 paperback
978-1-956440-44-7 ebook
Library of Congress Control Number: 2023933536

With thanks to family, friends, writers, readers and especially to all at the Corporeal Writing Center who are such a force of creative nurturing.

Prologue: A Decade of Denial

What do you do if the neighbor's dogs chase you back into your old Toyota truck, claws scratching at the windows while your own dogs are trapped safe within their yard, unable to protect you—not that you'd want them to—not with these dogs, a pack of six or seven inbred pit bulls, raised on too little food and abundant violence, they're full of fight to survive and that means they chased you at your gate, and you're unable to get home, it's only yards away, but you can't get out, not now, not while they're there, teeth bared at windshield, nails on glass, barking snarling scratching, trying to get to you and your dogs howl, Harold, an older Husky/Collie mix, and Rosie, a mini-Akita, both stuck on the other side of the fence, wanting to help and you cry, no, please no, don't fight these dogs, no, they'll kill you.

Contents

vii   Prologue: A Decade of Denial

1   Part I: Backwards

29   Part II: Towards

67   Part III: Away

103   Part IV: Both

131   Part V: A Coda of Sorts

138   Further Readings
140   Acknowledgments
141   About the Author

I

Backwards

"When are you coming home?"
"I don't know. I'm scared."
"You should be," and my brother put down the phone.

My mum lay in intensive care and I didn't know what to do.

I didn't know where to call home

and to be honest, I still don't, because what happens if as a kid or as an adult you've rarely felt safe?[1]

---

1   You move a lot.

Origin Stories #1

I was not funny.

No, I was serious, shy and a tomboy, one who was bullied or ignored all

 through middle and high school in small town England. I read the Famous Five, imagining myself as George. I wandered my gran's farm with her retriever, Jesse. Mum and I used to talk about the books we'd read while eating baked beans on toast, sitting at the wooden table under the kitchen clock.

On Tuesdays at six, Dad and I sat in the two armchairs, cats on our laps, munching on apples as we watched Laurel and Hardy, Charlie Chaplin, and Harold Lloyd.

My formative years were silent.

I'm often asked if I get homesick, do I go back to England?

In the beginning was Bromsgrove and living with my parents.

- I open the fridge door and Mum asks, "are you looking for something?"
  I put the kettle on, Dad says, "are you making a drink?"
- I do my laundry, Mum asks, "do you know how?"
- I walk in with a shopping bag of groceries, Dad says, "what have you got there?"
- I open the front door, they both ask, "where are you going now?"

I returned to Worcestershire for Christmas 2003.

After staying for a few days, I stumbled downstairs in the chilly brick farmhouse for a mug of something warming to start the day.

In the kitchen sat Mum in her thick maroon woolen housecoat. Without glancing up, she asked, "Don't you have a hairbrush?"

Time backtracked to my awkward teens, standing in front of her with a hand stuck in scruffy short hair but this time, at thirty-six, I muttered, "yes, do you need to borrow it?"

Mum put on her thick glasses to peer at me, halfway down the doorway's step. Silence but for the ticking clock. I offered, "or would you like a mug of tea?"

Mum half-smiled, saying, "No thanks, I wouldn't want to put you to all that trouble; I'll have half a cup instead."

I put the kettle on and sat down, my own grin hidden and passed her the shortbread.

Speak Up #11

I don't talk about how brains are wired one way and my rational mind knows I'm not trapped, caught in the corner of the room on my bed, stuck, trapped, terrified, teddy bear lost in the sheets, cats hiding underneath, with my mum screaming and yelling and shaking me so hard that my dad has a heart attack, unable to protect me, incapable of stopping her rage at this teenager who'd been busted for stealing from the supermarket, chocolate, nothing much, too much, how could I, the shame, the disgrace on the family she screeches, a wave of noise and motion that pins me in place and I can't escape, can't leave, can't breathe, and then she screams that I'm responsible for the doctor's call, the threat of losing dad, and it's true, it was my fault, and confused I don't talk about how my dad told me decades later that he'd faked that pain to save me.

I'm scared of stairs.

Vermont, 2017-18
Starting Over

In New Mexico, I'd gone as far as I could as a writer on my own: Wide open landscapes and limited writing opportunities. And as much my friends had kept me company, chatting and laughing and drinking beer over campfires on the weekends, it wasn't enough. I'd even ignored the stress of living with the threat of the neighbor's dogs attacking us and focused instead on new beginnings. I hadn't noticed the pattern of leaving home because of bullies, real and imagined. Bromsgrove. London. Ojo Caliente. And now again. If I'd wondered why I always had to move after a year or two, even though I'd come back head down, I'd focused on the idea it was my mum and dad's fault for making a Leaver. As a kid, home didn't always feel safe, not enough to relax and so therefore, I reckoned they were the reason why I couldn't stick around in any single community or keep a home for myself. That was the pattern wired into me. Nothing to do with mum's own problems, or the so-called teasing at school or those mainstream expectations on how women should act or even the straight world's dislike of anything queer, in all senses of the word. Nope. I blamed Mum and Dad.

Looking for somewhere to feel safe, to relax and belong, I drove 2415 miles across the country from Santa Fe to Montpelier with Harold, a sensitive sweet soul, Rosie my mischief maker, and Little Stevie, a reluctant brat of a cat, all of us living in a van. To start over. To get educated. To expand my creative world. Not in reaction to the neighbor's threats I lived with on a daily basis, not at all…because why did I call New Mexico home if I couldn't relax there?

What will you sacrifice in order to feel safe?

Or rather, who?

Origin Stories #2: Rosie

Dad once asked, why New Mexico? What's the draw?

A 1948 school bus, sage green on the outside, sits amongst the junipers and dead piñon trees in the Ortiz Mountains of New Mexico. The late afternoon suns tickles as I lie on the platform bed inside. With the cushion and pillow behind me, hours tick by and I spend my day reading, daydreaming, and writing. The usual. The dog naps on her blanket.

I make myself tea with milk and reach for a shortbread cookie. I just don't have any left, finished them yesterday. A homemade quilt covers the layers of blankets and sleeping bags. I sit on the bed with computer, books, and papers scrawled with notes and ideas. The t-shirt is inside out to hide the words *Made in Ireland* because I'm not. The socks are thick and a little too warm today. Next to the bed is a three-foot wide cabinet, with a sink, oil lamp, and books shelved above the cupboard of food and plates. I only have a few books these days: a dictionary, *Leyendas de Guatemala*, some erotica, and *The Tao of Pooh*. A mini globe holds the books against the window.

To my right is another cabinet, with clothes hidden on the shelves and a two-ring gas burner; with a skillet waiting for the eggplant curry I'm about to cook. When last in England, Claire and Rachel, a couple of my closest friends in London, took me to a local Indian restaurant on Brick Lane. We wandered those streets together, the old haunts of ours in Whitechapel and Hackney, although some twelve years had passed since we'd squatted in those council houses together. I didn't like to go back and there was no easy way to explain why not so I've kept quiet until now.

England, 1970s

It had all started with the questions,
usually said in anger or under the guise
of teasing:

What are you? A boy or a girl?

Brothers or sisters?

Vermont, 2017

Remember, I whispered to myself, pacing the small apartment, scribbling notes, sketching all those cartoons of driving across the country, but I was scaring my dogs, Harold and his bone and Rosie with her day-old apple, those easiest of friends, with my constant muttering, *"Remember what it took to get here and what I've left behind."*

London, 1992
  Surfacing

One Big Living Room

Too much too much too much thumping pounding echoing feet stomping deep voices screaming laughter sharp voices fighting to be heard, so bloody loud my ears bleed, my nose bleeds, toes bleed and the drum and bass booms through my feet and into my head and it's too much, too many voices pounding away at me, demanding attention, I'm edgy like a cat in heat, so Cate takes me across the stretched out legs, bodies sprawled on the dirty concrete, and there's place on the floor, against a wall, small, dusty, dirty, but so are we and we fold up heads on knees and stare, both grinning as we watch and eavesdrop eyes open/eyes closed, the thumping of boots on floor, dancing and pounding away, and we've filled the warehouse, everyone sitting and toking and chatting and laughing and I juggle, hands and wrists in time to the bass beat, the bounce in my hips, in my knees, I'm part drum, part guitar, and lost in the music, the moment, one two three one two three, over, behind, back, high, low, bounce, one two three, one two, eyes on the ball, ignore the crowds, all my friends, the squatters, musicians, painters and writers, we all sit around the pub like this is our home, one fucking big living room, and John's dogs run around between legs still looking still hungry.[2]

---

2   Listening to this reminds me of that spring in London. The soundtrack as it were, "Tubthumping" by Chumbawamba http://bit.ly/3XYJUYp

London, 1993
Breaking Another Promise

The sign above the old brick building said Police.

The Uniform pointed to a metal seat in the corner, make yourself at home, she'd said, they're taking care of someone else. There's a machine if you want a cuppa. Fifty pence.

You sat and stared out the window. A fat little robin perched on the tiniest of branches of a crab apple tree. Cate, Claire, Dale, Rachel, Lisa, none of them knew that today was the deciding day. Your fault, you could've told them but didn't. You turned back to the stack of old mags on the little table beside your chair, tucking in the t-shirt, it was pretty clean for once.

This was it. With the papers in your back pocket, the ones describing Squatters' Rights, the cops couldn't kick you out, not without a court order, and how since you'd had a lock and key when they'd nicked you, it wasn't breaking and entering. Technically. The hash and tools on you though? You didn't have an answer to that. You were bloody terrified. What if they threw the book at you? You'd never get into another country with a record, not legally anyway.[3]

---

3   I didn't get charged with anything in the end. The gift of the gab, a few lies, and some truth saved me. Nothing new. At high school, I rarely got put into detention despite some shenanigans. Lucky, I'd say.

England, 1997
Turning Twenty

One afternoon in the pub with Mum & Dad, at their local of course, you have a few quiet drinks together. Although you're not really allowed one. Doctor's orders. Makes sense but still. Your dad gets you a half instead of the usual pint. Mum has a chardonnay. Dad has his bottle of some oddly strong beer. You all eat salt and vinegar crisps. It's one you all used to go to, years ago when you still lived at home. Now though, you live in London. It's not the best time in your life. Broken teeth. You'd had been pregnant and now you're not. Failed college. Broken spirited. You quip, that at least it's sunny on your birthday. No one smiles. Your dad wears a striped shirt, a tie, top button undone, it's the weekend after all. His hair was cut recently, and no longer reminds you of Einstein. You miss his crazy white hair. Your mum tries hard to keep you all talking but it's not working. When it's time for another your dad goes to the bar, and you head to the bathroom. You do your business, flush, pick off a few stray cat hairs, and wash your hands. The door opens and closes. Same story, different day: A female voice looks at you in the mirror and then asks, am I in the wrong bathroom? Or are you? And when you turn, tall, scruffy, and pretty skinny these days, pale face, haunted eyes, and needle marks on your arm, she takes in your haggard angry expression and backs out, hands up, and slams the door. You stand there and dry your hands. Your mum asks you what's wrong. You tell her. Stumbling a bit in the telling. She stands up fast, in her thick dark glasses, storms over to the woman and tells her, my daughter is sick, she's getting poked and jabbed by doctors every day, blood drawn, pills to medicate, MRIs and CAT scans, and you dare judge my girl, she yells at the woman in slacks and a pale pink blouse. Your mum is relentless. She stands there. Full of a mum's fire and ice. She burns with her words. And this is why you hate your hometown. And why you love your mum.

New Mexico, Ongoing Regrets?

Ignoring these moments of how she stood up for me.

Speak Up #10

I don't talk about how as kids, we weren't that kind of family to have friends in and out, radio on, tick tock of the clock overhead, conversations in the kitchens over summer chatting about our days, but instead we retreated into our own rooms and wounds, hidden from each other, no, our home was silent, hushed and tense, and at ten, I never knew what to expect at school or at home, I couldn't relax, didn't feel safe except in the potato fields around town or at Gran's farm with her dog beside me, all because of that time, that first time, when I'd found my mum in the dark after another horrid day at middle school and there was nothing I could say to make it better.

Which makes me think about how my lovers yell in frustration when I shut down,

"You're just like your mother!" [4]

Also:

1. "Fucking clowns, can't take a joke."
    She stands in her kitchen on Canyon Road, arms crossed flat chest, skinny hips, angular chin, glaring black pupils, pissed at how I'd reacted when she'd suggested that her ex-lover share the bed with us.

2. "Don't you have anything to say for yourself?"
    She pushes her finger into my shoulder, again and again, poking, spitting, rage flies out of her when I hold Daisy's leash, ready to head out to work but saying nothing about how she's used me all these years, providing for us, driving her everywhere, buying supplies, watching her wake and bake back into cold oblivion.

3. "Where are you going now?"
    She watches me pack up my odds and ends, grab the dogs' bones from the blanket and step off the porch, out the gate, under the cottonwood, whistle for Harold and Rosie, then we load up into a beat up lifted red Toyota truck,[5] heading home to feed the kitten.

---

4   Note though that only one ever met my mum in all these years.
5   People. Houses. Fights.

1985-2009
What is it that makes me so bloody homesick?

It's my dreams, you see. They confuse me. I stand in the kitchen with Mum, Dad, and Pete. The huge willow tree outside droops low and thick with skinny leaves. Apple trees bend heavily toward the mown grass. The two calico cats are sleeping in the shade of the wild ragged roses underneath. We're all chatting, even me, the silent one. The lasagna is in the oven. Mum turns up the stereo. ABBA, Neil Diamond, Travelling Wilburys, and Rod Stewart blast out. We're dancing on the chairs, the wooden table, the steps to the living room, all of us, laughing and laughing and laughing.

It won't kill me, will it?

The cat flies off my lap, my head jerks to the side, a jolt of electricity zaps through from right to left ears. A thrum. A silence. Harold, looks worried, his tail low, eyes focused on me. Rosie, my mischief maker sleeps on, clutching an apple between front white paws.

Should I be scared?

I breathe out.

No, it's just what happens on a regular basis. Nothing to worry about. This brain of mine has been freaking out for decades now. A jolt, buzz, and done. It's just another injury haunting me. At least this one is physical.

Spain, In my Twenties

The first time I passed out, hit my head on a concrete table, was in a small sleepy but speedy town near Cuenca and three months after that episode, the doctors said I had brain farts (or in their terms, epilepsy).

I'm tired, fading in and out, confused, yes, kind of lost, so I look up and there's a circle of smiling heads staring at me, babbling away, shining teeth, smiling but not having fun and I'm number one because they're all looking at me, a crowd, and I don't know what's going on but a hand reaches down and your voice breaks through in English amongst the Spanish and you help me up, sitting up, but I'm having a hard time focusing and you're a trooper, holding on, getting the others to back off and give me room, to breathe you say to them and ease me up to standing while someone passes me water, your cousin I think and the radio plays in the background but I can't keep track like I usually do and words are muffled and my face feels funny but not hah-hah, there's more of a fuzzy metallic taste that lingers and I spit out blood onto my hand and my expression must have shown panic as a kid, your neighbor's son, all eight years old and soft with puppy fat, he comes up and holds my hand and takes me to the bathroom, shows me a mirror, saying, estas guapa, estas guapa, and the face in the mirror dribbles blood from a slash across my swelling chin, and then the mouth opens to see broken teeth, one sharp jagged knife of a tooth is a faded pink and my head fogs up, dizziness drops me to the cold concrete floor and the next time I wake up is in a small white room with bright lights overhead and I'm scared. I want my mum.

New Mexico, 1999
Song

Snow. Stuck. On the side of the Ortiz Mountains. Four miles to get home and it was late at night, eleven or maybe even later, and there was no choice. Rooting around in the back of the wagon, a two-wheel drive piece of shit, you layered up. Everything you had you wore, hats, scarves, two extra t-shirts, two pairs of socks, more gloves, one over the other, another coat, another sweater and that was that. Locking up, you tried not to think about it, the date. Your first proper date in ages, like with a dinner, wine, boobs, all of it, a real living date in the city. And now this. A snowstorm, at least the sky cleared up for exactly eight minutes, the moon lit the road ahead for you to stride up another mile, in theory stride but it was more of a shuffle, follow the tracks for another three miles, hope to find the gate under the drifts, climb it if needed, and struggle for that final quarter mile. So close, you were almost home, home to the cabin, no choice, so you walked, jeans tucked into boots, hands deep in jacket, you tromped through the untouched snowbanks, on the way home. Singing your mom's songs, rich and ripe with thoughts of warm beds and her smiling eyes and cool hands tucking you in, patting the hot water bottle, saying good night to the teddy bear peaking out of the covers, her pale blue eyes and shy soft voice singing to you. And so, deeply darkly chilled, you walk and sing, breathing hard. Four miles. In the wondrous storm of body and memory, comfort and cold, you walk home, but no one's there though, not now, it's just you and the dogs. And that's why you had to come home tonight, for them. Your sweet cold bored hungry lonely silly furry loyal loving dogs stuck inside and then, with door opened, they barrel past you, noses to snowsies and you laugh. In the midnight air, falling snow tickles your cheeks and your dogs run free. You sing for them. And just like a normal kid, you play.

England, As a Child
Keeping Mum

One day at middle school, I was standing out in the playground, on the edge of a grassy little slope down to the football field. As usual, the other kids didn't leave me alone, loving to pick on me, tease me, since I never reacted enough to get them in trouble. I didn't tell on them that is. I didn't have a voice. That day though, they pushed, I fell, and when I got back up, I ran away.

My dad found me a few hours later. He knew where to look; he knew to bring my teddy bear. After leaving the local hospital, we didn't talk of what happened, and Dad only asked that I not tell Mum. She was having a bad time, dealing with a deep depression. She'd worry. The extent of the bullying was kept just between me and my dad. And my bear, John.

England, 1998
Practical Advice

Mum tossed me over her hip, and I landed with a thump and a thunk. The cats ran for cover.

My friends all cheered. "Another win for Sallie!"

Mum and Dad had invited all my friends to camp out at the farmhouse for my birthday. That morning my parents had been driving through the local village when they saw a young couple wearing shorts and sandals, striding along with backpacks.

"Are you looking for our daughter?" Dad called out the rolled down window.

"Sleam? Yeah, we met in Spain. She said to stop by for her birthday."

"Hop in, we'll give you a ride."

We were quite an odd bunch, including these two from near Madrid, Brigitte from LA, and about ten friends from London. Once tents were set up and lunch served, Mum decided to teach us self-defense since so many of us hitched and wandered around Europe and beyond on our own. She loved every minute of it. So did we. At 5'8", the same as me but in much better shape, Mum was circled by a group of punk and hippie kids with beers and snacks in hand as she took us on, one at a time.

"Who's next?" she asked with a wide smile, sunglasses slightly askew, and her white hair wonderfully unkempt. Cate volunteered with a bit of a giggle. Rachel waited from a safe distance. Helen opened another beer. Brigitte wanted to take Mum on but had to wait her turn.

Toss. Oomph. Thunk. Cate landed with a grunt and a grin. And more cheers.

"Five-nil to Sallie!"

"Who's next?" Mum wiped her hands on faded jeans. "Or are you scared of me?"

II

Towards

Speak Up #9

I don't talk about why my legs twitch and push away. I don't talk about the claustrophobia of planes or trees or towns or the constant echo of radio, tv, voices, music, the overstimulation of noise or light or movement,

hyper alert and overly aware of everyone around me and I don't talk about the cramps in toes and calves, making my legs bounce in place as if I were juggling three pins, paddling in place, or still on speed or smoke, but I'm not, that's a long way behind me, yet that sensation of fire in my muscles and that uncontrollable urge to lash out, push off, fight and flight grabs me hard, but here I am on a plane, cramped in the middle seat, during that time of year, full of the shittiest of memories, and so with clenched jaw, closed eyes, I bite back another scream.

Vermont, 2017
Fighting Physical Limits

Sugar maple, beech, birch, poplar, and many kinds of evergreens, wildflowers such as trillium, bunchberry, lily, paintbrush, violets, orchids, black-eyed Susans, asters, clover, mushrooms, ferns, balsam fir, spruce, cedar, hemlock, mountain ash, white birch, blueberry, lichen, dandelions, poison sumac and poison ivy.

I'm trapped, this time it's within all these bloody trees.

Claustrophobia refers to a fear of closed spaces. Simple enough, I claim that for myself, but what would be the opposite? A fear of open spaces? Or a liking of closed spaces? Or more importantly for me, necessary for me, what's a liking of open spaces called? The thesaurus offers manias, phobias, and philias. So would it be agoraphobia? *Agora* comes from old Greek for open spaces, although it originally meant marketplaces. Was it then more suitable for a fear of crowds and groups of people instead of open land? So then would a liking of open space be called agoraphilia? Nope, that apparently refers to being sexually aroused in public. Not quite what I'm looking for. Not exactly the turned-on state that applies for me right now. It's not that I'm a prude, more like a prune. Kinda shut down in that department to be honest, this isn't a juicy time in my life although the writing community here feeds part of me but it's not enough and I don't know what to do.

New Mexico, December 2009
While Deciding Whether to Find a Flight Home During the Fucking Season of Good Grief

I'd needed a pint.

At the local pub, I sat in front of the open fireplace, ignoring my friends stringing up colorful streamers, red and green chile balloons, their idea of Christmas decorations, as they hummed with songs of fake cheer rattling through the room. With a pale ale in hand, I stared at the flames and something thawed inside me.[6] Shay, tall as me, bright blue eyes, a Southern Texas/New Mexican, stopped by the table. She's an ER nurse and friend. I blurted out how my niece had found my mum unconscious, at the foot of the stairs, face swollen, unresponsive.

—How long has she been like that?

—Overnight.

Shay rested a hand on my shoulder and with eyes shaded, saying nothing, she shook her head.

---

6   Breathe, sleam, breathe

Germany, 1998
Consequences

Brigitte came from Hollywood, a true L.A. lass, an editor from one of the big-name studios. She was a wild one, shorter than me at 5'3", tanned, dark eyes yet with long blond California hair tied back. One night, a few of us went out for Fasching, the big local spring festival of debauchery and trouble making. By 3:00 or 4:00 in the morning I decided to give Brigitte a ride home on a bike. For some reason, she decided to peddle, even though I was much bigger and well, heavier. My job was simply to not fall off.

"Sounds sensible to me," I thought. "I can do that."

We flew downhill from the city center, toward the zig-zag metal barrier next to the tramway bridge. Brigitte swerved through the zig and crashed on the zag. We slammed into the brick wall to the right. Brigitte dropped solidly on the pavement, her head, a thunk, followed by silence. Her splattered body frozen didn't move but suddenly shook, racked with internal messages of a miswired panic along twisted mental strings. Time to call an ambulance. An hour later, I pushed the bike back to her place in the student dormitory and waited there. In shock her friends and I sat smoking and terribly sober.

Early in the morning, Brigitte and her boyfriend arrived back, carrying headache painkillers and a diagnosis of concussion. Brigitte went to bed soon after, shaky but all right, although I now wonder what lasting effects the brain injury had on her life as mine did on me and my mum's on her.

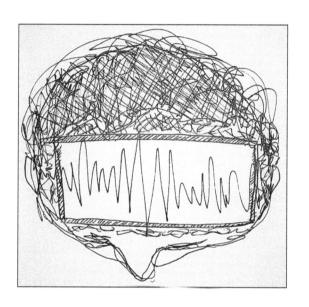

Speak Up #8

I don't talk about how the frontal lobe shows the cumulative effect of those years of micro-traumas in EEG scans and MRI and sleep studies, tracking my responses of broken nights with pulses flashing bouncing jumping juggling one two three one two three the beeps and dashes in my brain waves that keep waking me once an hour, every hour, or how a shock through muscles wakes each nerve and then takes another sixty minutes to fall back to sleep, every fucking night, just as the inner clock screams until I respond night after night and hope to cat nap during the day ahead, unable to let go of this crap in my head. Stuck.

New Mexico, 2006
Stick

I woke with swollen face, eyes smashed shut, barely able to see, a cut on my forehead red and burning. At work the day before, I'd picked up a snotty little kid, one who'd refused to get up after his snowplow moves planted him face down in yet another snowbank. He'd bonked me between the eyes with his gnarly helmet. A tiny red drop of blood. Now a tiny red mosquito bite of an owie. Should I go to a clinic? Nah, I didn't have insurance.

The next morning, I woke with a swollen face, eyes smashed shut, barely able to see, another morning passed and I waited. Went to work late.

The next morning, I woke with swollen face, eyes smashed shut.

I waited for my eyes to open, drove up the Sangre de Cristos to work at the ski basin.

The next morning, I woke. Same.

I called my ex. She took me to the ER. They rushed me back and shoved into a blank windowless room alone, sticked and pricked with huge needles to draw blood, the nurse read my stats, closed the door, and trapped me.

First MRI. A week of mornings with an IV of antibiotics. Another MRI. Brain waves monitored, the onetwothree blipblipblip reassuring no one. The ER nurses told me that I could die. A staph infection in my brain. I blinked. Then asked, Can I go home now?

2018
Time

The snow didn't melt, would not melt for another three months and you're scared, scared to sit with yourself, the memories slamming away, keeping you up at night, haunting your eyes so that the barista hands over the coffee with no chitchat, she takes the money and turns to the next in line with a glance of relief at his normality, the average build, short brown hair, brown eyes, pale skin, nothing unusual to him. Your Russian fur hat and ski instructor jacket from the seventies with the word *Polite* written across the back and your accent, that not-quite-right English accent, it's too much for casual conversation, so you sip a mug of rich dark coffee, perfectly roasted you admit, sitting alone and stare out the fogged window onto main street, unsure what to do with yourself for the next few months, next few days perhaps, because you're restless again. Why now when nothing is different but for that clock inside, the one with the loud ticking relentlessly reminding you that you live on borrowed time, too many died the last few months, eight to be exact, eight friends and you're only fifty, for fuck's sake, you're only fifty but you're scared that time is running out, speeding past and you'll never get all the words out before you die, never get the stories out and onto paper, onto screens, that they'd end up rattling around in the afterlife but as an atheist, that's no help, not for you so you sit and sip coffee, take notes of conversations around you, twist them up to make them warp and burn in your brain, and then you trudge home through the snow drifts in sub-freezing weather, up the hill and back to your desk. You're living on borrowed time and someone might knock on that door stop that clock inside and you'd be done. Words unspoken.

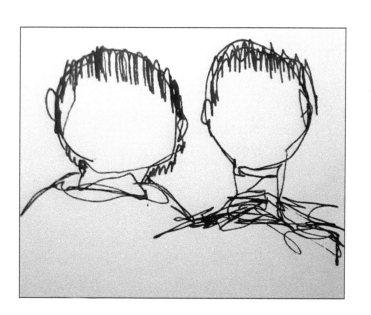

Speak Up #7

I don't talk about how the only time I felt safe or free was hitching across the States alone as a twenty-two-year-old with a backpack and my teddy bear, no money, and each day a struggle to find bread and cheese, having a smoke to kill the appetite, satisfied by only an apple, and I read now that constant chronic trauma wires our brains differently, and that what's safe to me isn't normal because as a kid inside those walls, behind those doors, were stilted words over Sunday dinner, a sudden rage of slammed doors, it was my fault or Pete's, it didn't matter, there was no escape, we were kids.

The States, 1989, early twenties
How Far Can I Go?

The diesel engine rumbles behind me as I adjust the red and grey rucksack on sweaty shoulders, unused to such July humidity. New York City, Day #1, it's too bright for my blue eyes and I squint. An empty sidewalk leads to a park if I can call this patch of littered concrete a destination; there are

three wooden benches with a single busker playing a shining brass horn, surrounded by bags of clothes, newspapers, bedding. He nods. A moment of relative quiet brings me closer, and I sit with a grunt, bone weary after the two flights, two trains and one bus from my hometown. I made it. I'm here. I collapse onto that bench and gulp in the fumes and soak up the heat under my feet, happy beyond words.

Origin Stories: Rosie

Driving. Dogs. Freedom.
We'd go far together.
For the time being.

London, my late twenties
You Can't Go Back

Bethnal Green. Stoke Newington. Cambridge heath. Whitechapel. All of my old haunts, all those favorite pubs, the places I used to love, had closed. And I don't mean just for the night. Metal grates covered windows. Huge padlocks clung to the doorframes. Seeing all of that confused me: Where was Rachel? Claire? Cate? Helen? How would I run into friends now? The answer was that I didn't.

The next day, I took a bus to the train station. I heard the weather forecast: *There's a possibility of icy roads and freezing fog. It's a little parky out there, ladies!* The woman forecaster's voice lilted in the same way all announcements are made, a joyful and friendly rise after every four words. From Birmingham, I took the number 145 bus back to my hometown, a place I didn't particularly like, then or now. I thought about my high school days and how our French teacher taught verb conjugations by repetition. She must have despaired of us. I hear us now, a class of ten-year-olds, intoning in our broad and bored Birmingham accents:

Je suis de Birmingham
Tu es de Birmingham

Mme Cook would sigh, a harsh out breath, and then repeat over and over again to herself, "Je suis de Birmingham," which I just recently found out is also French slang for "I'm bored to death."

England, Teenager
External Constraints

As a kid in the eighties, I was a wild warrior, no damsel in distress. I could climb the tallest trees and fight the greatest battles, but then came the lumps and bumps, the cramps and training bras. Tom and Chris and those other scrawny and pimply little boys in my class in North Bromsgrove High School pointed at my hairy legs and awkward gait.

"What is it?"

"Is it a boy or a girl?"

Tom grabbed at my school uniform, ripped the knee-length skirt off me, and then ran the playground, yelling, is it a boy or a girl? A boy or a girl? Jenny, Marcia, and Selma, all stood in their own pristine white and pink tennis skirts and sneakers, giggling, pointing at my sensible white-ish undies. Numb, saying nothing but thinking, I have to get out of here, fiddling, and thankful to be wearing my big brother's navy tee shirt, pulling it low over skinny hips, I walked back into the changing rooms alone but unhurt. Physically.

I never told Mum.

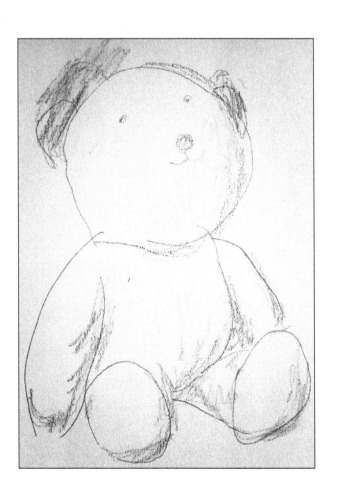

England, Middle School
First Day

Mum and I head down Stoney Hill Road in the morning. I'm in my new school uniform. It's okay, a dark green but how can I run or climb trees in this stupid skirt? A white shirt, nicely ironed by Mum, a tie, (Dad helped), and sensible brown shoes with white socks. My bag has sandwiches and an apple and notebook and pen and a book but Mum says I'll be playing and won't have time to read. At the bottom of the hill, we cross the High Street at the lights and Mum and I walk to the school. Her bus stop is right outside. It's my first day at Parkside Middle School. She hugs me and watches me go up the steps and to the right of the main entrance and through a green metal gate. The building is two-stories tall, lots of windows, and like a big brick T. The east side is for girls and the west side for boys. We have separate playgrounds, toilets, staircases, and even places to sit in the big hallway. I follow the other girls and find Sarah Wallis; we went to our first school together. I sit by her on the wooden floor and she smiles, curly haired with crooked teeth and bright green eyes. All the kids in school are in here, and I can smell carrots and baked beans, socks and smelly boys. The floor's clean though. Then the Headmaster gets up and talks for a stupidly long time, welcoming us new children, and telling us the rules. He wears a black cape over his grey suit, and then reads out a list of names and which classroom each should go to and one by one they all leave. At the end of the list, he notices me still sitting there. Alone.

He turns to another teacher and hisses, "where does she belong?"

It's a question that's haunted me for decades.
Where do I belong?

Earlier this winter, I left New Mexico—again. I'm homeless, living in my Dodge van with my pets, small propane heater, layers of bedding, lamps, and laptop. An Oregon winter rains softly on the roof, and sipping a local beer, I'm cozy even if ungrounded emotionally. I left New Mexico—after yet another dog attack. I left New Mexico—after being offered an opportunity to work with a writer I've admired. The heater kicks back on. The cat yawns. Harold muffle-barks in his sleep. I write. And I cry. Deep shaking wobbling chin, fists curled, thumbs rubbing, and scared, what am I doing here? I don't fucking know and wish I did. I gulp back the pale ale and stare at my notebook with the lists of synonyms, nomadic, wanderer, wanderlust, vagabond, and close my eyes, wishing that a life in motion came easier, but what does? It's not like anyone told me this was an option.

England, Teenager
Advice Ignored

When in high school, I trotted down to our local careers advisor. That squat three-story concrete building on the corner held a library, careers office, and fire department. It still does, thirty years on. The small square office overlooked Stoney Hill Road and the parking lot opposite next to the swimming pool. Shelves from floor to ceilings on three sides were all stuffed with pamphlets about courses, colleges, trainings, so much information. So much paper. Glorious! Overwhelmed and relieved to find someone full of answers, I rattled off all my questions, one after another, impatient to know my way out, my exit from this town I hated. What can I do next? Where can I go? Write? Travel? Both?

"Oh, honey, you've read too many books, haven't you? Well, given your background, you could be a teacher like your dad. He's at the college, isn't he? I recognize the name. Or, perhaps if you learnt to type, you could work as a manager like your mum. You'd need to smarten up though. Wear a skirt. Put on some lipstick. Do something with your hair. Brush it perhaps?"

That was that.

I found a job in France[7] as an au pair with two kids, and on that first day, a dead dog. I should've left then. No, that nanny job didn't work out and 6 weeks later they kicked me out with no money or plane ticket but I made it back by train-hopping from Nice to Calais, stealing bread from a supermarket, and even running through the Paris underground as the guards chased me. Don't believe what they tell you. There's more to life than those old school careers officers think.

---

7   Desire

Venice Beach, 1989, early twenties
Cash?

The man leaned in, bad breath, late forties, short salt and pepper hair, a tidy moustache. He was a slightly tanned white fella with cool blue eyes, wearing a starched white shirt, and after half an hour the tie was slightly loosened. With a soft low rumble, he asked, "Do you want to earn some extra cash? Mend my shirts?"

Up the stairs and through tall glass doors and into a modern white sterile room, the bedroom was to the right and the man took me straight there. The sheets on the bed and crystal white, almost too bright to look at. Out the double windows I stared, onto the Pacific Ocean and the slow-moving sunset. Not a cloud in the sky, just the trails of planes heading out. I walked to the balcony and stretched arms wide. He watched me, this twenty-two-year-old, and then said, "I don't mind that you're a girl if you know what I mean ... well, how much do you need? For your ticket back to London? I'll buy it. If…"

I'd told him earlier how I'd hoped to fly back in time for Christmas, to turn up as a surprise at my mum and dads' farmhouse. At the edge of his crisp and tidy bed, I stood tempted with his offer, held captive. No knife needed. I was stuck, staring at the sunset over Venice Beach and missed my family even though I was hanging out with Brigitte from that previous year in Germany. I grabbed his shirts and ran. Down the steps. Down the sidewalk and along the beach, still holding onto his shirts, I fled to Brigitte's place and waited for her to come home from work. On her steps, I relaxed into the heat of the afternoon and with my bag of apples juggled. Onetwothreeonetwothree.

Chicago, 1991, almost mid-twenties
Brave, not Fearless, at least in my dreams

You've been on the go since you were born, I wonder why, asked the bland middle-aged man in a shoddy suit, amber eyes slow panning across my dusty boots, baggy green jeans, suspenders, worn out bowler and sun-faded shirt.

Well, I replied, some of us are cave dwellers. Some live in houses. Some like to be loose footed. Quoting a song, I repeated, I'm a rambling man. He waited for more. I stared at him, making him nervous. It was payback for giving me shit about being so bloody androgynous. I'm a rambling man, I repeated, or woman if you prefer. And you? What are your regrets? I asked and the man, Call-Me-Jake, stared at me furiously behind a white toothy smile. I listed places I'd known or dreamt of: Paris. Tibet. Sydney. Gambia. Redditch. Rotterdam. Salwarpe. Santander. Haight Ashbury. Calais. The North Pole. Antwerp. Youtwerp. Toronto. Tokyo. Togo-yo. Damascus. Dumbaskus.

Juggling life and on the go since I was born, yes, with a chronic case of wanderlust, aiming towards and not from, I said, meaning it at the time.

I've told myself that

I'm a novelty seeking wide-eyed wanderer with a rucksack, teddy bear, juggling apples and wearing beat-up Doc Martins instead of a pantry full of canned regret.

And I'm alright with that.

But not everyone is.

Tennessee, 2003, my thirties
Why Do You Even Care?

You. Yes, You. You go to the bathroom. In public, you have to choose, men's or women's. You go to the women's because you are one. You do your business, flush, and wash your hands afterwards. It's nice in there, quiet after the chaos of Karaoke in small town Tennessee.[8] You wash your face finally and look up just as another woman trots in behind you. She steps back out, looks at the sign on the door and then at you, in the mirror. She looks you up and down, boots, jeans, and short brown hair. Amelia Earhart, you're told you look like, not that this woman seems to care. She stares at you. Am I in the wrong bathroom, she asks? You shrug, how would I know? And then you reach for a paper towel to dry off. She steps in and closes the door behind her sharply. Well, what are you, she asks. You shrug. I am, you say, I am myself, and then you ask, and you are? She doesn't like your tone, so she tries again, are you a man? No, you say, are you? I can't tell, you say and throw the towel down at her feet, at those shiny new cowboy boots at the tip of this tiny framework of denim and hairspray. How dare you? She yells at you, and that's it, she's off, and it's almost funny - but not quite - so you stand there and listen and wish you had a witty comeback or the gumption to slap her silly instead you wait until she's finished before offering, want me to prove it?—as you unbuckle your belt and drop your jeans.

---

8   I'd been living on an anarchist commune with two church ladies, Billy and Jacob.

Tennessee, 2003
You dropped
'em?

Not really.
I just wish I had.

England, 2004
Coding

As babies, the twins, my nephew and niece, were color-coded into pink for Emily and blue for Thomas. Despite the close confines of class and culture, Emily is a tiger, fierce and prickly. She pokes and prods me from a distance, running away when I roar and laugh with her. Her favorite color is purple though. Thomas, the fair-headed and blue-eyed one, is all affection. He holds my hand and crawls into my lap, forgetting to run as his sister does. His favorite color is orange not blue.

How will they grow up in a town where people are unnerved by the fact that I, a woman, know how to weld, build houses and fix cars, all on my spare time? When I learnt to fix up houses in London for us squatters, I was deemed "resourceful." Now in my (late) thirties, when I do what I like, traveling alone and building odd homes, I'm told I "should have been a boy." But why? Why does it matter what I do or wear just because of my body? I want to be left alone. I want to be a woman on my own terms. Why is that so fucking hard?

I want you to know that my favorite colors are green and blue. Striped preferably.

Another friend recently asked, Why did I become a clown?

Well, I'm more of a street-performer than circus clown. You might call me a fool. I do. An innocent stepping off into the unknown without worry or forethought. For me, the Fool is a child, outcast, the underdog and the wildcard. Lucky, unfazed, she heads out into the world, unconcerned or maybe oblivious. Judy Finelli, from the Clown Conservatory in San Francisco, told me, "The Fool, the truly curious, always tries something at least once." Well, I can say that's definitely true for me. At twenty, and living in Freiburg, Germany, I dated a juggler. Norbert. He was very, er, Germanic. Tall, blond, and serious about juggling. We practiced in the streets, we practiced at his place in the evenings, and we practiced at the college where I got a credit for taking his class. He was very disciplined about learning the craft of juggling. He introduced me to the idea of street performing and those friends of his that did it. I felt at home with them.

At twenty-three, another bullying incident in England sent me off with a backpack, a few hundred dollars and a flight to the States. I stayed in Maine to start with and then ended up in Madison, Wisconsin, where various street performers got to know me as I'd wander around, trying to sell bracelets and read tarot cards. I made money breathing fire, although people paid me to stop as I kept singeing my hair. They told me I was funny. Apparently, they liked my stream of consciousness monologues as I stood on street corners, making a buck or two. In the process of finding my way in this unfamiliar country, I'd found friends. They were other fire-breathers, stilt-walkers, circus performers, musicians and buskers. They took me in as one of their own, encouraged me, and challenged me to claim my place in the world. As in the archetypal journey, I'd found my mentors.

San Francisco, 2006, late thirties
Costumes

What was I thinking?

Living in a regular apartment for once, I looked though my wardrobe. After a decade without such a thing, (no room in the school bus) I enjoyed hanging all my clothes and seeing what I owned. T-shirts, boxers, socks, hats, filling my own closet, with coat hangers no less. Focus, I told myself, you need to decide what to wear for your first day at Clown School.

Let's see. Tails. One is black, too small. One is grey, but too patched and raggedy.

Trousers. Pinstripes? Or was that too formal? The baggy blue-and-white-striped pants were too patched and yes, raggedy. Ah, the stretchy and stripy jeans I'd worn for years, going for comfort value here. T-shirts? Something plain I thought was best. Grey? Purple? Blue. Yes, the blue one. Striped socks. Yellow hand-made hat. What else? A stripy fleece sweatshirt. Yep, I felt good now. Familiar. That's it. Like myself, at home in this skin I'm in.

I walked along Haight Street to the Circus Center on a bright sunny morning, sipping delicious coffee and snacking on a fresh donut from the corner shop.

Judy, our new juggling teacher, introduced me to the other students, Kelsey (in tight jeans), and Suzanne (loose sweatpants), we'd met at the audition in May. The other ten or so new students were in a mix of clothes, from one man who reminded me of Oliver Hardy in a suit and tie, to the rest in sweats, with a couple of us in jeans. A few stripes were to be seen. Most, though, made simple, plain, comfortable and, yes, practical choices. Do they know something I don't? Do I look alright?

New Mexico, 2019
How Not to Write a Memoir

Bury yourself at home with the curtains closed as you wear your dad's shirt, the only one you still own, and your mum's pink woolen hat (the one you all laughed at as kids) but it feels just right even though it's 93 degrees and you wish you were soaking naked in a crispy snow-melted lake instead of inside a dark adobe cabin, obsessing about everyone you've lost, and you decide to write about your family and then freak out because of the pressure so you fall asleep at one o'clock in the afternoon clutching your bear and wake up an hour or two later with one fluffy bugger of a cat called Stevie as well as both Harold and Rosie, all squished against slick feverish skin and you haven't written a thing but you've remembered the silences that framed and the voices that shaped you.[9]

---

9   Beck, "Loser," http://bit.ly/3kvrMb0

Is it a boy? Is it a girl? What is it?

Speak Up #6

I don't talk about the time me and mum hid in a doorway in a village on the coast of Wales, licking vanilla ice cream out of sight of Pete and Dad, giggling as we saw them head our way, and how we hid our treats, filling our mouths and dumping the rest, best friends holding hands in the afternoon shade that one hot summer.

Spain, 1970s, kid me
I wouldn't Get Out #1

A fish, my mum called me a fish when I was little because we were in a bright sunny swimming pool in the mountains and I had my sunflower hat on but had ditched the red armbands and I wore a mustard coloured swim shorts and Mum was in the water with me and everything was blue and green and silvery and slippery and she said trust me and I did and I let go of the side and aimed for her and I couldn't reach her and so I splashed and thrashed and suddenly she smiled and said you just swam, Sarah, look how far you swam and I'd gone all the way across and no one was holding me and I'd done it on my own and then they couldn't stop me and I went back and kept splashing and paddling and swimming towards Mum.

Wales, 1987, twenties
It's not the end of the road after all

Lambs bleat and frolic together in fields as you sit alone with your rucksack, and you eat the last of the cheese sandwiches. A sign lies at your feet, ready for the next car or truck willing to pick up a lone scruffy boy-girl hitchhiker. It's late and you've already come over two hundred miles, from London to Swansea. Now there's just one more country lane meandering along the coast of Southwest Wales, finally calming on your frazzled nerves. Far from doctors and dentists, poking at you every week while asking even more invasive questions. Far from college professors handing out exams in large silent halls full of other students scribbling furiously as you stare out the window. Waiting for the minimum time allowed before you hand in a blank sheet of paper with no insightful essay comparing and contrasting the work of Heine and Durrenmatt. Instead, here you are alone on the road again. You put the empty lunch bag into a much-loved rucksack, an a-frame tent, stove and socks, books of notes and knickknacks, extra jeans, and a sweatshirt and little else. You breathe in wet grass, the mix of dampness and dung. The sheep are everywhere, young and playful lambs soon off to the slaughterhouse. You though, not you, no, you escaped, you climbed out the window and ran for the fields. So, you stand, munching on that last apple, ready to hitch the final twenty miles needed to reach where your mum and dad are camped – with JohnBear. On the coast, camping, no walls holding in the tensions. No, that was your happy place. And they waited there for you. You pick up the sign: *Help Me. Please.*

England, 1985
High School Lunches

School bored me. No wonder. Our high school was a three-story concrete building along the road by the swimming pool. A dead-end. Twelve hundred happy students and me. As soon as the lunch bell rang out, I changed out of the school uniform and into jeans in the bathroom, grabbed my helmet and after checking the corridor was free of teachers, I made a run for it. My moped, a red Honda C50, was parked out front. I rode through the small town and turned down a country lane, pulling in after a few minutes, walked up the steps to the black and white building with hanging flowerpots and pushed open the heavy wooden door with a grunt. It always stuck in those September rains.

"Hello, Mum."

Mum took off her dark glasses and smiled. So sweet and childlike with watering blue eyes, pale hair, even paler skin, she wore a soft grey cotton shirt that made her eyes shine. I smiled.

"My round," she said and handed over a tenner. "Chardonnay. A double. And crisps, let's have some cheese and onion crisps."

Neil Diamond[10] played over the speakers in the quiet pub. The Cross was not so far from home, a nice walk along Burcot Lane to Blackwood Street and across the main road heading to Redditch. Mum had walked there, bored at home, still waiting to find another job, and I was bored at school where I kept my head down while planning my escape. We both looked forward to Wednesdays in our own awkward way, scanning the room for people to watch. We sat next to each other, facing out, expressions blank, quiet yet comfortable together.

---

10   Neil Diamond, "Sweet Caroline," http://bit.ly/3EEXz09

England
Advice Given

When my mother was depressed—which was often—she'd tell me that I should "never have children."

I almost did, or could have, at age twenty, when I was into drinking stupid amounts of beer and shots, smoking, toking, and speed, when I'd passed out in Spain from too much coke and broke my front teeth and then I'd come back to England with a lisp, cut mouth, and drowning in occasional blackouts. My friend felt sorry for me, or that's what I tell myself, a handsome fella I'd been crushed out on for years, we had sex in my bedroom next to the kitchen and my brother walked in on us in a drunken stupor, took a moment, went "Oh, right," and left us to it. Pregnant. Yes, well. Not good timing, was it? Nope, but the bloke helped pay for the abortion, my brother took me to the clinic and brought me home, mute as I was. It had been the final straw in a rough few months. The blackouts had continued and doctors took my blood, stuck me in MRI machines, and covered my head in wires and read the wobbling lines across their screens, all the while shaking their heads. Trying to work out what was wrong with my brainwaves. Epilepsy they said, take these pills, be safe out there. My brother read the labels for me, frowning then reassuring.

I never did have kids. I listened to my mum after all. In some things that is. The queer lifestyle, the clothes I wear, traveling alone, being broke, not settling down, not getting a proper job, not getting too involved anywhere or with anyone were all my own but her warnings echo still.

I was listening, Mum, but I wish I'd asked you why? Why were you so unhappy? Was it really me?

England, 1970-2009
Unaccompanied[11]

My cousins referred to
Mum
as
Scary Sallie.

11   Yoyo Ma, J.S. Bach, *Cello Suite No. 1* in G Major, BWV 1007: I. "Prélude"
      http://bit.ly/41mFNsh

III

Away

Manchester, 1991, early twenties
Free to be me

A bass a deep beat drove up through my legs into my smile and my eyes broke open and there we were in a club in the warehouses in the city in the north and we were on a mission to be to claim our own lives. You're free to do what you want whenever you want, Helen said, you're free. Her blue eyes didn't blink–they didn't need to since they couldn't focus on more than the floor overhead and the beer in hand that Saturday night, or was it a Sunday morning, in that cavern that old factory that brick barren packed echoing dark thumping warehouse in a city we didn't know, well, we heard the bass and the beat and with stomping feet, we shouted, Am I? Free? Yes! I am! I am! And I stood up there on the dance floor, like a right prat, a right happy prat, singing along with the Soup Dragons, it was Manchester after all, Madchester, acid house, drum and bass, words we loved and we sang and danced and pranced and the blues were gone so gone even in the morning when hungover and broke, when we left, packed up all our sleeping bags, we were free, free like a bee in the rose garden shooting love down into our veins and we were on the prowl and we strode down the middle of the little streets and past the brick homes with washing lines and kids' toys laughing still, a crazy gleam in our eyes and we wouldn't stop singing, I'm free to be whoever I want, and it was our theme our world and we ran it and sold it and played it and we weren't afraid, we had no reason to be afraid, it was ours, we were free to be what we chose, to get our booze any old time, and thirty years later, it's true, it's true, I'm free to be me.[12]

---

12   Well, this would be an example of the things we did that messed with my brain chemically-speaking but did wonders for my sense of joy and playfulness. Soup Dragons, "I'm Free," http://bit.ly/3Y3Zq5s

—although all these years I've also been running on autopilot, and I've often wondered what would it take for me to stand up for myself? To find a sense of belonging and home that works for me?

Bromsgrove, Late 1980s, my early twenties
Swallowing Down

I shrugged and ate my eggs on toast, I didn't know what to say to Mum about how it's life to be scared but you carry on because what's the choice, there isn't one, and I tried to explain between mouthfuls but she left me alone and I shrugged and crunched on toast because how could I get it across about the fight or flight of being in the world beyond this safe little enclave and how exploring cities and towns and back roads and mountains and deserts on my own is safer than being smothered mothered in our little home town in small minded england of the eighties and I gulped down the thought of a life here working for the next how many years—too many—and so I finished up and shouted down the hall I'm off and she called back don't forget to call and I promised but I did—not forget exactly—and it was months later when I'd picked up a phone and the relief in her voice fed my guilt and I choked on the words, sorry sorry sorry. It's alright, she said, where are you?

Speak Up #5

I don't talk about coming home from middle school that chilled winters' afternoon, scared and tired, wanting to curl up with my bear or run in the fields alone but instead finding home lay shushed, a dark energy submerged, cats hiding under my bed, and all those closed curtains and the horrid sobbing muttering coming in waves from my mum's room, and how I crept inside to find her half passed out, with empty bottles of pills, drowning in booze, cigarette smoldering in the ash tray, hearing her murmuring in the dark, Sarah, please promise me, don't have kids.

New Mexico
Population Studies

121, 589 square miles

17 people per each of those wonderfully empty miles

Lots of space.

It's quiet here.

There's no one to take care of.

England, 2000
Rituals

Dad put on the kettle, stared out the small window onto the back garden. The grass needs cutting, he probably said. Sundays were the days for all of us to do things around the house. Mum did the clothes and cooked lunch. Dad mowed the grass. I picture him at the counter, pouring hot water into the stainless-steel teapot, the one I now have. The sunshine bright in the square white walled kitchen. I'd be sitting at the wooden table with a book. He wore slippers, blue and white pajamas, and a thick red and black dressing gown, it's one we've all worn. I still do. His blue eyes, so bright and light, almost painful to look into for the openness, vulnerability, you couldn't lie to those eyes, or I never could. He noticed things but didn't judge me, a gentle man was my dad. I would watch as he'd put two mugs on the tray, a chocolate digestive biscuit for each of them, and head back upstairs. Every day, it didn't matter what had happened within our walls, Dad made tea for Mum. They'd sit in bed and sip, start the day with a quiet moment, at home with each other.

In an ideal world
Home = Safety

It's something we're taught to believe, that this is the one place where we can truly and completely relax, especially as kids or perhaps more so as adults since we made a home for ourselves, settled as per social expectations and yes, I fell for the notion, tried to do exactly that, recreate that dream or memory, and it's true, I loved it, for a while, coming home to the pets after working at Trader Joes in Santa Fe, worn out yet welcomed back with wagging tails and rumbling tummies, and for them, I let my guard down.

Breath Meditation

in: I've arrived
out: I'm home

New Mexico, in my forties
Breathing Hard,

I stumbled up hill. Falling over rocks and into cacti made for a slow progress. Finally, I stopped and turned slowly three hundred and sixty degrees. The silhouettes of trees and shrubs filled the landscape eerily. I saw neither houses nor lights and had heard no traffic. Only in the far distance, the interstate showed a stream of cars' headlights as they drove north to Santa Fe and beyond. Hearing a single howl, I stood stock-still, and stared. With Harold and Rosie at my side, we waited for an echo.

England, 1997, thirties
You Can't Go Back #2

I was deported at thirty, handcuffs and papers that took me from my lover my dog my job my friends my beat-up Subaru and a cabin in the Ortiz Mountains with the view of the mesa across to the Sangre de Cristos to the north, back in a town of dreams, or rather nightmares, with no grounding no clothes of my own no money of my own calling immigration each week only to be told soon soon soon but maybe not though, he'd said then, you were married? you did all the paperwork? And only weeks before, I'd been holed up in the hills in the trees and comfortable with the footprints of black bears hidden and hunched up on the oak tree overhead as I'd crossed the creek to get to my cabin with my pup Charlie following along unaware and the owl had hooted just as lightening crashed in front and I cringed in fear, put down the phone, burst into tears, Mum's cats scattered, and with no markers of my own, I was a lost kid back in my hometown, an immigrant in my own family.

London, 1993
Pivot #1

In my mid-twenties I'd lived in East London and even in that great cosmopolitan city, I was hassled for being a gender-bender. It started with the questions *what is it?* I tried really hard to ignore these kids behind as Claire and I walked home one evening along the canal. These kids got closer and closer, still taunting me, *"Is it a boy? Is it a girl? What is it?"* Then I was hit with a rock. I turned and screamed with rage, threw my bike towards them and chased the little fuckers. Needless to say they never forgot my face. I came home one day to find them sitting on a wall. In front of them was my motorbike. They had torched it. Set fire to the gas tank, and watched it burn. I looked at them, at the bike, and walked inside. What would you have done? Talked? Fought? This had been building up over the last year I didn't tell anyone. What would I say? "I'm being terrified by a gang of ten-year olds?" I couldn't speak up for myself as a kid and I still couldn't at 25.

When I bought a one-way ticket to the States, I'd left everything. Everyone.[13]

---

13 Even though now, as an old school tomboy in stripes, I still carry my family with me.

Weren't you scared? asked a good friend.

Yes, but the want was greater than the fear. Just.

New Mexico, 1993, mid-twenties
Committed

Living in Pacheco Canyon, one winter morning, I stood, looked at the clouds, watched the winds surf across the cottonwoods and breathed deeply. Smelled the air through the junipers and pinons.

Snow in the afternoon, I predicted.

Around the cabin, I picked kindling before the storm came. Charlie, a six-month-old pittie and Husky pup, played at my feet, full of energy, and so we hiked through the narrow valley. He was my first puppy, a big commitment to living in the States, one I never regretted. He ran around wildly, chasing the ravens through the pinons whilst I bent and scrabbled under the trees looking for more dead and down branches. Back at the cabin, I chopped wood, enough for a few days ahead, getting better and better at swinging the axe. Inside by the wood stove, I stacked a pile of twigs whilst trying to distract Charlie from chewing on them all. On the porch I'd built, I stored the piñion, juniper, and few pieces of oak cut at 12 to 18 inch-lengths. Charlie and I shuffled inside, closed the doors. I gave him a bone, made myself a cup of tea, and lay down as the snowflakes fell outside.

England, 1998, early thirties
Needing

I'd been heading back to the States or so I'd thought, except the Texan immigration officers had decided my home wasn't in the Southwest and had sent me back, to "your country" as they said with a tip of the hat and a stamp in my passport, and Dad picked me up from the airport, the first and only time he managed to do that, and back at the farm house, Mum gave me valium and a cuppa, the two cats kneaded my lap, and neither of my parents could help me this time because we didn't know what to say, we'd never learned how.

London, 1998, at thirty-ish
The Things You'll Do When You're Stuck in England (without work, and you want to get back to your dogs in the Southwest but are held away by bureaucrats while supported by your friends)

At the Duke of Wellington one Friday night, Lisa and I were trying to think of ways for me to bring in some cash. I had been in town for a few weeks by then. On the wall next to our table, a poster advertised a competition with a prize the equivalent of $75. "No telling anyone though, right, Lisa? You promise?" Lisa nodded, smiled, and lit her smoke with a grin wider than the pint glass. Two weeks later, I walked back into the Duke with my bag of props. The pub teemed with friends from years ago, from college, from my jobs in the different pubs in East London. There was Claire (the princess) and Clare (the teacher). Jane. Gina. Suzette. Maggie. Fiona. Rachel. John. Everyone grinned, bought me drinks, and said how glad they were to hear from Lisa.

The DJ came and told me I had a few moments before my turn. The last young woman had wowed the pub full of dykes with her strip show. I went upstairs and changed. The opening strands of Rod Stewart began, and I shuffled on stage. I wore a seventies-style blue boy's suit, complete with flairs, waistcoat, and wide-bottomed tie, a striped shirt, white vest, and as many layers as possible. I danced a half-hearted wiggle or two. A few women laughed at me, whispering loudly, *what is it?* Then the chorus began. Lighting my torches and breathing fire, I stripped, full on, claiming the stage on my own terms. The other women in the competition cheered in surprised delight. My gang went wild, screaming, laughing, and full on riotous when I ended with a ten-foot flame and in striped boxer shorts, nothing else, I stood full of tomboy power and fuck-yous.

England, 1996, late twenties
Dad said, you should've been born a boy.

The Christmas party's chitchat paused and then my cousins and aunts and uncles all laughed at the comment as I stood there in my jeans and red plaid shirt, scruffy short hair and the big boots. Just let me be, I thought but smiled at my dad in his shirt and tie, blue eyes twinkling with cognac, knowing that he'd protected me the best he could. He didn't understand what it meant to be such a tomboy in a traditional small town and I had no words to explain, not then, and all I wished for was to disappear back into our cabin in the hills, with my dog and girlfriend, my first of each, where we lived next to a trickling creek and far away from both family and strangers.

Learning Curves

It's been a bit of a challenge, discovering women, how to talk to them, be with friends with them, and even harder if lovers, and yes, I know I  am one, was raised as one, kind of look like one but I didn't get it, had limited friendships because I didn't bring anyone home, not knowing if the curtains would be drawn with a heavy silence covering the tension of a suicidal parent and so I didn't learn how to chat and gossip and tease and spend time with others supposedly like me which meant that dating women has been a bit of a non-starter (or rather non-laster) since it's the unavailable ones I drown within even though I still prefer to be, continue to be, silent and alone.[14]

---

14   human-wise

The Art of a Solo Life

1. Behind the wheel, window open, thoughts drifting as I drive down narrow highways.

2. On the side of a mountain meadow with no one around but for my dogs and cat.

3. Swimming in pools or skinny-dipping in lakes, oceans, rivers, waterfalls, all of it.

4. Listening to a breeze in the valley or a distant train heading south echoing in the valley.

5. Watching Rosie, Harold, and Stevie sleep and dream, paws skipping, tails barely flicking.

6. Street-performing and juggling with a bunch of strangers or friends, it didn't matter, there's a freedom there, a looseness in me.

7. Writing even as I'm terrified of what the scribblings will spew out, all the secrets I'd kept underwater.

Maine, early twenties
First Date

How was Maine? The first time, you mean, in 1989? When I showed up at the bus station with my backpack and boots and a few letters from Liz? We'd not met. I didn't know her. One of the many friends of friends who took me in when I hitched across the States at twenty-two. Portland, Maine, the depot was smaller than expected but busy still, and after a long bus ride through Worcester, I'd jumped off the bus. Do you have any postcards for sale? No. Nothing to show Mum in Worcester that her daughter was in Worcester: Home to home. No, instead, the humidity stuck to my skin like those fantasies I'd had. Liz, a flirtation over letters for months. I waited for her. Two women approached me, one tall and dark, the other stocky and fair skinned, both nervous-like, asking, are you? Yes, are you? Yes we were. Liz's girlfriend drove us, pale eyes flickering between me and Liz as we headed from city to an island down east but really up north and the air conditioning cranked and Liz and I talked all the way, catching up on life and ideas and books and writing. Then weeks spent together, with fishing boats passed us by as we walked across rocky shores. Naps stolen in the cool wooden house in the dense woods. Grass constantly underfoot. Rocks slick. Lobster fighting to get out the pot in the kitchen and how I couldn't eat it after that. Buttery fingers. Reading aloud to each other. Mist. Hidden views. Lost. Awake. Coffee on the porch. Fresh muffins baked. Newspapers, stories, and secrets shared. And now, thirty years later, I come back to Maine, this time with two dogs and no lover. The tourists gather around the dock, and I walk in a haze, holding a coffee and fresh blueberry muffin and I'm distracted by thoughts of that first kiss with a woman and how she was married, and that I hadn't cared and now I'm sorry.

Tennessee, mid-thirties
First Date #5

The only time we danced together, Lisa, you were barefoot. It was New Year's Eve in Tennessee, and I wore a blue silk shirt that matched my eyes. You were in a skin-tight black dress and yes, all those curves caught my attention. You were a familiar face, but I barely knew you. I was shy as usual. Your husband, Tim, was dancing up close with another woman and you grabbed my hand, dragging me onto the wooden floor, so perfectly obvious in your own flirtations. The both of you were unfazed and open with these attractions. Poly, you said, not that I knew what that really meant. Later that week, you invited me over on the weekend to see your place, stick around for dinner—all together—you, me, Tim, and even his latest lover. I turned up at your rustic cabin, a few miles away from mine, and Tim was cooking dinner. He said, she's in the shower, expecting you, and he winked at me just as a truck pulled up, and Tim headed out to meet his girl. I went to find you and yes, there you were in the bathroom, with all those Mexican tiles and mosaics covering curved walls, with sweaty saltillos underfoot, the window ledges were full of thick leafy plants, moist from the steamy shower. Water flowed over your tanned shoulders and pale hips and you talked through the fog and came out reaching for a warm towel. I handed one over as you stood in front of me, skin glistening, both of us dripping. You dried off and chatted to me. You reached for nail polish, handed it to me. I unscrewed it and gave it back. No, you said, I want you to paint my nails, and you placed your bare foot on the tub. For the first time, I knelt before you.

New Mexico, in my thirties
Doing my best to resist because getting crushes on unavailable women was wearing me down

She folds up her long legs into the front seat of the old Toyota truck,[15] windows rolled down, one silky arm draped out touching the trees as we drive down narrow rocky back roads mid-morning and her other hand holds a tall mug of creamy coffee, clasping it carefully with feline fingers that trace the curves, and I drive with eyes averted, focused on the dangers ahead, the the flash of wild-woods, and the the valley as we and deeper into vate land and all vague sense of truck trundles flinching and re-steady churning and slower and rockier and my with determi-  rocks unseen, ness in the sun creeps into head deeper unknown pri-with only a direction, the onwards un-liable with the of gears slower the world gets hands clench nation not to wander too far off course and we're barely breathing, hardly moving, but covering so much ground as we catch up and laugh out loud and tease and I drive, ignoring the hand on my lap, and squinting in the bright light, past ponds that tempted, and then our mountain track opens up to a meadow of sunflowers as tall as this woman beside me and she turns and says, Stop.

---

15   "Yellow," by Coldplay, http://bit.ly/3kBnvTg

Ebb and Flow

Connect.
Need.[16]
Leave.

Repeat.
Repeat.
Repeat.
Repeat.
Repeat.
Repeat.
Repeat.
Repeat.
Repeat.
Repeat.
Repeat.
Repeat.
Repeat.

ad nauseum

and yeah, I can't stop but I'm sick of running

---

16   her wanting something from me, that is

Vermont, 2017, turning fifty
Brave Enough to Walk not Run

That first week in town, I had crossed Main Street ignoring the flashing lights, chomping down an organic apple and a UPS driver slammed on his brakes. I'm not exactly a small woman, and who couldn't see me in the crosswalk in a yellow rain jacket and cowboy hat? Oh, right, after fifty, no men see me, no men under fifty that is. I gave him the finger and carried on up the hill to the new college, a graduate degree at my age? Oh bloody hell, what have I done now? It had been a while. What, thirty years or more? Yep. Thirty-two years. Finally the June rains had eased and with a smile up to the blue above, I nodded. The brief splash of sunshine was a grating contrast to the dark memories of middle school, singing, *Hey Teacher, leave those kids alone, I'm just another brick in the wall,* Tum de tum. Oh, yeah, that last day at Parkside Middle School with the kids all singing out the Pink Floyd songs but we hadn't got a clue what any of it meant, and those school bullies echoed deep inside and my head snapped back like no time has passed. I dropped to the ground, knees on pavement, a wave of fear slammed into me. Not again, please no, not another panic attack, not here. Yes, here. Head down, between knees, breathe in, out, in and out, slow and steady, onetwothree, onetwothree. A couple in their sixties stepped around me and the chill in the air wasn't imagined after all. Alone, I gulped, forced myself to stand, muttering, and then walked to school because fuck 'em, I wouldn't quit, I'd make friends, I'd stick it out. I belonged here too.

Vermont, 2017
Where are you from?

"Did you say New Mexico?"
 "Yes," and tilt the cowboy hat back.
"But your accent...?"

Vermont, 2017

At college, all those writing exercises spewed up memories and questions and patterns and decisions and regrets and images and never-ending conversations, all that lead me there, to study to become a better writer, to create a career, but what had I given up?[17] I turned off the laptop, grabbed the truck keys, needing to clear my head, the only way I knew how, behind the wheel.

The Green Mountains, part of the Appalachian Mountain Chain, run north to south in Vermont, a spine holding together this dense state. The forest closes in, thick branches fold overhead to form a tunnel along this winding country road as we drive towards Lake Champlain. Rain beats down on this summer's afternoon and the wipers slap side to side. The sound of wet tires on paved roads pokes at my patience, already as worn as my favorite shirt with ripped seams and not at its prettiest. The weather turns even darker or is it the bloody trees? The signs are hidden by thick heavy branches. Traffic backs up behind me, braking at my NM plates to give me the Look, too polite to give me the Finger. Rain thumps on the roof. The wipers swoosh over and over. I snap at Rosie for sitting on Harold's tail. When I reach for them to apologize, they cringe and stare out the windows quietly. We come out of the forest finally and follow a few softly rounded hills the locals call mountains. My favourite colours greet me, blue and green, striped across the horizon. The landscape opens up across waves of knee-deep grass, with hints of ponds flickering and reflecting in the distance. I pull over at what looks like a welcome trailhead only to see a sign: NO TRESPASSING.

Fuck it. The dogs lean away from me. Cursing, I drive off, tension like body odor filling the Toyota relentlessly. Where next?

---

17   Space. Solitude. Open skies. Sunshine.

Rewired

A story describes a death, decaying bodies, crematoriums, and it's over, I'm done, a wreck, carefully holding in, holding on, but today it's too much and I can't function, can't help, can't do much but write and read and stare and I'm back in that time, the time of clearing out rooms, a home, the photos, the clothes and shoes and mugs and music and hats and plates and tea and scarves and cutlery and pictures and paintings and blankets and coats and letters and and and it's too much. They say, those doctors and counselors all, they tell me that the cumulative effect of never knowing how to relax as a kid rewired my brain and her death is just like all those taunts and terrors from before and too stressful and even now as I write this swallowing is hard, words in my throat drown me, and I'm stuck, trapped in that bedroom again, and the music the beer the dogs the grey day it doesn't help, nothing helps. How many years? I'd thought, I'd hoped, grief would lesson its grip and it did, really it did, but all it takes is another violent death to bring me back, tackle me to the dirt and hold me down, face in the earth, breathe in, death and decay, dust to dust, she's gone, they're gone, breathe out. It doesn't matter, it's quick or short or neither and it's never enough, time is never enough, and I'm on my knees, done in once again.

Vermont, 2018
Mary

This first one was an Edward, an IPA, not my usual choice but you like them. That's good enough for me. A pint of course - what else is there? The second was a pale ale, a Susan it's called. Local brewery. We like our local breweries. Vermont has so many breweries. You'd like trying them out. Hill Farm is one, like where I grew up, Hill Farm House. The third pint was a lager, a Lion's Heart that I don't have. Then the fella next to me, mid-thirties, short beard, smiling soft eyes, well, he made a mistake. It'd been easy until then, talking books, college, what we like to read, what we like to write. He said something. I said something back. Silence. I paid up. Left. Not his fault, he didn't know I was drinking with you, one of my closest friends. Didn't know you were in hospice, terminal, fatal, a fighter even now. He'd asked if I'd go back to New Mexico over winter break.

I said, it'd be too late.

Speak Up #4

I don't talk about keeping track of all my fuck-ups, with my mum and dad, and all those friends and lovers I've failed, when I've run away from any sense of responsibility, and I'm also haunted by all who've died without me nearby and there's too many and I have to ask, why am I still here despite all the reckless risks I took over the years because I'm alive still/ somehow and they're not and I'm told that with faith these questions ease, and somehow this belief's founded not in science or facts, or even experience direct or not, but I don't get it- although it's true, I call my old beat-up 4Runner Faith because in her I trust, to a point ,and then again, in Dog I trust but in god not so much, and then what am I meant to say when yet another message comes, and it's a fucking Facebook message, saying how another friend from New Mexico is dead and it's suicide this time by handgun, Oh to be in America, yes, Fuck Facebook and there's nothing worse than grieving for a friend when those around you don't know her, him, them and well, I, with no shared stories, memories, laughter, tears, I've nothing to say anyway.

Hill Farm House
Quiet Places

1. The clock over the fridge ticks loudly and Mum sits at the table with a coffee and a cigarette. Viv's opposite her facing the kitchen window above the sink. The willow tree fills the view. Mum and Viv chat but go silent when they see me, mischievous sisters talking badly of someone probably. Mum stands, turns on the cassette for Neil Diamond, Rod Stewart, oldies even then. She laughs and jigs in place, pouring out a shot of something dark brown into two little glasses, a snifter she says, passing it over. Her eyes are bright blue sparkles of summer and I love these times, sitting on the step between kitchen and living room. Just the three of us.

2. The clock ticks loudly and Mum sits with her head in her hands, breath so soft. Quiet. Deadly so but for the fucking clock. [18]

3. Now, it's in a corner by the woodstove at my New Mexican home, and on the wall, I've hung this monster, and it's a good 18" tall, made of dark wood, with grapes chiseled into the circle around the face itself.

I have it now they're all gone and it's as quiet as me.

---

18 Dad and Mum bought it one summer on one of their holidays. After we'd both left home, me first, Pete next. They'd go to Spain, take tons of photos of the beaches, of picnics, of views. Mum kept the envelopes of photos on the kitchen tables, any of our kitchens, at Hill Farm or the house they later moved to in town. The kitchen made the home, it was the heart, the place we all sat. With that clock. Marking the days until I'd leave again.

England, 1992
He Simply Couldn't Ask

I'd been flying in and out of the country since I was 18 and then after five or so years, my dad came to meet me—the once—as I'd come back from camping in the Midwest with friends where I'd dislocated my shoulder and it had taken us about 4 or 5 hours driving in the dark thick forested landscape before Dawn found a hospital open that night and my shoulder was severely messed up from being out of joint for so long and when I called home, asking for help, not easy for me to do, well, that's why Dad was coming to the airport, three and a half hours away, you see, Dad wanted to help because it comes easy to him, but, then he went to the wrong terminal and he was in his sixties, a traditional man of his era, in his suit, tie and mild manners and so he wandered around Gatwick airport looking for me, forgetting my flight details and unable, physically unable to ask

for help, only able to give it, and meanwhile I'm at the other terminal with a backpack full of camping gear that I can't move on my own and I called my mum to see if she could help but she was having one of her moments and I hung up, took a deep breath, and waited before calling my brother who told me the latest that Dad was on his way home...he'd left me.

Guatemala, 2005
Gone in Antigua

Through the peeling peach plaster of the hotel room, I listened to the English couple discuss their wedding. *It's not a loan, we'll tell him it's a gift because we can't get married without him, right? Whenever he can, he's to get a flight to meet us in Honduras, right?* The man's voice annoyed me, too childish and whiney for a grown up, do all British men sound so young? I didn't remember. It had been twelve years since last living there, and I thought of Dad, Mum, and Pete, as we all sat around the kitchen table, drinking wine, and telling each other stories.

The next day, while getting ready to leave town, I spent the spring afternoon in the clothes shop on Sixth Avenue, to the west of the central park where I looked through the racks of women's trousers and blouses. These aren't the things I know how to buy, I was muttering to herself when the lady offered to help. We spoke in Spanish, with me describing the need for black, for baggy yet formal if possible, saying, look at me, I prefer men's loose trousers to these high waists. We found a selection of black clothes for the occasion coming. Which is, she asked. My dad died. There, I said it. The silence though inevitable was not awkward but natural, as the lady looked at me with sympathy and touched me briefly on the shoulder. She understood. I said nothing else as the wave of sudden tears came fast. I took refuge in a chilled dressing room.

IV

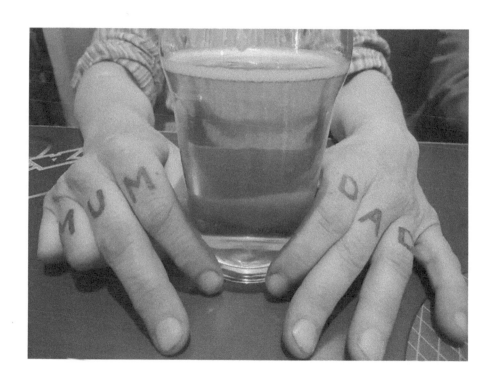

Both

Vermont, 2018
Responsibility Fatigue

Her eyes lit up. Blue. Pale. Her skin was dirty, skin weathered, chin sunburnt, and she had a huge genuine smile. Linda, you'd chatted with her a few times on Main Street over the months. You waved at her this morning. She was walking slowly up State, the farmers' market out in force. She stopped at your voice. Smiled. Then she asked you for money. Instinct kicked in and you said no, I can't help.

"I'm going home to my mom. I need to catch the bus today, that's what she said. She worries about me for some reason."

"They do that," you joked.

She again asked for help. You lied. You fucking lied to her. In your back pocket was $25 in cash. You never have cash. The sun beat down. Hot day ahead. You thought of your cool apartment. Fans blurring the edges. Fridge full. Cash in pocket. Croissant crumbs on your tee shirt. You walked around Bear Pond Bookstore, tempted by another collection of essays that you don't need. Outside, Linda sat on a concrete bench in the shade of an Ash tree, stretching out one leg, pack at her feet. You called her name and her face lit up. Wishing her a safe trip home, you gave her all she needed, but it wasn't you, it was me, I turned home and I'm so fucking angry, someone asked for my help, and I didn't want to be responsible for anyone else but I couldn't shut down because I've been there: broke. Reaching out. Trying to go home. And helped by others for their own reasons.

Speak Up #3

I don't talk about the loneliness of coming back from school as a kid and teen, needing to hold misery at bay, somehow, always checking on Mum, making sure she made it through another day without a job or reason to live, or how I learned that life was fucking hard for us all which lead to my own suicidal tendencies and how after witnessing months of my pained silence as a twenty-three year old, Mum sat me down one winter's day at the wooden table under the kitchen clock and pulled out paper and pen and asked me what did I want to do with my life, what could I do to make it better, and hours later we had a map of action, it was full of classes to take, in photography and pottery and art, and we found ways to challenge those times when I struggled with months of no work in London even though I had a great circle of friends, Cate and Claire and Rachel and Lisa and everyone else, but not one of them could help me, not really, it had to come from within me, didn't it, and Mum asked the right questions and we played with ideas and it made it all the difference, that one afternoon with her at home in the kitchen together, I'd needed her and she was there.

England, 1977
Doing his Best

That time in middle school when I ran away? My shoulders had been strapped up as I'd recently fallen and broken my collar bone, and so I had avoided the other kids, protective of my pain. I stood near the tennis courts, munching on my lunchtime apple and watching the back and forth of the ball, lost in the thwack and bounce. One of the boys, Mick or Mike or Mark or something, he couldn't leave me alone. He ran up and shoved into me from behind and I crashed down onto my broken shoulder and screamed bloody murder. A teacher ran over, for once noticing me, grabbing my arm, not seeing the bandages and sling. I screamed again, and when she let go, I ran. Dad had found me. He knew where to look. He took me home to the teddy bear and kittens.

Do the dead have memories?

Do they
remember
our mistakes?

My mistakes? [19]

---

19   Don't tell me, I can't bear to hear.

I prefer the silence

—we both did—

Although There were Sounds that Soothed

Harold's tail
thump thump thump
you're
home, he
mumbled
over the
crackle of the
woodstove

and
a
bubbling
green chile
stew

with a cat called Stephen slurping cream
and Rosie licking her apple
perhaps there's a lone cello
on the radio, heard over
the winters' snow sizzling down the metal stovepipe
as I faced my past

Guatemala, 2005
Echoes

Rucksack. Boots. Teddy bear. Shirts (two), jeans, and undies. A sweatshirt, a jacket, a pair of shorts. You had a one-way ticket in your pocket, a few hundred dollars in cash and no credit cards—yes, some things never changed, you were still broke, awake, and a tad terrified to fly into another strange country. You did it anyway. Once in Antigua, you found a room off the plaza with tall ceilings, huge windows facing a church and park, the adobe walls covered with ochre and maroon peeling paint, a rickety wooden table and hard-backed chair. You dropped the pack and then headed out to explore the neighbourhood, so different from your small close community in New Mexico, one you'd left once again, restless as usual, weren't you? A fella was selling mangos and avocados, and you began juggling in the afternoon sun whilst nearby families waited to visit others in the overcrowded and run-down hospital. And then suddenly a circle of girls, barefoot and shy in traditional Mayan shirts and skirts, wanted to play catch and so you did. With you in the middle, playing the fool, you all ran around the park, tossing balls high and mighty, free in the afternoon. Juan, a shoe-shine boy with blackened fingers and feet, threw one tennis ball up so far into the blue sky that it fell onto the roof of an ancient stone church and the kids all froze in fear and when you just laughed and pulled out another ball, the whole plaza erupted in cheers and laughter and you all played until the sun dropped and the families went home and you left for your room with the yells of happy kids echoing through the cobbled streets of Antigua; "Payasa! Payasa! Hasta mañana, Payasita!"

Guatemala, 2005
Insomnia

Dad had died in his bed, a week before the call, and my brother had tried to track me down for days, and well, fuck, once I heard that, sleep fought me and held me down, unable to breathe. My body ached with the need for a child of my own. A boy, so I could call him Tony after Dad. I thought of all the kids I loved in New Mexico and England, and how they'd light up when they see me. Thomas. Emily. Zoë. Kate. Freya. Dasen. Vivian. Ely.

I packed, unpacked, and packed again. Non-stop I fiddled, looked for something, then forgot what, in particular, then replaced it all in the small green backpack on the other bed, a bed empty and unused by friend or lover. Or dog.

Outside in Antigua, an orchestra pulled together wandering tourists and locals and I found myself drawn in, listening to Dolor Con Suenos de Alegria. All around me, the stonework of the sixteenth century, the architecture of Spanish colonial times, the arches and pillars and fountains reminded me of our family holidays in northern Spain and coastal Wales.

Dad taking photos, drinking a cold local beer, making sandwiches, Peter eating them while I simply loved to swim with Mum, we'd fling ourselves into huge waves, squealing with delight. We were braver together.

Wales, 2005
Rage #2

Once I'd made it back for the funeral, and grieving for my dad, I took a weekend away on the Gower coast of Wales, a place we'd all loved as a family growing up. Listening to REM, Losing My Religion, play over the tinny speakers, I sat in a pub, staring out the window over craggy cliffs and high tides, missing my family, yet craving the company of my dog. An old bloke with dappled pale skin, thick glasses and a dangerous-to-ego bald spot, sat next to me and started the interrogation. *Where you from, lass? Where's your husband? Kids? Family?* He grabbed at my hand. I shook him off and then I answered his questions truthfully. There was a pause. And then he stormed at me; *you live in America, eh? Too good for us, are you? Why aren't you married, eh? Think that men aren't good enough either, eh? Fucking arrogant shit, go back then, go back to your kind of friends, to that country; we don't want your sort here anyway...* He smashed his pint down on the table between us.

The pub went silent. I had to leave

before I threw my pint of Carlsberg in his florid face.

The song had ended.

Vermont, 2018

It was too loud. The fridge. I seriously considered unplugging the fridge.

After twenty-five years spent in the Southwest, I'd needed that kind of deep quiet. I missed those horizons as broad as the Oregon Coast. I missed sticking my nose in the bark of a juniper in New Mexico and taking a big whiff of vanilla. I missed striding across the Ortiz Mountains with Harold and Rosie roaming free through pinons, cacti, junipers and jackrabbits. Millions of acres all around, the sun overhead, and a dry desert heat that relaxes the muscles like a good massage: I missed sitting on the bench overlooking the Rio Grande valley next to a friend or lover, with only the ticking of a wristwatch, the crackling craw of ravens bickering with the blue jays, and ignoring the barking dogs next door as my own ran free, yipping in chase of a cottontail, yeah, these were the sounds surrounding me for years and one of the reasons why I kept going back despite all the times I'd left, swearing to be done with the place if not the people.

New Mexico, 2016
Danger Signs

Rosie, Rosie, Give me your answer do. I'm half crazy all for my love of you. It won't be a stylish marriage. I can't afford a carriage. But you'll look sweet, upon a seat, of a bicycle made for two.

Driving to the emergency vet, Rosie's scalp swollen, bloody and torn after another dog fight, I sang to her over and over this little rhyme, one my mum used to sing to me, making me laugh. Rosie shook on the seat next to me in the 4Runner, her white fur a mess, her eyes wide. On the highway, the roads empty, I petted my lap, once twice and she crept over, all forty pounds of akita/lab mix. She nestled in, shaking still. I sang the ditty again, *Rosie, Rosie, give me your answer do*, and she stopped shaking, her head pressed against the rumble in my chest. When I stopped, well, ran out of lyrics, she shook so I sang it again and she relaxed. For 45 minutes, I sang those three lines over, and my girl leaned in for more. Safe.

Clean Up on Aisle Twenty-Three

Shut up. Drink up. Throw up. It's all the same. You're not the first. You're not the first to bury a mum or a dad, a friend, or even a pet. You're not the only one gulping hard, smothered, with eyes so raw you can't see the price tag of the shirt you really don't need or the dog treats you do. Swallow it down, hold it in, smile. No one cares, not really, no one cares. No one cares that you can't breathe, can't sleep, want to throw up, right here on aisle twenty-three. Shut up. Drink up. Hold up. Please insert cash or select payment type. Shut up. Shut up.

Vermont, 2018
Eight Years Later to the Day

Ice. Blue. Dark sky. Well below zero. A blizzard across the staircase. The wooden steps were old and worn slippery. Red PJs blue snow boots and dad's red dressing gown thick and warm. The dogs ran down, Harold had a case of the runs, woke me up at four in a snowstorm raging outside. I followed the two dogs down the stairs through snow drifts but my boots slipped out from under me and I smashed onto my back and slid down crunch thump yell fuck shit shit. My arm grabbed the rail, one on the left, and yanked me to a stop halfway down in the snow in the freezing black ice snow drifts on worn out stairs outside my home in town and the neighbors were out and lights off and I grabbed the rail and stood up shaky lonely. My back and arms were bruised and muscles torn but not dislocated like years before and oh shit don't think about it. Struggling back upstairs, I let us all in and lay on my back feeling bruised scared and my heart hurts and burst into tears. Eight years ago to the night, my mum fell down a flight of stairs. At her home. I'm alive. Bruised. Breathing. She's not.

in breath

Vermont, 2018
The shower didn't help.

The stink lingered. The pain stuck around. The bathtub overflowed. The hot water ran out. The mirror fogged up. The toothpaste had dried up. The jeans and tee-shirt got soaked. The dogs begged. The clock ticked. You left. The sandwiches forgotten.

Walking outside was hot. The headache didn't help. The aspirin didn't help. Not enough. The monsoons didn't help either and quite frankly, you were cranky.

The hangover didn't help.

It was a long morning but lunch at the pub helped. The first beer helped. The quiet helped. The walk back to work was pleasant. The frog in the puddle croaked. The nod hello from the old lady and her poodle helped.

The day ended. The dogs were waiting. The sandwiches untouched. The beer was cold. The phone was silent. The dinner was cooked. The dogs walked. The cat fed. The clock said nine. You said, bedtime.

Stevie sulked. Harold nestled on the bed beside you. Your other dog wagged her tail, knocked over the phone, and you smiled, finally, saying, ah Rosie, thank you, you're right, I don't need to hear from anyone now.

Rosie sucks socks before kibble.

My socks.

I hate soggy socks.

1983-2009
Responsibility Fatigue #2

- Caring for my mum's depressions by making her tea and toast, starting as a ten-year-old.
- Babysitter for three girls at fifteen.
- Worrying about Mum constantly as a teenager.
- Housecleaner and odd jobs for a housebound crotchety elderly woman in the village up the hill at sixteen.
- Nanny for a family in South of France for two months at eighteen.
- Returning home from college because of mum's struggles and threats at twenty.
- Elderly residential caregiver for a bunch of strangers over a few months to save up decent money for more traveling, in my early twenties.
- Caregiver for an elderly partially paralyzed Santa Fe woman when I was in my mid-twenties.
- Caregiver for my teacher with MS, completely paralyzed, while at clown school in my late thirties.

But then when I was 42, Mum was in a coma and I did nothing.[20]

---

20   And there lies my guilt. Ten years later. I hadn't wanted to go home after all —although I did.

Speak Up #2

I don't talk about acute trauma of the brain shutting the wiring between the frontal lobes, severing the ability to breathe, move, think, or speak.

I'd never told Mum about how scared I was as a kid.

How then can I blame her for not keeping me safe?

New Mexico, 2019
No Words

It's been almost ten years since we cleared out mum and dad's house and there I was back in New Mexico when riffling through a suitcase of photos from our family holidays on the coast, I came across a letter from Dad to Mum, and he spoke of her grief for the death of her two cats, Kiki and Smudge (yes, I'd named them as a kid) and how touched he was by the love and loss in her eyes and how much he'd wanted to say something but hadn't known how.

New Mexico, 2019
A Good Day to Die

Tuesday morning was chilly after the monsoons, and a mustard yellow Mexican blanket was tucked around bare shoulders. You lay in bed with Rosie curled up against your belly, her apple tucked under paws. Harold lay along the length of your back. Little Stevie walked along the ridge between, purring to himself. You didn't move. The dreams faded. The cat licked your nose. There was no better way to wake up from a nap. You can relax now.

No rush. No rush.

Speak Up #1

I don't talk about that first time seeing her in the hospital, swollen and smashed, in a coma, and how I fell to the floor before the nurse could grab me, the sobbing slump that I was, unable to look mum in the eyes and how I sat beside her, stroking pale skin and slender fingers, silent.

I don't talk about how on Christmas a week later, when I sat next to mum in a deserted ICU, I talked to her, nonstop for hours, telling her how much she'd given me, the fun we'd had, all those silly times at the beach, her teaching me to swim and to face the waves, braver together.

I don't talk about explaining to Mum's blank eyes that I had a home now, with Harold, with friends and neighbors, a local pub of my own and how I'd be okay, I could relax now, I was safe. She could let go.

I don't talk about how her vitals spun out of control, beeping, bouncing, and how I yelled for the nurses but they dismissed it as a bump, instinctive, and that it didn't mean Mum could hear me but I knew better, she could, she heard me, I know it. **I know it.**

I don't talk about any of this but my legs cramp on the plane and I'm gasping for fresh air yet trapped by these memories and it's that time of year when she fell–nine years ago–and here I am, once again stuck on another plane, just like I did then, when I'd had to fly back to the ICU and this plane pulls into gate number 2 back in New Mexico and I stand released into motion and able to relax finally, and I buy a banana for my legs and coffee for my brain at 5:42 am but still I wonder if I'll ever be able to forgive myself for leaving you and I'm sorry Mum, I'm sorry, I'm sorry for not knowing you better.

I don't talk about that final act of responsibility for Mum was to say

– Yes, turn off the life support system. She's not coming back.

out breath

England, 2008
Heading Out

Mum sat at the kitchen table with her back to the window. We'd just been out on the Welsh Coast together for a few days, staying in a hotel, a treat said Mum, let's see all the places we used to go as a family. We did just that, the two of us. You see, Dad had been gone for three years. Pete was probably at his house, nearby, taking care of the kids before coming over. Mum and I listened to Radio Two playing The Traveling Wilburys, one of her favorites, and we sipped tea, awkward and somehow easy. Mostly.

The cats dozed on armchairs in the living room and Mum stared at them. We didn't know what to say, we rarely did, but it was worse that day. I was off to the States again, for who knew how long. Rucksack was propped by the front door, waiting on Pete to pick me up.

"When's the flight?"

She knew though. We both did. I finished my tea, washed the mug, stared out the kitchen window onto the trimmed lawn, apple trees, wild roses, a couple of chairs and a table nestled in the shade of the weeping willows, and thought this is home, it's not enough yet I belong here too.

"Soon," I replied and sat back down for my mum, quiet but comfortable together.[21]

---

21   "Hello Again," by Neil Diamond, the song that breaks me each time now. Mum's favourite. http://bit.ly/3ZeK1Ao

V

A dog. An apple.
A nap.
This is a Sunday poem.

A Coda of Sorts

New Mexico, 2019
Consequences

One August afternoon, after we'd gone for a meandering hike across the rough cactus filled hills, Harold, Stevie, Rosie and I had a nap together, no rush, and then I headed out for an hour or so, dinner in town, having a beer with my friends, listening to Lori and Erik play at the cantina as we do on a sunny afternoon, and while there, the neighbor's dogs broke into my yard and fuck, those dogs from next door, they did just as I'd feared all these years, they attacked and killed my girl Rosie, left her broken and bloodied body inert in the dirt, and finding her, my legs cramped, knees crumpled and my screams, I'll fucking kill you, came as if a hand strangled my throat but then no more pain could escape, I had no words, only muffled yells and a sickened whimpering, and there was no way to stick around and so in the dim flicker of a headlamp, with a hole dug in the rocks, I buried Rosie with an apple and her own stuffed toys under a thick blanket of stars, threw Harold and Stevie in the van, grabbed my teddy bear, and drove away up north to a place we'd camped together as a family, me and my dogs and my cat and we'd spent summers there and so that's where I needed to be, a place to remember.

We'd had fun together, Harold, Rosie, Stevie and I, traveling from New Mexico around the Southwest, into Vermont and Maine, and even heading across to the Northwest, playing on the beaches of Oregon together. I need to remember her this way, Rosie as mischief maker, playmate, and the great apple protector.

and she's off

One Life. Love it.

A Life in Motion

My understanding of home is different—I think—and I'm most relaxed, behind the wheel yet tethered to a community, although I'm still struggling to find the right balance of people, place and purpose that works for me because with Rosie's death, no, there's no happy ending, but this time I know that I did my best, for all of us, 'cos I came back to New Mexico, fought for her, for some semblance of justice, and I spoke up and I can live with that, and since then my concept of leaving has changed too, it's no longer an act of avoidance or cowardice, but one of opportunity, and with that in mind, and after spending winter in Oregon to work on this story of mine with a writer I admire, I came back to New Mexico, to my home in the hills, the silence of the mountains and yes, the easy comradery of our small rural community, living near those friends of mine who understand my need to come and go, and simply let me be. So for now, that's the best I can do.

Further Readings

Complex Trauma and Children:
https://www.nctsn.org/what-is-child-trauma/trauma-types/complex-trauma

How complex ptsd can gain ground even decades later:
https://www.nhs.uk/conditions/post-traumatic-stress-disorder-ptsd/complex/

The effects and roles of bullying, of being hidden, androgynous and how there's a lack of our stories in mainstream literature:
https://www.academia.edu/38372281/Leamy-A_Conversation-CriticalThesis.pdf

Brain Zaps are a thing:
It's true. As a twenty year old, I took quite a few of the various things you don't want your kids to inhale or taste and then I had a bit of a breakdown as you read earlier. I was researching "brain zaps" and came across this. The doctors had prescribed me some strong drugs for the supposed epilepsy which I stopped cold turkey.

> "Because SSRIs, benzodiazepines, ecstasy and Adderall are all associated with an increase in the brain's level of GABA, discontinuing these drugs are likely associated with low brain levels of GABA. As low levels of GABA can trigger seizures, this hypothesis leaves open the possibility that the reported brain zaps are instances of brief, localized seizures." https://www.psychologytoday.com

On epilepsy:
In an atonic seizure (or *drop attack*) the person's muscles suddenly relax and they become floppy. If they are standing they often fall, usually forward, and may injure the front of their head or face. Like tonic seizures, atonic seizures tend to be brief and happen without warning.
https://www.epilepsysociety.org.uk

#JusticeforRosie
I've done all that I could. Collected evidence, created a paper trail, filed

court cases, talked on television[22] about the ongoing lack of protection from Santa Fe County, been quoted on Newsweek,[23] local papers,[24] articles,[25] petitions,[26] attended community meetings with sheriffs and friends, fixed gates, worked with an EMDR[27] therapist to rewire my brain's reactions, micro-dosing[28] with Indica for anxiety, added more fencing, had target practice, and (sometimes) even carried a 9mm Glock and pump actions shotgun but nothing changed. And then the idiot neighbor burned down his own house. Problem gone. Temporarily.

The court case took eighteen months and the neighbor was allowed more dogs, so I sold. I've been living in my van since then. Although I just bought a casita in Mexico. It's a different ending…

22   Television KRQE News, https://www.krqe.com/news/new-mexico/santa-fe-county-woman-claims-neighbors-dogs-are-threatening-neighborhood/
23   Newsweek, https://www.newsweek.com/new-mexico-neighborhood-has-gone-dogs-says-neighbor-1473663
24   Santa Fe Reporter, https://www.sfreporter.com/news/2019/09/11/the-wild-dog-road-situation/
25   On the Lack of Protection from the County, https://sarahleamy.com/2019/10/29/on-the-lack-of-protection-from-santa-fe-county/
26   https://www.change.org/p/santa-fe-county-animal-control-santa-fe-county-commissioners-justice-for-rosie-and-lulu-dealing-with-owners-of-problem-dogs
27   Benefits of EMDR, https://www.forbes.com/health/mind/what-is-emdr-therapy/
28   Medical Cannabis in NM, https://www.nmhealth.org/about/mcp/svcs/info/

Acknowledgments

Thanks to these anthologies and journals where some of this work was previously published:

- "As If" (*Hidden*, Finishing Line Press, 2020)

- "Blue for Pints" (*Passengers Journal* 2021/*Best Short Fiction Anthology*, 2022)

- "Eight Years" (*Los Angeles Review*, 2020)

- "An Immigrant in My Own Family" (*Immigrant Report*, 2020)

- "The Shower" (*Los Angeles Review*, 2020)

About the Author

Sarah Leamy is a gender-queer writer, editor, and publisher, currently based in New Mexico. Born in England, she has spent most of her life in the Southwest of the USA after exploring Europe in her early twenties and the States in her thirties. *Hidden*, a narrative prose poetry collection, came out in 2021 with Finishing Line Press, and in 2022, they published *G'dog*, a selection of fables. Her travel books, novels, and shorter hybrid work have been published in the States and England, most recently in *LARB*, *Ad Alta Literary*, *Dunes Review*, *Hunger Mountain*, *Santa Fe Project Quarterly*, *National Book Review Circle*, *Bunbury Magazine*, and was a finalist and honorable mention with *Glimmer Train* twice.

CPSIA information can be obtained
at www.ICGtesting.com
Printed in the USA
BVHW061808180423
662584BV00017B/198

9 781956 440430

QUESTIONS
ABOUT
JESUS CHRIST

QUESTIONS ABOUT
JESUS CHRIST

THE 100 MOST FREQUENTLY ASKED
QUESTIONS ABOUT JESUS CHRIST

S. MICHAEL HOUDMANN
GENERAL EDITOR

WESTBOW
PRESS
A DIVISION OF THOMAS NELSON

WestBow Press books may be ordered through booksellers or by contacting:

WestBow Press
A Division of Thomas Nelson
1663 Liberty Drive
Bloomington, IN 47403
www.westbowpress.com
1-(866) 928-1240

ISBN: 978-1-4497-9329-6 (sc)
ISBN: 978-1-4497-9328-9 (e)

Library of Congress Control Number: 2013907749

Printed in the United States of America.

WestBow Press rev. date: 06/12/2013

CONTENTS

Acknowledgements vii

Preface ix

Introduction—The Ultimate Question. xi

   1. Questions about Who Jesus Is. 1

   2. Questions about Jesus' Deity 29

   3. Questions about Jesus' Humanity 55

   4. Questions about Jesus' Birth and Life 63

   5. Questions about Jesus' Ministry 97

   6. Questions about Jesus' Crucifixion 119

   7. Questions about Jesus' Resurrection and Ascension. . .151

   8. Questions about Jesus in the Old Testament. 171

   9. Miscellaneous Questions about Jesus 179

Appendix—Statement of Faith. .195

Endnotes 201

Scripture Index. 205

ACKNOWLEDGEMENTS

THIS BOOK IS dedicated to the more than 500 individuals who have served as volunteer writers for Got Questions Ministries in the past ten years. Their hard work, commitment, and passion are what make this ministry possible.

Special thanks goes to Kevin Stone, Rebekah Largent, and Gwen Sellers, who contributed greatly to this volume in writing, editing, organizing, and indexing.

All the glory goes to God, "For from him and through him and to him are all things. To him be the glory forever! Amen." (Romans 11:36)

PREFACE

EVERY DAY, MORE and more people turn to the Internet to find answers to their questions about spiritual matters. Topics related to spirituality are the second-most searched subjects online. Sadly, websites that present false teachings far outnumber those that proclaim the truth of God's Word.

In February of 2002, www.gotquestions.org was launched to help fill this gap and meet the needs of millions of spiritually-minded Web surfers. Since our launch, we have personally answered over 340,000 questions that have been submitted to us. Tens of millions of people have found answers to their questions via our Frequently Asked Questions archives, giving us a unique understanding of what questions are truly on people's minds.

This volume is a collection of the most important and/or most frequently asked questions about Jesus Christ. Each question is answered directly from the Bible, if the Bible specifically addresses the particular issue. Where the Bible is silent on an issue, biblical principles are used to lead to a solid and correct understanding. The Lord Jesus Christ is our passion, and declaring His Word is our mission.

Mission Statement of Got Questions Ministries

Got Questions Ministries seeks to glorify the Lord Jesus Christ by providing biblical, applicable, and timely answers to spiritually-related questions.

INTRODUCTION— THE ULTIMATE QUESTION

Question: What does it mean that Jesus saves?

Answer: "Jesus saves" is a popular slogan on bumper stickers, signs at athletic events, and even banners being pulled across the sky by small airplanes. Sadly, few who see the phrase "Jesus saves" truly and fully understand what it means. There is a tremendous amount of truth packed into those two words.

Jesus saves, but who is Jesus?

Most people understand that Jesus was a man who lived in Israel approximately 2,000 years ago. Virtually every religion in the world views Jesus as a good teacher, a prophet, or a moralist. And while Jesus was most definitely all of those things, the descriptions do not capture the full picture of who Jesus is, nor do they explain how or why Jesus saves. Jesus is God in human form (John 1:1, 14). God became a human being in the person of Jesus in order to save us. That raises the next question:

Jesus saves, but why do we need to be saved?

The Bible declares that every human being who has ever lived has sinned (Ecclesiastes 7:20; Romans 3:23). To sin is to do something, in thought, word, or deed, that contradicts God's perfect and holy character. Because of our sin, we all deserve judgment from God (John 3:18, 36). God is perfectly just, so He cannot allow sin to go unpunished. Since God is infinite and eternal, and since all sin is ultimately against God (Psalm 51:4), only an infinite and eternal punishment is sufficient. Eternal death is the only just punishment for sin. That is why we need to be saved.

Jesus saves, but how does He save?

Because we have sinned against an infinite God, either a finite person (you) must pay for your sin for an infinite amount of time, or an infinite Person (Jesus) must pay for your sin one time. There is no other option. Jesus saves us by dying in our place. In the person of Jesus Christ, God sacrificed Himself on our behalf, paying the infinite and eternal penalty that only He could pay (2 Corinthians 5:21; 1 John 2:2). Jesus took the punishment that we deserve in order to save us from a horrible eternal destiny, the just consequence of our sin. Because of His great love for us, Jesus laid down His life (John 15:13), paying the penalty that we owed but could not pay. Jesus was then resurrected, demonstrating that His death was indeed sufficient to pay the penalty for our sins (1 Corinthians 15).

Jesus saves, but whom does He save?

Jesus saves all who will receive His gift of salvation. Jesus saves all those who fully trust in Him—in His death and resurrection—as the payment for sin (John 3:16; Acts 16:31). While Jesus' sacrifice was perfectly sufficient to pay for the sins of all humanity, Jesus only saves those who personally receive, by faith, His most precious gift (John 1:12).

If you now understand what it means that Jesus saves, and you want to trust in Him as your personal Savior, make sure you understand and believe the following. Then, as an act of faith, communicate with God:

"God, I know that I am a sinner, and I know that because of my sin I deserve to be eternally separated from you. Even though I do not deserve your love, thank you for loving me and providing the sacrifice for my sins through the death and resurrection of Jesus Christ. I believe that Jesus died for my sins and I trust in Him alone to save me. From this point forward, help me to live my life for you instead of for sin. Help me to live the rest of my life in gratitude for the wonderful salvation you have provided. Thank you, Jesus, for saving me!"

Have you made a decision to receive Jesus Christ as your Savior because of what you have read here? If so, please send us an email at questions@gotquestions.org.

Chapter 1

QUESTIONS ABOUT WHO JESUS IS

Contents

Who is Jesus Christ?

What is Christology?

Did Jesus really exist? Is there any historical evidence of Jesus Christ?

Is Jesus a myth? Is Jesus just a copy of the pagan gods of other ancient religions?

How is Jesus Christ unique?

How is Jesus different from other religious leaders?

What are the different names and titles of Jesus Christ?

Who was the real, historical Jesus?

What does it mean that Jesus Christ is the cornerstone?

What does it mean that Jesus is the "firstborn" over creation?

What does it mean that Jesus is King of kings and Lord of lords?

Question: Who is Jesus Christ?

Answer: Unlike the question "Does God exist?" very few people question whether Jesus Christ existed. It is generally accepted that Jesus was truly a man who walked on the earth in Israel 2,000 years ago. The debate begins when the subject of Jesus' identity is discussed. Almost every major religion teaches that Jesus was a prophet or a good teacher or a godly man. The problem is that the Bible tells us that Jesus was infinitely more than a prophet, a good teacher, or a godly man.

In his book *Mere Christianity* C. S. Lewis writes, "I am trying here to prevent anyone from saying the really foolish thing that people often say about Him [Jesus Christ]: 'I'm ready to accept Jesus as a great moral teacher, but I don't accept his claim to be God.' That is the one thing we must not say. A man who was merely a man and said the sort of things Jesus said would not be a great moral teacher. He would either be a lunatic—on a level with a man who says he is a poached egg—or else he would be the Devil of hell. You must make your choice. Either this man was, and is, the Son of God, or else a madman or something worse. You can shut him up for a fool, you can spit at him and kill him as a demon; or you can fall at his feet and call him Lord and God. But let us not come up with any patronizing nonsense about his being a great human teacher. He has not left that option open to us. He did not intend to."[1]

So, who did Jesus claim to be? Who does the Bible say He is? First, let's look at Jesus' words in John 10:30, "I and the Father are one." At first glance, this might not seem to be a claim of deity. However, the Jews' reaction was to attempt to stone Jesus "for blasphemy, because you, a mere man, claim to be God" (John 10:33). The Jews understood Jesus' statement as a claim to be God. Jesus does not retract His statement and never corrects the Jews by saying, "I did not claim to be God." This indicates Jesus truly meant to say He was God.

John 8:58 is another example: "'I tell you the truth,' Jesus answered, 'before Abraham was born, I am!'" Again, in response, the Jews took up stones in an attempt to stone Jesus (John 8:59). Jesus' use of "I am" is a direct application of the Old Testament name for God (Exodus 3:14). Again, those who heard Jesus' statement recognized He was claiming deity, and Jesus did not amend His words in the slightest.

John 1:1 says, "The Word was God." John 1:14 says, "The Word became flesh." These statements clearly indicate that Jesus is God in the flesh. Thomas the disciple declared to Jesus, "My Lord and my God" (John 20:28). Jesus does not correct him. The apostle Paul describes Jesus as "our great God and Savior" (Titus 2:13). The apostle Peter says the same in 2 Peter 1:1. God the Father is witness of Jesus' full identity as well: "But about the Son he says, 'Your throne, O God, will last forever and ever, and righteousness will be the scepter of your kingdom'" (Hebrews 1:8). Old Testament prophecies of Christ also announce His deity, "For to us a child is born, to us a son is given, and the government will be on his shoulders. And he will be called Wonderful Counselor, Mighty God, Everlasting Father, Prince of Peace" (Isaiah 9:6).

So, as C. S. Lewis argued, believing Jesus to be only a good teacher is not an option. Jesus undeniably claimed to be God. If He is not God, then He is a liar, and therefore not a prophet, good teacher, or godly man. Some modern "scholars" claim that the "historical Jesus" did not say many of the things the Bible attributes to Him. But who are we to argue with God's Word concerning what Jesus did or did not say? How can a "scholar" two thousand years removed from Jesus have better insight into what Jesus did or did not say than the eyewitnesses who lived with, served with, and were taught by Jesus Himself (John 14:26)?

Why is the question of Jesus' true identity so important? Why does it matter whether or not Jesus is God? Most importantly, Jesus has to be God because, if He is not God, His death would not have been sufficient to pay the penalty for the sins of the whole world (1 John 2:2). Only God could pay such an infinite penalty (Romans 5:8; 2 Corinthians 5:21). Jesus had to be God in order to pay our debt, and He had to be a man in order to die. Salvation is available only through faith in Jesus Christ. Jesus' deity is why He proclaimed, "I am the way and the truth and the life. No one comes to the Father except through me" (John 14:6).

Question: What is Christology?

Answer: The word *Christology* comes from two Greek words meaning "Christ/Messiah" and "word"—which combine to mean "the study of Christ." Christology is the study of the Person and work of Jesus Christ. There are numerous important questions that Christology answers.

Who is Jesus Christ?

Almost every major religion teaches that Jesus was a prophet or a good teacher or a godly man. But the Bible tells us that Jesus was infinitely more than a prophet, good teacher, or godly man.

Is Jesus God? Did Jesus ever claim to be God?

Although Jesus never uttered the exact words, "I am God," He made many other statements that can't be properly interpreted to mean anything else.

What is the hypostatic union? How can Jesus be both God and man at the same time?

The Bible teaches that Jesus is both fully human and fully divine, that there is no mixture or dilution of either nature, and that He is one united Person, forever.

Why is the virgin birth so important?

The virgin birth is a crucial biblical doctrine because it accounts for the circumvention of the transmission of the sin nature and allowed the eternal God to become a perfect man.

What does it mean that Jesus is the Son of God?

Jesus is not God's Son in the sense of how we think of a father/son relationship. God did not get married and have a son. Jesus is God's Son in the sense that He is God made manifest in human form (John 1:1, 14).

A biblical understanding of Jesus Christ is crucial to our salvation. Many cults and world religions claim to believe in Jesus Christ. The problem is that they do not believe in the Jesus Christ presented in the Bible. That is why Christology is so important. It helps us to understand the significance of the deity of Christ. It demonstrates why Jesus is the atoning sacrifice for our sins. Christology teaches us that Jesus had to be man so that He could die, but also had to be God so that His death would pay for our sins. It is perhaps the most important area of theology. Without a proper understanding of who Jesus Christ is and what He accomplished, all other areas of theology will be errant as well.

An in-depth study of Christology has incredible personal impact on the believer's daily life. As we delve into the heart of Jesus, we begin to grasp the amazing concept that He, being fully Man and fully God, loves each of us with a never-ending love—the extent of which is hard for us to imagine. The various titles and names of Christ in the Scriptures give insight into who He is and how He relates to us. He is our Good Shepherd, leading, protecting, and caring for us as His own (John 10:11, 14); He is the Light of the world, illuminating our pathway through a sometimes dark and uncertain world (John 8:12); He is the Prince of Peace (Isaiah 9:6), bringing tranquility into our tumultuous lives; and He is our Rock (1 Corinthians 10:4), the immovable base whom we can trust to keep us safe and secure.

Question: Did Jesus really exist? Is there any historical evidence of Jesus Christ?

Answer: Typically, the person asking this question qualifies it with "outside of the Bible." We do not grant this idea that the Bible cannot be considered a source of evidence for the existence of Jesus. The New Testament contains hundreds of references to Jesus Christ. There are those who date the writing of the Gospels to the second century AD, more than 100 years after Jesus' death. Even if this were the case (which we strongly dispute), in terms of ancient evidences, writings less than 200 years after events took place are considered very reliable. Further, the vast majority of scholars (Christian and non-Christian) will grant that the Epistles of Paul (at least some of them) were in fact written by Paul in the middle of the first century AD, less than 40 years after Jesus' death. In terms of ancient manuscript evidence, this is extraordinarily strong proof of the existence of a man named Jesus in Israel in the early first century AD.

It is also important to recognize that in AD 70, the Romans invaded and destroyed Jerusalem and most of Israel, slaughtering its inhabitants. Entire cities were literally burned to the ground. We should not be surprised, then, if much evidence of Jesus' existence was destroyed. Many of the eyewitnesses of Jesus would have been killed. These facts likely limited the amount of surviving eyewitness testimonies of Jesus.

Considering that Jesus' ministry was confined to a relatively unimportant area in a small corner of the Roman Empire, a surprising amount of information about Jesus can be drawn from secular historical sources. Some of the more important historical evidences of Jesus include the following.

The first-century Roman Cornelius Tacitus, who is considered one of the more accurate historians of the ancient world, mentioned superstitious "Christians" (from *Christus*, which is Latin for "Christ"), who suffered under Pontius Pilate during the reign of Tiberius.[2] Suetonius, chief secretary to Emperor Hadrian, wrote that there was a man named Chrestus (or Christ) who lived during the first century.[3]

Flavius Josephus is the most famous Jewish historian. In his *Antiquities of the Jews* he refers to James, "the brother of Jesus, who was called Christ." There is a controversial verse (18:3) that says, "Now there was about this time Jesus, a wise man, if it be lawful to call him a man. For he was one who wrought surprising feats...He was [the] Christ...he appeared to them alive again the third day, as the divine prophets had foretold these and ten thousand other wonderful things concerning him." One version reads, "At this time there was a wise man named

6

Jesus. His conduct was good and [he] was known to be virtuous. And many people from among the Jews and the other nations became his disciples. Pilate condemned him to be crucified and to die. But those who became his disciples did not abandon his discipleship. They reported that he had appeared to them three days after his crucifixion, and that he was alive; accordingly he was perhaps the Messiah, concerning whom the prophets have recounted wonders."[4]

Julius Africanus quotes the historian Thallus in a discussion of the darkness that followed the crucifixion of Christ.[5]

Pliny the Younger recorded early Christian worship practices, including the fact that Christians worshipped Jesus as God and were very ethical, and he includes a reference to the love feast and Lord's Supper.[6]

The Babylonian Talmud (Sanhedrin 43a) confirms Jesus' crucifixion on the eve of Passover and the accusations against Christ of practicing sorcery and encouraging Jewish apostasy.[7]

Lucian Samosata was a second-century Greek writer who admits that Jesus was worshipped by Christians, introduced new teachings, and was crucified for them. He said that Jesus' teachings included the brotherhood of believers, the importance of conversion, and the importance of denying other gods. Christians lived according to Jesus' laws, believed themselves to be immortal, and were characterized by contempt for death, voluntary self-devotion, and renunciation of material goods.[8]

Then we have all the Gnostic writings (The Gospel of Truth, The Apocryphon of John, The Gospel of Thomas, The Treatise on Resurrection, etc.) that all mention Jesus.

There is overwhelming evidence for the existence of Jesus Christ, both in secular and biblical history. Perhaps the greatest evidence that Jesus did exist is the fact that literally thousands of Christians in the first century AD, including the 12 apostles, were willing to give their lives as martyrs for Jesus Christ. People will die for what they believe to be true, but no one will die for what they know to be a lie.

Question: Is Jesus a myth? Is Jesus just a copy of the pagan gods of other ancient religions?

Answer: There are a number of people claiming that the accounts of Jesus as recorded in the New Testament are simply myths borrowed from pagan folklore, such as the stories of Osiris, Dionysus, Adonis, Attis, and Mithras. The claim is that these myths are essentially the same story as the New Testament's narrative of Jesus Christ of Nazareth. As Dan Brown phrases it in *The Da Vinci Code*, "Nothing in Christianity is original."[9]

To discover the truth about the claim that the Gospel writers borrowed from mythology, it is important to 1) unearth the history behind the assertions, 2) examine the actual portrayals of the false gods being compared to Christ, 3) expose any logical fallacies being made, and 4) look at why the New Testament Gospels are trustworthy depictions of the true and historical Jesus Christ.

The claim that Jesus was a myth or an exaggeration originated in the writings of liberal German theologians in the nineteenth century. They essentially said that Jesus was nothing more than a copy of popular dying-and-rising fertility gods in various places—Tammuz in Mesopotamia, Adonis in Syria, Attis in Asia Minor, and Horus in Egypt. Of note is the fact that none of the books containing these theories were taken seriously by the academics of the day. The assertion that Jesus was a recycled Tammuz, for example, was investigated by contemporary scholars and determined to be completely baseless. It has only been recently that these assertions have been resurrected, primarily due to the rise of the Internet and the mass distribution of information from unaccountable sources.

This leads us to the next area of investigation—do the mythological gods of antiquity really mirror the person of Jesus Christ? As an example, the *Zeitgeist* movie makes these claims about the Egyptian god Horus:

1. He was born on December 25 of a virgin: Isis Mary
2. A star in the East proclaimed his arrival
3. Three kings came to adore the newborn "savior"

4. He became a child prodigy teacher at age 12
5. At age 30 he was "baptized" and began a "ministry"
6. Horus had 12 "disciples"
7. Horus was betrayed
8. He was crucified
9. He was buried for three days
10. He was resurrected after three days

However, when the actual writings about Horus are competently examined, this is what we find:

1. Horus was born to Isis; there is no mention in history of her being called "Mary." Moreover, "Mary" is our Anglicized form of Jesus' birth mother's real name, Miryam or Miriam. "Mary" was not even used in the original texts of Scripture.
2. Isis was not a virgin; she was the widow of Osiris and conceived Horus with Osiris.
3. Horus was born during the month of Khoiak (Oct/Nov), not December 25. Further, there is no mention in the Bible as to Christ's actual birth date.
4. There is no record of three kings visiting Horus at his birth. The Bible never states the actual number of magi that came to see Christ. Further, the visit of the Magi likely occurred up to two years after His birth.
5. Horus is not a "savior" in any way; he did not die for anyone.
6. There are no accounts of Horus being a teacher at the age of 12.
7. Horus was not "baptized." The only account of Horus that involves water is one story where Horus is torn to pieces, with Isis requesting the crocodile god to fish him out of the water.
8. Horus did not have a "ministry."
9. Horus did not have 12 disciples. According to the Horus accounts, Horus had four demigods that followed him,

and there are some indications of 16 human followers and an unknown number of blacksmiths that went into battle with him.

10. There is no account of Horus being betrayed by a friend.
11. Horus did not die by crucifixion. There are various accounts of Horus' death, but none of them involve crucifixion.
12. There is no account of Horus being buried for three days.
13. Horus was not resurrected. There is no account of Horus coming out of the grave with the body he went in with. Some accounts have Horus/Osiris being brought back to life by Isis and then becoming the lord of the underworld.

When compared side by side, Jesus and Horus bear little, if any, resemblance to one another.

Jesus is also compared to Mithras by those claiming that Jesus Christ is a myth. All the above descriptions of Horus are applied to Mithras (e.g., born of a virgin, being crucified, rising in three days, etc.). But what does the Mithras myth actually say?

1. He was born out of a solid rock, not from any woman.
2. He battled first with the sun and then with a primeval bull, thought to be the first act of creation. Mithras killed the bull, which then became the ground of life for the human race.
3. Mithras's birth was celebrated on December 25, along with winter solstice.
4. There is no mention of his being a great teacher.
5. There is no mention of Mithras having 12 disciples. The idea that Mithras had 12 disciples may have come from a mural in which Mithras is surrounded by the 12 signs of the zodiac.
6. Mithras had no bodily resurrection. Rather, when Mithras completed his earthly mission, he was taken to paradise in a chariot, alive and well. The early Christian writer Tertullian did write about Mithraic cultists re-enacting

resurrection scenes, but this occurred well after New Testament times, so if any copycatting was done, it was Mithraism copying Christianity.

More examples can be given of Krishna, Attis, Dionysus, and other mythological gods, but the result is the same. In the end, the historical Jesus portrayed in the Bible is unique. The alleged similarities of Jesus' story to pagan myths are greatly exaggerated. Further, while tales of Horus, Mithras, and others pre-date Christianity, there is very little historical record of the *pre-Christian* beliefs of those religions. The vast majority of the earliest writings of these religions date from the third and fourth centuries AD. To assume that the *pre*-Christian beliefs of these religions (of which there is no record) were identical to their *post*-Christian beliefs is naive. It is more logical to attribute any similarities between these religions and Christianity to the religions' copying Christian teaching about Jesus.

This leads us to the next area to examine: the logical fallacies committed by those claiming that Christianity borrowed from pagan mystery religions. We'll consider two fallacies in particular: the fallacy of the false cause and the terminological fallacy.

If one thing precedes another, some conclude that the first thing must have caused the second. This is the fallacy of the false cause. A rooster may crow before the sunrise every morning, but that does not mean the rooster *causes* the sun to rise. Even if pre-Christian accounts of mythological gods closely resembled Christ (and they do not), it does not mean they caused the Gospel writers to invent a false Jesus. Making such a claim is akin to saying the TV series *Star Trek* caused the NASA Space Shuttle program.

The terminological fallacy occurs when words are redefined to prove a point. For example, the *Zeitgeist* movie says that Horus "began his ministry," but the word *ministry* is being redefined. Horus had no actual "ministry"—nothing like that of Christ's ministry. Those claiming a link between Mithras and Jesus talk about the "baptism" that initiated prospects into the Mithras cult, but what was it actually? Mithraic priests would place initiates

11

into a pit, suspend a bull over the pit, and slit the bull's stomach, covering the initiates in blood and gore. Such a practice bears no resemblance whatsoever to Christian baptism—a person going under water (symbolizing the death of Christ) and then coming back out of the water (symbolizing Christ's resurrection). But advocates of a mythological Jesus deceptively use the same term, "baptism," to describe both rites in hopes of linking the two.

This brings us to the subject of the truthfulness of the New Testament. No other work of antiquity has more evidence as to its historical veracity than the New Testament. The New Testament has more writers (nine), better writers, and earlier writers than any other document from that era. Further, history testifies that these writers went to their deaths claiming that Jesus had risen from the dead. While some may die for a lie they think is true, no person dies for a lie they know to be false. Think about it—if someone was about to crucify you upside down, as happened to the apostle Peter, and all you had to do to save your life was renounce a lie you had knowingly told, what would you do?

In addition, history has shown that it takes at least two generations to pass before myth can enter a historical account. That's because, as long as there are eyewitnesses to an event, errors can be refuted and mythical embellishments can be exposed. All the Gospels of the New Testament were written during the lifetime of the eyewitnesses, with some of Paul's Epistles being written as early as AD 50. Paul directly appeals to contemporary eyewitnesses to verify his testimony (1 Corinthians 15:6).

The New Testament attests to the fact that, in the first century, Jesus was not mistaken for any other god. When Paul preached in Athens, the elite thinkers of that city said, "'He seems to be a proclaimer of strange deities,'—because he was preaching Jesus and the resurrection. And they took him and brought him to the Areopagus, saying, 'May we know what this new teaching is which you are proclaiming? For you are bringing some strange things to our ears; so we want to know what these things mean'" (Acts 17:18–20, NASB). Clearly, if Paul were simply rehashing stories of other gods, the Athenians would not have referred to his doctrine as a "new" and "strange" teaching. If dying-and-rising gods were plentiful in the first century, why, when the apostle Paul preached Jesus rising from the dead, did the Epicureans and Stoics not remark, "Ah, just like Horus and Mithras"?

In conclusion, the claim that Jesus is a copy of mythological gods originated with authors whose works have been discounted by academia, contain logical fallacies, and cannot compare to the New Testament Gospels, which have withstood nearly 2,000 years of intense scrutiny. The alleged parallels between Jesus and other gods disappear when the original myths are examined. The Jesus-is-a-myth theory relies on selective descriptions, redefined words, and false assumptions.

Jesus Christ is unique in history, with His voice rising above all false gods' as He asks the question that ultimately determines a person's eternal destiny: "Who do you say I am?" (Matthew 16:15).

Question: How is Jesus Christ unique?

Answer:
1. He is the only Son of God (Psalm 2:7; John 1:14; Luke 1:35).
2. He is eternal. He existed from eternity past, He exists in the present, and He will exist for all eternity in the future (John 1:1–3; John 8:58; Revelation 1:8).
3. Jesus alone is the One who bore our sins so that we could have forgiveness and be saved from them (Isaiah 53; Matthew 1:21; John 1:29; 1 Peter 2:24; 1 Corinthians 15:1–3).
4. Jesus is the only way to the Father (John 14:6; Acts 4:12; 1 Timothy 2:5); there is no other way to salvation. He is the only righteous One who exchanged that perfect righteousness for our sin (2 Corinthians 5:21).
5. Jesus alone had power over His own death and the ability to take back His life (John 2:19; 10:17–18). Note: His resurrection was not a "spiritual" one, but physical (Luke 24:39). His resurrection from the dead distinguished Him as the unique Son of God (Romans 1:4).

6. Jesus alone accepted worship as an equal with the Father (John 20:28–29; Matthew 28:9–10), and indeed, God the Father states that the Son is to be honored as He is honored (John 5:23). All others rightly reject that worship, whether they are Jesus' disciples or angelic beings (Acts 10:25–26; Acts 14:14–15; Matthew 4:10; Revelation 19:10; 22:9).

7. Jesus has the power to give life to whom He will (John 5:21).

8. The Father has committed all judgment to Jesus (John 5:22).

9. Jesus was with the Father and directly involved in creation, and it is by His hand that all things are held together (John 1:1–3; Hebrews 1:8–10; Colossians 1:17).

10. It is Jesus who will rule the world at the end of this present age (Hebrews 1:8; Isaiah 9:6–7; Daniel 2:44; Revelation 19:11–16).

11. Jesus alone was born of a virgin, conceived by the Holy Spirit (Isaiah 7:14; Matthew 1:20–23; Luke 1:30–35).

12. It is Jesus who demonstrated that He had the attributes of God [e.g., the power to forgive sins and heal the sick (Matthew 9:1–7); to calm the wind and waves (Mark 4:37–41; Psalm 89:8–9); to know us, being perfectly acquainted with us (Psalm 139; John 1:46–50; 2:23–25); to raise the dead (John 11; Luke 7:12–15; 8:41–55); etc.].

13. There are a great number of prophecies concerning the Messiah's birth, life, resurrection, person, and purpose. All were fulfilled by Jesus and no other (Isaiah 7:14; Micah 5:2; Psalm 22; Zechariah 11:12–13; 13:7; Isaiah 9:6–7; Isaiah 53; Psalm 16:10).

Question: How is Jesus different from other religious leaders?

Answer: In a sense, asking this question is similar to asking how the sun differs from other stars in our solar system—the point being that there are no other stars in our solar system!

There is no other "religious leader" who even compares to Jesus Christ. Every other religious leader is either alive or dead. Jesus Christ is the only one who was dead (He died in our place, for our sins) and is now alive (1 Corinthians 15:1–8). Indeed, He proclaims in Revelation 1:17–18 that He is alive forevermore! No other religious leader dares make such a claim, since it is either true or utterly preposterous.

Another important difference is found in the very nature of Christianity. The essence of Christianity is Christ—crucified, resurrected, ascended into heaven, returning someday. Without Him—and without His resurrection—there is no Christianity. Compare that with other major religions. Hinduism, for example, can stand or fall apart entirely from any of the "great Swamis" who founded it. Buddhism is the same story. Even Islam is based upon the sayings and teachings of Mohammed, not upon the claim that he came back to life from the dead.

In 1 Corinthians 15:13–19, the apostle Paul says that if Christ was not raised from the dead, then our faith is empty and we are still in our sins. What he is saying is that the truth claims of Christianity are based simply and solely upon the resurrected Christ. If He did not come back from the dead, then there is no truth to Christianity whatsoever. Over and over again throughout the New Testament, the apostles and evangelists base the truth of the gospel on the Resurrection.

One other significant point is the exceedingly important fact that Jesus Christ claimed to be the Son of God (a Hebraism meaning "characterized by God") as well as the Son of Man ("characterized by man"). In many passages, Jesus makes claims to be equal with the Father (see, for example, John 10:29–30). To Him are ascribed all of the prerogatives and attributes of deity. Yet He was also a man, born of a virgin (Matthew 1:18–25; Luke 1:26–38). Having lived a sinless life, He was crucified in order to pay for the sins of all men: "He is the atoning sacrifice for our sins, and not only for ours but also for the sins of the whole world" (1 John 2:2). He was then resurrected from the dead three days later. He is fully God and fully man; yet He is one person.

The very Person and work of Christ pose for us a question that we cannot avoid: What will we do with Jesus? We cannot simply dismiss Him. We cannot ignore Him. He is the central figure in all of human history, and if He died for the sins of the whole world, then He died for yours as well. The apostle Peter tells us in Acts 4:12, "Salvation is found in no one else, for there is no other name under heaven given to men by which we must be saved." If we believe on the Lord Jesus Christ as our Savior from sin, we will be saved (Acts 16:31).

Question: What are the different names and titles of Jesus Christ?

Answer: There are at least 200 names and titles of Christ found in the Bible. The following are some of the more prominent ones, organized in three sections relating to names that reflect the nature of Christ, His position in the tri-unity of God, and His work on earth on our behalf.

The Nature of Christ

Chief Cornerstone: (Ephesians 2:20)—Jesus is the cornerstone of the building that is His church. He cements together Jew and Gentile, male and female—all saints from all ages—and places them into one structure built on Him through faith.

Firstborn over All Creation: (Colossians 1:15)—Not the first thing God created, as some incorrectly claim; Colossians 1:16 says all things were created through and for Christ. The "firstborn," in both Jewish and Greek cultures, was one who had the right to an inheritance. Therefore, Christ possesses the rank and pre-eminence of the "firstborn" over everything, and He occupies the most exalted position in the universe. He is at the head of all things.

Head of the Church: (Ephesians 1:22; 4:15; 5:23)—Jesus Christ, not a king or a Pope, is the only supreme, sovereign ruler of the church, which is comprised of those for whom He died and who have placed their faith in Him alone for salvation.

Holy One: (Acts 3:14; Psalm 16:10)—Christ is holy, both in His divine and human natures, and is the fountain of holiness to His people. By His death we are made holy and pure before God.

Judge: (Acts 10:42; 2 Timothy 4:8)—God appointed the Lord Jesus to judge the world and to dispense the rewards of eternity.

King of Kings and Lord of Lords: (1 Timothy 6:15; Revelation 19:16)—Jesus has dominion over all authority on the earth, and none can prevent Him from accomplishing His purposes. He directs them as He pleases.

Light of the World: (John 8:12)—Jesus came into a world darkened by sin and shed the light of life and truth through His work and His words. He opens the eyes of those who trust in Him so they can walk in the light.

Prince of Peace: (Isaiah 9:6)—Jesus came to bring peace between God and man, who was separated from God by sin. Jesus died to reconcile sinners to a holy God.

Son of God: (Luke 1:35; John 1:49)—Jesus is the "only begotten of the Father" (John 1:14, NASB). "Son of God" affirms the deity of Christ and is used 42 times in the New Testament.

Son of Man: (John 5:27)—This title affirms the humanity of Christ, which exists alongside His divinity.

Word: (John 1:1)—The Word is the second Person of the triune God, who said it and it was done, who spoke all things out of nothing in the first creation, who was in the beginning with God the Father and the Holy Spirit, who was God, and by whom all things were created.

Word of Life: (1 John 1:1)—Jesus not only spoke words that lead to eternal life, but He is the very word of life. This title refers to the eternal life of joy and fulfillment that He provides.

His Position in the Trinity

Alpha and Omega: (Revelation 1:8; 22:13)—Jesus declared Himself to be the beginning and end of all things, a statement of eternality that applies only to God.

I Am: (John 8:58, with Exodus 3:14)—When Jesus ascribed this title to Himself, the Jews tried to stone Him for blasphemy.

They understood that He was declaring Himself to be the eternal God, the unchanging Jehovah of the Old Testament.

Immanuel: (Matthew 1:23)—Literally, "God with us." Both Isaiah and Matthew affirm that the Christ who would be born in Bethlehem would be God Himself, who came to earth in the form of a man to live among His people.

Lord of All: (Acts 10:36)—Jesus is the sovereign ruler over the whole world and everything in it—creation and all the nations of the world, and particularly of the people of God's choosing, both Jew and Gentile.

True God: (1 John 5:20)—This is a direct assertion that Jesus, the true God, is not simply divine; He is *the* Divine. Since the Bible teaches there is only one God, this can only mean Jesus is one Person of the triune God.

His Work on Earth

Author and Perfecter of our Faith: (Hebrews 12:2)—Every aspect of our salvation is a gift from God (Ephesians 2:8–9). Jesus is the founder of our faith, and the finisher of it as well. From first to last, He is the source and sustainer of the faith that saves us.

Bread of Life: (John 6:35; 6:48)—Just as bread sustains life in the physical sense, Jesus is the Bread that gives and sustains eternal life. God provided manna in the wilderness to feed His people, and He provided Jesus to give us eternal life through His body, broken for us.

Bridegroom: (Matthew 9:15)—The picture of Christ as the bridegroom and the church as His bride reveals the special relationship we have with Him. We are bound to each other in a covenant of grace that cannot be broken.

Deliverer: (Romans 11:26)—Just as the Israelites needed God to deliver them from bondage to Egypt, so we need Christ to be our Deliverer from bondage to sin.

Good Shepherd: (John 10:11, 14)—A good shepherd is willing to risk his own life to protect his sheep from predators. Jesus laid down His life for His sheep, and He cares for and nurtures and feeds us.

High Priest: (Hebrews 2:17)—The Jewish high priest entered the temple once a year to make atonement for the sins of the people. The Lord Jesus performed that function for His people once for all at the cross.

Lamb of God: (John 1:29)—God's Law called for the sacrifice of a spotless, unblemished lamb as an atonement for sin. Jesus fulfilled the type and became the Lamb led meekly to the slaughter, showing His patience in His sufferings and His readiness to become the perfect sacrifice.

Mediator: (1 Timothy 2:5)—A mediator is one who goes between two parties to reconcile them. Christ is the one and only Mediator who reconciles men and God. Praying to Mary or the saints is idolatry because it bypasses Christ and ascribes the role of mediator to another.

Rock: (1 Corinthians 10:4)—Just as life-giving water flowed from the rock Moses struck in the wilderness, Jesus is the Rock from whom flow the living waters of eternal life. He is the Rock upon whom we build our spiritual house, and no storm can shake us there.

Resurrection and Life: (John 11:25)—Jesus has life in Himself, and He is the means to resurrect forgiven sinners to eternal life. He proved His right to this title by raising Lazarus and by His own resurrection from the grave. Our sin is buried with Him, and we are resurrected to walk in newness of life.

Savior: (Matthew 1:21; Luke 2:11)—Jesus saved His people by dying to redeem them and by giving the Holy Spirit to renew them. He enables believers to overcome their spiritual enemies, sustains them in trials and in death, and will raise them up at the last day.

True Vine: (John 15:1)—The True Vine supplies all that the branches (believers) need to produce the fruit of the Spirit. His supply includes the living water of salvation and nourishment from the Word.

The Way, the Truth, and the Life: (John 14:6)—Jesus is the only path to God, the only Truth in a world of lies, and the only source of eternal life. No one comes to the Father except through Him.

Question: Who was the real, historical Jesus?

Answer: Without a doubt, one of the most frequently asked questions is "Who was Jesus?" Jesus has, by far, the highest name recognition throughout the world. Fully one third of our world's population—about 2.5 billion people—call themselves Christians. Islam, which comprises about 1.5 billion people, recognizes Jesus as the second greatest prophet after Mohammed. Of the remaining 3.2 billion people (roughly half the world's population), most have at least heard of the name of Jesus.

If one were to put together a summary of the life of Jesus from His birth to His death, it would be somewhat sparse. He was born of Jewish parents in Bethlehem, a small town south of Jerusalem, while the territory was under Roman occupation. His parents moved north to Nazareth, where He grew up; hence, He was commonly known as "Jesus of Nazareth." His father was a carpenter, so Jesus likely learned that trade in His early years. Around thirty years of age, He began a public ministry. He chose a dozen men of dubious reputation as His disciples and worked out of Capernaum, a large fishing village and trading center on the coast of the Sea of Galilee. From there He traveled and preached throughout the region of Galilee, often moving among neighboring Gentiles and Samaritans with intermittent journeys to Jerusalem.

Jesus' unusual teachings and methodology startled and troubled many. His revolutionary message, coupled with astonishing miracles, garnered a huge following. His popularity among the people grew rapidly, and the well-entrenched leaders of the Jewish faith quickly noticed. Soon, these Jewish leaders became jealous and resentful of Jesus' success. Many of these leaders found His teachings offensive and felt that their established religious traditions and ceremonies were being jeopardized. They soon plotted with the Roman rulers to have Him killed. It was during this time that one of Jesus' disciples betrayed Him to the Jewish leaders for a paltry sum of money. Shortly thereafter, the leaders arrested Jesus, engineered a hastily arranged series of mock trials, and made sure the Roman government crucified Him.

But, unlike any other person in history, Jesus' death was not the end of His story. Christianity exists only because of what happened after Jesus died. Three days after His death, His disciples and many others began to claim that He had returned to life. His grave was found empty, the body gone; and many different groups of people witnessed numerous appearances at different locations and involving dissimilar circumstances.

People began to proclaim that Jesus was the Christ, or the Messiah. They claimed His resurrection validated the message of forgiveness of sin through His sacrifice. At first, they declared this good news, known as the gospel, in Jerusalem, the same city where He was put to death. This new following soon became known as the Way (see Acts 9:2; Acts 19:9; Acts 19:23; Acts 24:22), and it expanded rapidly. In a short period of time, this gospel message spread beyond the region, expanding as far as Rome and to the outermost reaches of its vast empire.

Dr. James Allan Francis aptly described the influence of Jesus through the history of mankind:

"Here is a man who was born in an obscure village, the child of a peasant woman. He grew up in another village. He worked in a carpenter shop until He was thirty. Then for three years He was an itinerant preacher.

"He never owned a home. He never wrote a book. He never held an office. He never had a family. He never went to college. He never put His foot inside a big city. He never traveled two hundred miles from the place He was born. He never did one of the things that usually accompany greatness. He had no credentials but Himself...

"While still a young man, the tide of popular opinion turned against Him. His friends ran away. One of them denied Him. He was turned over to His enemies. He went through the mockery of a trial. He was nailed upon a cross between two thieves. While He was dying His executioners gambled for the only piece of property He had on earth—His coat. When He was dead, He was laid in a borrowed grave through the pity of a friend.

21

"Nineteen long centuries have come and gone, and today He is a centerpiece of the human race and leader of the column of progress.

"I am far within the Mark when I say that all the armies that ever marched, all the navies that were ever built; all the parliaments that ever sat and all the kings that ever reigned, put together, have not affected the life of man upon this earth as powerfully as has that one solitary life."[10]

George Buttrick, recognized as one of the ten greatest preachers of the twentieth century, wrote, "Jesus gave history a new beginning. In every land he is at home...His birthday is kept across the world. His death-day set a gallows against every skyline."[11]

Even Napoleon himself admitted, "I know men and I tell you that Jesus Christ was no mere man: between him and whoever else in the world there is no possible term of comparison."

Question: What does it mean that Jesus Christ is the cornerstone?

Answer: In ancient building practices, the cornerstone was the principal stone placed at the corner of the edifice. The cornerstone was usually one of the largest, most solid, and most carefully constructed of any in the structure. Jesus describes Himself as the cornerstone that His church would be built upon—a unified body of believers, both Jew and Gentile (Mark 12:10).

The Book of Isaiah has many references to Jesus, the Messiah. In several places He is referred to as "the cornerstone," such as in Isaiah 28:16–17a: "So this is what the sovereign LORD says: 'See, I lay a stone in Zion, a tested stone, a precious cornerstone for a sure foundation; the one who trusts will never be dismayed. I will make justice the measuring line and righteousness the plumb line.'" God is speaking to scoffers and boasters when He refers to the cornerstone—His precious Son—who provides the firm foundation for their lives, if they would but trust in Him. In keeping with the reference to a cornerstone, Isaiah uses other construction terminology (measuring line and plumb line) to make his point.

The cornerstone metaphor continues in the New Testament. Isaiah's words are quoted in 1 Peter 2:6 and applied specifically to Jesus. In Ephesians 2:19–21, the comparison is made again between Jesus and a cornerstone: "Consequently, you are no longer foreigners and aliens, but fellow citizens with God's people and members of God's household, built on the foundation of the apostles and prophets, with Christ Jesus himself as the chief cornerstone. In him the whole building is joined together and rises to become a holy temple in the Lord."

What a marvelous book is the God-inspired Bible! Peter uses construction terms for his readers, just as Isaiah did. They both use "cornerstone" to represent the Messiah, whom Peter knew personally and whom Isaiah only knew through the heavenly Father's promise. Their words bear out what Jesus said in the Gospel of John: "I am the way and the truth and the life. No one comes to the Father except through me" (John 14:6).

Question: What does it mean that Jesus is the "firstborn" over creation?

Answer: In a letter to the church at Colossae, the apostle Paul gave an intriguing description of Jesus as the firstborn of creation. Some have claimed that Paul means that Jesus was created—not eternal, not God. Such a doctrine, however, conflicts with the rest of the Bible. Christ could not be both Creator and created, and John 1 clearly names Him Creator. Let's take a careful look at the passage where Jesus is called the firstborn.

Colossians 1:15–20

"He is the image of the invisible God, the firstborn over all creation. For by him all things were created: things in heaven and on earth, visible and invisible, whether thrones or powers or rulers or authorities; all things were created by him and for him. He is before all things, and in him all things hold together. And he is the head of the body, the church; he is the beginning and the firstborn from among the dead, so that in everything he might have the supremacy. For God was pleased to have all his fullness dwell in him, and through him to reconcile to himself all things, whether things on earth or things in heaven, by making peace through his blood, shed on the cross."

Jesus is God

First, Christ's relationship to His Father is described by the phrase "the image of the invisible God." The word *image*, meaning "copy or likeness," expresses Christ's deity. This word involves more than a resemblance or representation, however. Jesus *is* God! Although He took on human form, He has the exact nature of His Father (Hebrews 1:3).

The "Word" of John 1:1 is a divine Person, not a philosophical abstraction. In the incarnation, the invisible God became visible in Christ; deity was clothed with humanity (John 1:14). God is in Christ: visible, audible, approachable, knowable, and available. All that God is, Christ is.

Jesus is Lord of Creation

The description "firstborn of all creation" speaks of Christ's preexistence. He is not a creature, but the eternal Creator (John 1:10). God also redeemed the world through Christ (Hebrews 1:2–4).

Note that Jesus is called the "firstborn," not the "first-created." The word *firstborn* (Greek *prototokos*) signifies priority. In the culture of the ancient Near East, the firstborn was not necessarily the oldest child. "Firstborn" referred not to birth order but to rank. The firstborn possessed the inheritance and the right of leadership in a family.

Therefore, the phrase expresses Christ's sovereignty over creation. After resurrecting Jesus from the dead, God gave Him authority over the earth (Matthew 28:18). Jesus created the world, saved the world, and rules the world. He is the self-existent, acknowledged head of creation.

Finally, the phrase recognizes Him as the Messiah: "I will also appoint him my firstborn, the most exalted of the kings of the earth" (Psalm 89:27).

Six times the Lord Jesus is declared to be the firstborn of God (Romans 8:29; Colossians 1:15, 18; Hebrews 1:6; 12:23; Revelation 1:5). These passages declare the preexistence of Christ, His sovereignty, and the redemption that He offers.

Thus, the phrase "firstborn of all creation" proclaims Christ's preeminence. As the eternal Son of God, He created the universe and all of creation is His inheritance.

Question: What does it mean that Jesus is King of kings and Lord of lords?

Answer: The phrase "king of kings" is used in Scripture six times, three of which refer to the Lord Jesus (1 Timothy 6:15; Revelation 17:14; 19:16). The other three instances (Ezra 7:12; Ezekiel 26:7; Daniel 2:37) refer to either Artaxerxes or Nebuchadnezzar, kings who used the title to express their absolute sovereignty over their respective realms (Persia and Babylon). The phrase "Lord of lords" is used in Scripture five times, and only in reference to God (Deuteronomy 10:17; Psalm 136:3; 1 Timothy 6:15; Revelation 17:14; 19:16). When "King of kings" and "Lord of lords" are used together, it refers only to the Lord Jesus Christ.

Paul wraps up his first letter to Timothy by telling him to fight the good fight and keep his faith. He tells Timothy that he is to do this "until the appearing of our Lord Jesus Christ" (1 Timothy 6:14). Paul then calls Christ "the blessed and only Ruler, the King of kings and Lord of lords, who alone is immortal and who lives in unapproachable light, whom no one has seen or can see" (verses 15b–16). The title is used to indicate someone who has the power to exercise absolute dominion over all His realm. In the case of the Lord Jesus, the realm is the totality of creation. Paul emphasizes the singular nature of Christ's rule, calling Him the "only" Ruler, who is "alone" and "unapproachable." The rule of Jesus is unique and above that of all other rulers.

The other two uses of "King of kings and Lord of lords" refer to the final conquest and return of Jesus. In the end all other rulers will be conquered or abolished, and Christ alone will reign supreme as King and Lord of all creation. There is no power, no king, and no lord who can oppose Him and win. There are myriad references to this absolute rule of Jesus and His preeminence over other rulers throughout Scripture—some subtle, some overt. To mention just a few, Isaiah 40:23–24 says that the Lord brings "princes to naught" and makes earth's rulers "nothing." The mere breath of the Lord will "sweep them away like chaff." Daniel's vision of the son of man in Daniel 7:13–14 is of one whom he calls "the Ancient of Days," whose everlasting dominion is over all people, nations, and languages. In the New Testament, we get a better view of the One to whom these passages refer. The writer of Hebrews says of the Lord Jesus, "The Son is the radiance of God's glory and the exact representation of his being, sustaining all things by his powerful word" (Hebrews 1:3). The next verse speaks of Jesus being "much superior" to the angels. Clearly, His rule over creation is absolute.

Paul makes the point that Jesus' sovereign rule is derived from His sacrifice on the cross. In Philippians 2:5–11, he discusses Jesus' suffering for sinners and concludes that this is the reason that "God exalted him to the highest place and gave him the name that is above every name, that at the name of Jesus every knee should bow, in heaven and on earth and under the earth, and every tongue confess that Jesus Christ is Lord, to the glory of God the Father" (verses 9–11).

Finally, in the book of Revelation we see the kingship of Jesus made manifest. In chapter 5, the Lamb (Jesus) is the only one in all creation found worthy to open the scroll containing the judgments of God (verses 2–7). In chapter 11, voices in heaven proclaim that the kingdom of the world has become the kingdom of Christ, and that He will reign for all eternity (verse 15). In chapter 12, we read that Satan is thrown down to earth through the authority of Christ (verses 9–10). In Revelation 17:12–14, the Lamb conquers all those arrayed against Him, and John stresses that He conquers *because* He is King of kings and Lord of lords. Finally, in chapter 19, we see Christ's triumphant coming to strike the nations and tread the winepress of the wrath of God.

Jesus has the authority to do so because He is King of kings and Lord of lords (verses 11–16).

Fundamentally, the idea of Jesus as King of kings and Lord of lords means that there is no higher authority. His reign over all things is absolute and inviolable. God raised Him from the dead and placed Him over all things, "far above all rule and authority, power and dominion, and every title that can be given, not only in the present age but also in the one to come. And God placed all things under his feet and appointed him to be head over everything for the church, which is his body, the fullness of him who fills everything in every way" (Ephesians 1:21–23).

Chapter 2

. . . .

QUESTIONS ABOUT JESUS' DEITY

Contents

Is the deity of Christ biblical?

What are the strongest biblical arguments for the divinity of Christ?

Is Jesus God? Did Jesus ever claim to be God?

What is the hypostatic union? How can Jesus be both God and man at the same time?

What does it mean that Jesus is the Son of God?

What did Jesus mean when He said, "I am"?

What does it mean that Jesus is God's "only begotten son"?

What is the doctrine of eternal generation, and is it biblical?

What is the doctrine of eternal Sonship, and is it biblical?

If Jesus was God, why did He say, "No one is good but God alone"?

What does it mean that Jesus is the Alpha and the Omega?

Does the Bible support the pre-existence of Jesus?

What is the supremacy of Christ, and what are its implications?

29

Question: Is the deity of Christ biblical?

Answer: In addition to Jesus' specific claims about Himself (John 10:30), His disciples also acknowledged His deity. They claimed that Jesus had the authority to forgive sins—something only God can do, as it is God who is offended by sin (Acts 5:31; Psalm 130:4; Jeremiah 31:34). Thomas cried out to Jesus, "My Lord and my God!" (John 20:28). Paul calls Jesus "great God and Savior" (Titus 2:13) and points out that He is "in very nature God" (Philippians 2:5–8). God the Father says regarding Jesus, "Your throne, O God, will last forever and ever" (Hebrews 1:8). John states that "in the beginning was the Word [Jesus], and the Word was with God, and the Word was God" (John 1:1).

Jesus is also given titles that are unique to YHWH (the formal name of God) in the Old Testament. In the Old Testament, YHWH has the title of "Redeemer" (Psalm 130:7; Hosea 13:14); in the New Testament, Jesus is the One who redeems (Titus 2:14; Revelation 5:9). Jesus is called Immanuel—"God with us"—in Matthew 1:23. In Psalm 23, YHWH is the "Shepherd" who leads His sheep; Jesus is the Shepherd in John 10:11; 1 Peter 2:25; and Revelation 7:17. Other titles shared by YHWH and Jesus are "Rock" (Psalm 18:46; 1 Corinthians 10:4) and "Light" (Psalm 27:1; John 1:9).

In Zechariah 12:10, it is YHWH who says, "They will look on me, the one they have pierced," but the New Testament applies this to Jesus' crucifixion (John 19:37; Revelation 1:7). Paul interprets Isaiah 45:22–23 as applying to Jesus (Philippians 2:10–11). In Isaiah 6, the prophet sees YHWH on His throne, but in John 12:41, the apostle makes it abundantly clear that the Person Isaiah saw was Jesus Himself.

Further, Jesus' name is used alongside God's in prayer: "Grace and peace to you from God our Father and the Lord Jesus Christ" (Galatians 1:3; Ephesians 1:2). This prayer would be blasphemous if Christ were not deity. The name of Jesus is equated with God's in the command to baptize "in the name [singular] of the Father and of the Son and of the Holy Spirit" (Matthew 28:19; see also 2 Corinthians 13:14).

Actions that can be accomplished only by God are credited to Jesus. Jesus forgave sins (Matthew 9:2; Acts 5:31; 13:38), and He created and sustains the universe (John 1:2; Colossians 1:16–17). Jesus' deity becomes even clearer when one considers YHWH said He was alone during creation (Isaiah 44:24). Jesus is also said to be the one who will "judge the living and the dead" (2 Timothy 4:1). Further, Christ possesses attributes that only deity can have: eternality (John 8:58), omnipresence (Matthew 18:20; 28:20), omniscience (Matthew 16:21), and omnipotence (John 11:38–44).

Now, it is one thing to *claim* to be God or to fool someone into believing you are God, but it is something else entirely to *prove* it to be so. Christ offered many miracles as proof of His claim to deity. Just a few of Jesus' miracles include turning water to wine (John 2:7–9); walking on water (Matthew 14:25); multiplying physical objects (John 6:11); healing the blind (John 9:7), the lame (Mark 2:3–12), and the sick (Matthew 9:35; Mark 1:40–42); and even raising people from the dead (John 11:43–44; Luke 7:11–15; Mark 5:35–42). Moreover, Christ Himself rose from the dead. Nothing like the resurrection is seriously claimed by any other religion.

There are at least 12 historical facts about Jesus that even non-Christian critical scholars will admit:

1. Jesus died by crucifixion.
2. He was buried.
3. His death caused the disciples to despair and lose hope.
4. Jesus' tomb was discovered (or was claimed to be discovered) to be empty a few days later.
5. The disciples believed they experienced appearances of the risen Jesus.
6. After this, the disciples were transformed from doubters into bold believers.
7. This message was the center of preaching in the early Church.
8. This message was preached in Jerusalem.
9. As a result of this preaching, the Church was born and it grew.

10. Resurrection day, Sunday, replaced the Sabbath (Saturday) as the primary day of worship.
11. James, a skeptic, was converted when he also believed that he saw the resurrected Jesus.
12. Paul, an enemy of Christianity, was converted by an experience that he believed to be an appearance of the risen Jesus.

Even if someone were to object to this specific list, only a few of the facts are needed to establish the gospel: Jesus' death, burial, resurrection, and appearances (1 Corinthians 15:1–5). While there may be theories to explain away one or two of the above facts, only the resurrection accounts for them all. Critics admit that the disciples claimed they saw the risen Jesus. Neither lies nor hallucinations can transform people the way the resurrection did. First, what would the disciples have had to gain by lying? Christianity was not popular, and it certainly did not benefit the apostles monetarily. Second, liars do not make good martyrs. There is no better explanation than the resurrection for the disciples' willingness to die horrible deaths for their faith. Yes, many people die for lies that they think are true, but people do not die for what they know is untrue.

In conclusion, Christ claimed He was YHWH, that He was deity (not just "a god" but the one true God); His followers (Jews who would have eschewed idolatry) believed Him and referred to Him as God. Christ proved His claims to deity through miracles, including the world-altering resurrection. No other hypothesis can explain these facts. Yes, the deity of Christ is biblical.

Question: What are the strongest biblical arguments for the divinity of Christ?

Answer: It is hard to deny that the New Testament is full of references to the divinity of Christ. From the four canonical Gospels through the Book of Acts and the Pauline Epistles, Jesus is presented not only as the Messiah (or Christ), but also as God

Himself. The apostle Paul refers to the divinity of Christ when he calls Jesus our "great God and Savior" (Titus 2:13). He also says that Jesus existed "in the form of God" prior to His incarnation (Philippians 2:5–8, KJV). God the Father says regarding Jesus, "Your throne, O God, will last forever and ever" (Hebrews 1:8). Jesus is referred to as the Creator Himself (John 1:3; Colossians 1:16–17). Many other passages teach Christ's deity, such as Revelation 2:8, 1 Corinthians 10:4, and 1 Peter 5:4.

While these direct statements are sufficient to establish the biblical claim that Jesus is divine, a more indirect approach may prove more powerful. Jesus repeatedly identified Himself as Yahweh in some of the titles He applied to Himself and by assuming the Father's divine prerogatives. He was often doing and saying things that only God has a right to do and say. Some of these instances provide us with the strongest proof of Jesus' divine self-understanding.

In Mark 14, Jesus stands accused at His trial before the high priest, who asked him, "'Are you the Christ, the Son of the Blessed One?' 'I am,' said Jesus. 'And you will see the Son of Man sitting at the right hand of the Mighty One and coming on the clouds of heaven'" (Mark 14:61–62). The high priest immediately charged Jesus with blasphemy; he understood that Jesus was harking back to the book of Daniel, which states, "There before me was one like a son of man, coming with the clouds of heaven. He approached the Ancient of Days and was led into his presence. He was given authority, glory and sovereign power; all peoples, nations and men of every language worshipped him. His dominion is an everlasting dominion that will not pass away, and his kingdom is one that will never be destroyed" (Daniel 7:13–14). Jesus was indeed claiming Godhood.

Jesus' use of the title "Son of Man" from the Daniel 7 passage has strong apologetic value, for a skeptic of Christ's deity cannot dismiss this particular self-designation of Jesus very easily. Jesus calls Himself "Son of Man" in every Gospel; apart from the Gospels, the title is used of Jesus only a few times (Acts 7:56; Revelation 1:13; 14:14). Given its scarce usage by the early apostolic church, it is unlikely that the title "Son of Man" would have been read back into the lips of Jesus if, in fact, He had not used it Himself. Jesus' application of this title to Himself indicates that He considered Himself to have everlasting power and a unique authority beyond that of a mere mortal. Jesus taught that He, the Son of Man, will ultimately judge humanity (Matthew 25:31–46) and that our eternal destinies depend on our response to Him (Mark 8:34–38).

Sometimes it was Jesus' actions that revealed His identity. Jesus' healing of the paralytic in Mark 2 was done to demonstrate His authority and ability to forgive sins (Mark 2:3–12). Forgiving sins, of course, is God's business. When Jesus forgave sin, He was performing a divine task. Jesus also receives worship several times in the Gospels (Matthew 2:11; 28:9, 17; Luke 24:52; John 9:38; 20:28). Never did Jesus reject such adoration. Rather, He regarded the worship as well placed. Such behavior is further indication that Jesus understood Himself to be divine.

Jesus also stated that His forthcoming resurrection from the dead would vindicate the special claims that He made for Himself (Matthew 12:38–40). After His crucifixion and burial, Jesus did, in fact, rise from the dead, establishing His claim to deity.

The evidence for the resurrection is compelling. Numerous contemporary sources report Jesus' post-crucifixion appearances to both individuals and groups under various circumstances (1 Corinthians 15:3–7; Matthew 28:9; Luke 24:36–43; John 20:26–30; 21:1–14; Acts 1:3–5). Many of these witnesses were willing to die for this belief, and several of them did! Clement of Rome and the Roman historian Josephus provide us with first-century reports of several of their martyrdoms. All of the theories used to explain away the evidence for the resurrection (such as the hallucination theory) have failed to explain all of the known data. The resurrection of Jesus is an established fact of history, and this turns out to be the strongest evidence for Jesus' divinity.

Question: Is Jesus God? Did Jesus ever claim to be God?

Answer: The Bible never records Jesus saying the precise words, "I am God." That does not mean, however, that He did not proclaim that He is God. Take for example Jesus' words in John 10:30, "I and the Father are one." We need only to look at the Jews' reaction to His statement to know He was claiming to be God. They tried to stone Him for this very reason: "You, a mere man, claim to be God" (John 10:33). The Jews understood exactly what Jesus was claiming—deity. When Jesus declared, "I and the Father are one," He was saying that He and the Father are of one nature and essence. John 8:58 is another example. Jesus declared, "I tell you the truth...before Abraham was born, I am!" Jews who heard this statement responded by taking up stones to kill Him for blasphemy, as the Mosaic Law commanded (Leviticus 24:16).

John reiterates the concept of Jesus' deity: "The Word [Jesus] was God" and "the Word became flesh" (John 1:1, 14). These verses clearly indicate that Jesus is God in the flesh. Acts 20:28 tells us, "Be shepherds of the church of God, which he bought with his own blood." Who bought the church with His own blood? Jesus Christ. And this same verse declares that God purchased His church with His own blood. Therefore, Jesus is God!

Thomas the disciple declared concerning Jesus, "My Lord and my God!" (John 20:28). Jesus does not correct him. Titus 2:13 encourages us to wait for the coming of our God and Savior, Jesus Christ (see also 2 Peter 1:1). In Hebrews 1:8, the Father declares of Jesus, "But about the Son he says, 'Your throne, O God, will last forever and ever, and righteousness will be the scepter of your kingdom.'" The Father refers to Jesus as "O God," indicating that Jesus is indeed God.

In Revelation, an angel instructed the apostle John to only worship God (Revelation 19:10). Several times in Scripture Jesus receives worship (Matthew 2:11; 14:33; 28:9, 17; Luke 24:52; John 9:38). He never rebukes people for worshipping Him. If Jesus were not God, He would have told people not to worship Him, just as the angel in Revelation did. There are many other passages of Scripture that argue for Jesus' deity.

The most important reason that Jesus has to be God is that, if He is not God, His death would not have been sufficient to pay the penalty for the sins of the world (1 John 2:2). A created being, which Jesus would be if He were not God, could not pay the infinite penalty required for sin against an infinite God. Only God could pay such an infinite penalty. Only God could take on the sins of the world (2 Corinthians 5:21), die, and be resurrected, proving His victory over sin and death.

Question: What is the hypostatic union? How can Jesus be both God and man at the same time?

Answer: The *hypostatic union* is the term used to describe how God the Son, Jesus Christ, took on a human nature, yet remained fully God at the same time. Jesus always has been God (John 1:1; 8:58), but at the incarnation Jesus became a human being (John 1:14). The addition of the human nature to the divine nature is Jesus, the God-man. This is the hypostatic union: Jesus Christ, one Person, fully God and fully man.

Jesus' two natures, human and divine, are inseparable. Jesus will forever be the God-man, fully God and fully human, two distinct natures in one Person. Jesus' humanity and divinity are not mixed, but are united without loss of separate identity. Jesus sometimes operated with the limitations of humanity (John 4:6; 19:28) and other times in the power of His deity (John 11:43–44; Matthew 14:18–21). Always, Jesus' actions were from His one Person. Jesus has two natures, but only one personality.

The doctrine of the hypostatic union is an attempt to explain how Jesus could be both God and man at the same time. It is ultimately a doctrine we are incapable of fully understanding. It is impossible for us to fully grasp how God works. We, as human beings with finite minds, should not expect to totally comprehend an infinite God. Jesus is God's Son in that He was conceived by the Holy Spirit (Luke 1:35). But that does not mean Jesus did not exist before He was conceived. Jesus has always existed (John 8:58).

When Jesus was conceived, He became a human being in addition to being God (Colossians 2:9).

Jesus became a human being in order to identify with us in our struggles (Hebrews 2:17) and, more importantly, in order to die on the cross to pay the penalty for our sins (Philippians 2:5–11). In summary, the doctrine of the hypostatic union teaches that Jesus is both fully human and fully divine, that there is no mixture or dilution of either nature, and that He is one united Person, forever.

Question: What does it mean that Jesus is the Son of God?

Answer: Jesus is not God's Son in the same sense that a human father has a son. God did not get married and have a son. God did not mate with Mary and, together with her, produce a son. Jesus is God's Son in the sense that He is God made manifest in human form (John 1:1, 14). Jesus is God's Son in that He was conceived in Mary by the power of the Holy Spirit. Luke 1:35 declares, "The angel answered, 'The Holy Spirit will come upon you, and the power of the Most High will overshadow you. So the holy one to be born will be called the Son of God.'"

During Jesus' trial before the Jewish leaders, the High Priest demanded of Him, "I charge you under oath by the living God: Tell us if you are the Christ, the Son of God" (Matthew 26:63). "'Yes, it is as you say,' Jesus replied. 'But I say to all of you: In the future you will see the Son of Man sitting at the right hand of the Mighty One and coming on the clouds of heaven'" (Matthew 26:64). The Jewish leaders responded by accusing Jesus of blasphemy (Matthew 26:65–66). Later, before Pontius Pilate, "The Jews insisted, 'We have a law, and according to that law He must die, because He claimed to be the Son of God'" (John 19:7). Why would Jesus' claiming to be the Son of God be considered blasphemy and worthy of death? The Jewish leaders understood exactly what Jesus meant by the phrase "Son of God." To be the Son of God is to be of the same nature as God. The Son of God is "of God." The claim to be of the same nature as God—to, in fact, *be* God—was blasphemy to the Jewish leaders; therefore, they demanded Jesus' death, in keeping with Leviticus 24:16. Hebrews 1:3 expresses this clearly: "The Son is the radiance of God's glory and the exact representation of His being."

A "son" of something shares the qualities of that something. Our modern idiom "like father, like son" expresses the same idea. In Acts 4:36, a man named Joseph is nicknamed "Barnabas," which means "son of encouragement." Being the "son" of encouragement meant that Joseph possessed that quality in abundance; he was encouragement personified. In the same way, to say that Jesus is the "Son of God" is to say that He has the qualities of God; He is God in the flesh.

It may also be helpful to consider John 17:12 (NAS), where Judas is described as the "son of perdition." We know from John 6:71 that Judas was the son of Simon. What, then, does John 17:12 mean by describing Judas as the "son of perdition"? The word *perdition* means "destruction, ruin, waste." Judas was not the literal son of "ruin, destruction, and waste," but those things were associated with him. Judas was ruin personified. In this same way, Jesus is the Son of God. The Son of God is God. Jesus is God made manifest (John 1:1, 14).

Question: What did Jesus mean when He said, 'I am'?

Answer: When the Pharisees asked Jesus, "Who do you think you are?" (John 8:53), Jesus replied, "'Your father Abraham rejoiced at the thought of seeing my day; he saw it and was glad.' 'You are not yet fifty years old,' the Jews said to him, 'and you have seen Abraham!' 'I tell you the truth,' Jesus answered, 'before Abraham was born, I am!' At this, they picked up stones to stone him, but Jesus hid himself, slipping away from the temple grounds" (John 8:56–59). The violent response of the Jews to Jesus' "I am" statement indicates the Jews clearly understood what He was declaring: that He was the eternal, incarnate God. Jesus was equating Himself with the "I Am" title God gave Himself in Exodus 3:14.

If Jesus had merely wanted to say He existed before Abraham's time, He would have said, "Before Abraham, I was." The Greek words translated "was" in the case of Abraham and "am" in the case of Jesus are quite different. The words Jesus chose make it clear that Abraham was created but Jesus existed eternally (see John 1:1). There is no doubt that the Jews understood what He was saying, since they took up stones to kill Him for making Himself equal with God (John 5:18). Such a statement, if untrue, was blasphemy, and the punishment prescribed by the Mosaic Law was death (Leviticus 24:11–14). But Jesus committed no blasphemy; He was and is God, the second Person of the Godhead, equal to the Father in every way.

Jesus used the same phrase "I am" in seven declarations about Himself. In all seven, He combines "I am" with tremendous metaphors that express His saving relationship with the world. All appear in the book of John. They are *I am* the bread of life (John 6:35, 48, 51); *I am* the light of the world (John 8:12); *I am* the gate for the sheep (John 10:7, 9); *I am* the good shepherd (John 10:11, 14); *I am* the resurrection and the life (John 11:25); *I am* the way and the truth and the life (John 14:6); and *I am* the true vine (John 15:1, 5).

Question: What does it mean that Jesus is God's "only begotten son"?

Answer: The phrase "only begotten Son" occurs in John 3:16, "For God so loved the world, that he gave his only begotten Son, that whosoever believeth in Him should not perish, but have everlasting life" (KJV). "Only begotten" is a translation of the Greek word *monogenes*. This word is variously translated into English as "only," "one and only," and "only begotten."

It's this last phrase ("only begotten," used in the KJV, NASB, and NKJV) that causes problems. False teachers have latched onto this phrase to try to prove their false teaching that Jesus Christ isn't God; i.e., that Jesus isn't equal in essence to God as the second Person of the Trinity. They see the word "begotten" and say that Jesus is a created being because only someone who had a beginning in time can be "begotten." This overlooks the fact that "begotten" is an English translation of a Greek word. As such, we have to look at the original meaning of the Greek word and not transfer English meanings into the text.

So what does *monogenes* mean? According to the *Greek-English Lexicon of the New Testament and Other Early Christian Literature*, *monogenes* has two primary definitions.[12] The first definition is "pertaining to being the only one of its kind within a specific relationship." This is the meaning attached to its use in Hebrews 11:17 (KJV) where the writer refers to Isaac as Abraham's "only begotten son." Abraham had more than one son, but Isaac was the only son he had by Sarah and the only son of the covenant.

The second definition is "pertaining to being the only one of its kind or class, unique in kind." This is the meaning implied in John 3:16. In fact, John is the only New Testament writer who uses this word in reference to Jesus (see John 1:14, 18; 3:16, 18; 1 John 4:9, KJV). John was primarily concerned with demonstrating that Jesus was the Son of God (John 20:31), and he uses the word *monogenes* to highlight Jesus as uniquely God's Son, sharing God's divine nature. This sets Jesus apart from other "sons" of God—believers who are God's sons and daughters through faith (John 1:12).

The bottom line is that terms such as "Father" and "Son," which are descriptive of God and Jesus, are human terms used to help us understand the relationship between the different Persons of the Trinity. If we can understand the relationship between a human father and a human son, then we can understand, in part, the relationship between the first and second Persons of the Trinity. The analogy breaks down if we try to take it too far. Some cults (such as the Jehovah's Witnesses) teach that Jesus was literally "begotten," as in "produced" or "created," by God the Father, but this is not what John 3:16 says.

Question: What is the doctrine of eternal generation, and is it biblical?

Answer: The doctrines of eternal generation and eternal procession are associated with the doctrine of the Trinity. The doctrine of eternal generation teaches that God the Father eternally and by necessity *generates* or *begets* God the Son in such a way that the substance (divine essence) of God is not divided. The doctrine is codified in the Nicene Creed, the Belgic Confession (Articles X and XI), and the Westminster Confession of Faith (Chapter II.3).

As finite, created beings, we never will be able to fully comprehend the doctrine of the Trinity; it is simply beyond our ability. All human analogies used to explain the Trinity break down at some level. With that said, let's review the common evangelical belief in regard to the Trinity. This doctrine makes four basic assertions:

1. There is only one true and living God.
2. This one God eternally exists in three Persons—God the Father, God the Son, and God the Holy Spirit.
3. These three Persons are completely equal in attributes, each with the same divine nature.
4. While each Person is fully and completely God, the Persons are not identical.

Each of these four claims can be defended from Scripture. Thus, we can compare the doctrine of eternal generation against these to see if it holds up.

The Person of God the Son derives His deity from this "eternal generation." In other words, there is a communication of the whole, indivisible substance of the Godhead so that God the Son is the exact representation (or express image) of God the Father (Hebrews 1:3). There is still one divine essence that eternally exists in two Persons through eternal generation. Reformed theologian Louis Berkhof explains the doctrine of eternal generation this way: "It is that eternal and necessary act of the first person in the Trinity, whereby He, within the divine Being, is the ground of a second personal subsistence like His own, and puts this second person in possession of the whole divine essence, without any division, alienation, or change."[13]

So we see that eternal generation is an act performed by the First Person of the Trinity. Furthermore, this act by the First Person is necessarily and eternally performed, without interruption. Finally, the result of this act is the generation of the Second Person of the Trinity in such a way that the entire divine essence is communicated from the First Person to the Second Person.

Because of this act of eternal generation, the relational terms "Father" and "Son" come to describe the First and Second Persons of the Trinity. The Father eternally generates the Son, and the Son is eternally generated by the Father. We have an illustration in human generation (which, however, is not eternal). We know a human father "generates" or "begets" a human son; the divine Father eternally and necessarily "begets" the divine Son. The Son is the *only* Person so begotten (John 3:16).

The analogy of a human father and son has weaknesses, of course. The idea of begetting implies a creation in time, but Jesus is eternal (John 1:1). Generation also implies an ontological dependence, but the Son is one with the Father (John 10:30). In response to this, we repeat that all human analogies regarding the mystery of the Trinity eventually break down. We don't want to carry an analogy too far. Also, the qualifiers "eternally" and "necessarily" should remove any concerns of a temporal or subordinate relationship between the Father and the Son. The qualifier "eternal" exempts this relationship from the constraints of time and space; there is neither beginning nor end to the generation of the Son by the Father. The qualifier "necessarily" removes any ontological dependence between the Father and the Son; the Son *must* be generated from the Father, and the Father *must* generate the Son.

Not only do the terms "Father" and "Son" help us to analogize this relationship, but they also help explain another truth regarding the Trinity. There is a hierarchical and functional order described here—one that defines the activity of Father and Son in creation and salvation. The Father "speaks" the universe into existence, and the Son is the agent of that creation (Genesis 1:3; Colossians 1:16). In salvation, the Father elects the chosen, and the Son provides the necessary atonement (Romans 8:29; Romans 3:25). The Father sends the Son into the world; the Son never sends the Father (John 5:36). This hierarchy of role and function in no way diminishes the ontological equality between the Father and the Son; i.e., they are equal in nature. Both Father and Son are God, sharing equally in the full divine essence (John 11:14). So the terms "Father" and "Son," far from being a mere anthropomorphism to help us understand the relationship between the First and Second Persons, goes to the heart of defining this necessary and eternal relationship. As such, the doctrine of eternal generation is clearly in line with the biblical teaching of the Trinity.

We should not expect every believer to have a full grasp of this doctrine. However, as we study the Bible, we will come to a more mature understanding of the Trinity and the eternal relationship between the Father and the Son.

Question: What is the doctrine of eternal Sonship, and is it biblical?

Answer: The doctrine of eternal Sonship simply affirms that the second Person of the triune Godhead has existed eternally as the Son. In other words, there was never a time when He was not the Son of God, and there has always been a Father/Son relationship within the Godhead. This doctrine recognizes that the idea of Sonship is not merely a title or role that Christ assumed at some specific point in history, but that it is the essential identity of the second Person of the Godhead. According to this doctrine, Christ is and always has been the Son of God.

Most Christians throughout history have believed that Jesus existed as God's eternal Son before creation. The Nicene Creed (AD 325) affirms this: "We believe in one Lord, Jesus Christ, the only Son of God, eternally begotten of the Father, God from God, Light from Light, true God from true God, begotten, not made, of one Being with the Father. Through him all things were made." The pre-existence of Christ was later reaffirmed in the Athanasian Creed of the fifth century.

There is considerable biblical evidence to support the eternal Sonship of Christ. First of all, there are many passages that clearly identify the Son as He who created all things (Colossians 1:13–16; Hebrews 1:2). The most normal and natural meaning of these passages is that, at the time of creation, Jesus was the Son of God, the second Person of the Triune Godhead.

Second, there are numerous verses that speak of God the Father sending the Son into the world to redeem sinful man (John 20:21; Galatians 4:4; 1 John 4:10; 1 John 4:14) and giving His Son as a sacrifice for sin (John 3:16). These passages imply that Jesus was the Son before God sent Him into the world. Galatians 4:4–6 uses the phrase "sent forth" both of the Son and the Spirit. Just as the Holy Spirit did not "become" the Holy Spirit when He was sent to empower the believers at Pentecost, neither did the Son "become" the Son at the moment of His incarnation. He was *already* the Son. All three Persons of the Triune Godhead have existed for all eternity, and their names reveal who they are, not simply their title or function.

Third, 1 John 3:8 speaks of the "appearance" or manifestation of the Son of God: "The reason the Son of God appeared was to destroy the devil's work." The verb *appeared* means "made visible" or "brought to light something previously hidden." The idea communicated here is not that the second Person of the Trinity suddenly became the Son of God, but that the already existing Son of God was made visible to us. He appeared in order to fulfill God's predetermined purpose. This idea is also taught in John 11:27 and 1 John 5:20.

Fourth, Hebrews 13:8 says that "Jesus Christ is the same yesterday and today and forever." The fact that Jesus' divine nature is unchanging indicates that He was *always* the Son of God because Sonship is an essential part of His Person. At the incarnation Jesus took on human flesh, but His divine nature did not change, nor did His relationship with the Father. This truth is also implied in

John 20:31, "Jesus is the Christ, the Son of God." John does not say that Jesus *became* the Son of God but that He *is* the Son of God. The fact that Jesus was and is the Son of God is essential to who He is and His work in redemption.

Fifth, one of the strongest evidences for the eternal Sonship of Christ is the triune nature of God and the eternal relationship that exists among the Father, Son, and Holy Spirit. Particularly important is the unique Father/Son relationship that can only be understood from the perspective of Christ's eternal Sonship. This relationship is key to understanding the full measure of God's love for those He redeems through the blood of Christ. The doctrine of Sonship helps us understand that God the Father took His Son, the very Son He loved from before the foundation of the world, and sent Him as a sacrifice for our sins. What an amazing act of grace and love!

We believe that the doctrine of eternal Sonship is indeed biblical. However, not all Christians will agree. While it has been the view of the majority of Christian commentators throughout history, there have been several prominent Christians on the other side of the issue as well.

Those who deny the doctrine of eternal Sonship hold a view often referred to as "Incarnational Sonship," which teaches that, while Christ pre-existed, He was not always the Son of God. Those that hold this view believe Christ became the Son of God at some point in history, such as His incarnation. Others believe Christ did not become the Son until some time after His incarnation, such as His baptism, resurrection, or exaltation. It is important to realize that those who deny the eternal Sonship of Christ still recognize and affirm His deity and His eternality.

Those who hold to Incarnational Sonship see the Sonship of Christ as not being an essential part of who He is. Instead, they see Sonship as a role, title, or function that Christ assumed at His incarnation. They also teach that the Father became the Father at the time of the incarnation (because if Christ was not yet called the Son, then there could be no role of "Father"). Throughout history many conservative Christians have denied the doctrine of eternal Sonship. Some examples are Ralph Wardlaw, Adam Clarke, Albert Barnes, Finis J. Dake, Walter Martin, and at one time John MacArthur. However, several years ago MacArthur changed his position on this doctrine, and he now affirms the doctrine of eternal Sonship.

One of the verses commonly used to support Incarnational Sonship is Hebrews 1:5, which appears to speak of God the Father's begetting of God the Son as an event that takes place at a specific point in time: "You are my Son; today I have become your Father...I will be his Father, and he will be my Son." Those who hold to the doctrine of Incarnational Sonship point out two important aspects of this verse: 1) that "begetting" normally speaks of a person's origin, and 2) that a son is normally subordinate to his father. They reject the doctrine of eternal Sonship in an attempt to preserve the perfect equality and eternality of the Persons of the Triune Godhead. In order to do so, they must conclude that "Son" is simply a title that Christ took on at His incarnation and that "Sonship" refers to Christ's humble obedience and voluntary submission to the Father when He was made flesh (Philippians 2:5–8; John 5:19).

One of the problems with the Incarnational Sonship view is that this teaching confuses or destroys the internal relationships within the Trinity. If the Father does not eternally beget the Son, then neither does the Spirit eternally proceed from the Father through the Son. Instead of having a triune God eternally existing in three distinct Persons with three distinct names—Father, Son, and Holy Spirit—we have a nameless Trinity prior to the incarnation. Also, we would be forced to say that God has chosen not to reveal Himself as He truly is, but only as He was to become. In other words, instead of actually revealing who He is, the Triune God instead chose to reveal Himself by the titles He would assume or the roles that He would take on. This is dangerously close to modalism and could easily lead to false teachings about the nature of God.

Taken to its logical conclusion, denying the eternal Sonship of Christ reduces the Trinity from Father, Son, and Holy Spirit in relationship to simply Number One, Number Two, and Number

Three Persons—with the numbers themselves being an arbitrary designation. In essence, Incarnational Sonship destroys the God-given order and relationship that exists among the Persons of the Trinity.

Question: If Jesus was God, why did He say, "No one is good but God alone"?

Answer: Those who reject the deity of Christ often claim that Jesus Himself denies His divinity by rejecting the notion that He is good. Jesus' statement is found in Mark 10:17–22: "As Jesus started on his way, a man ran up to him and fell on his knees before him. 'Good teacher,' he asked, 'what must I do to inherit eternal life?' 'Why do you call me good?' Jesus answered. 'No one is good—except God alone. You know the commandments: "Do not murder, do not commit adultery, do not steal, do not give false testimony, do not defraud, honor your father and mother."' 'Teacher,' he declared, 'all these I have kept since I was a boy.' Jesus looked at him and loved him. 'One thing you lack,' he said. 'Go, sell everything you have and give to the poor, and you will have treasure in heaven. Then come, follow me.' At this, the man's face fell. He went away sad, because he had great wealth."

Is Jesus rebuking the man for calling Him good and thereby denying His deity? No. Rather, He is using a penetrating question to push the man to think through the implication of his own words, to understand the concept of Jesus' goodness and, more especially, the man's lack of goodness. The young ruler "went away sad" (Mark 10:22) because he realized that, although he had prided himself in keeping the commandments, he had failed to keep the first and greatest commandment—"love the Lord your God with all your heart and with all your soul and with all your mind" (Matthew 22:37–38). The man's riches were of more worth to him than God; thus, he was not "good" in God's eyes.

Jesus' fundamental lesson here is that goodness flows not from a man's deeds, but rather from God Himself. Jesus invites the man to follow Him, for faith in Christ is the only means of becoming "good" by God's standard (Romans 3:22). Jesus describes to the young ruler what it means to follow Him—to be willing to give up everything, thus putting God first. When one considers that Jesus is drawing a distinction between man's standard of goodness and God's standard, it becomes clear that following Jesus is good. The command to follow Christ is the definitive proclamation of Christ's goodness. Thus, we see that Jesus is good by the very standard He is exhorting the young ruler to adopt. And it necessarily follows that, if Jesus is indeed good by this standard, Jesus is implicitly declaring His deity—for only God is good.

Jesus' question to the man is designed not to deny His deity but to lead the man to recognize His deity. Such an interpretation is substantiated by passages such as John 10:11, wherein Jesus declares Himself to be the "good shepherd." Similarly, in John 8:46, Jesus asks, "Can any of you prove me guilty of sin?" Of course, the answer is "no." Jesus was without sin (Hebrews 4:15), holy and undefiled (Hebrews 7:26), the only One who knew no sin (2 Corinthians 5:21).

The logic can thus be summarized as follows:

1. Jesus claims only God is good.
2. Jesus claims to be good.
3. Therefore, Jesus claims to be God.

Such a claim makes perfect sense in Mark's narrative of the unfolding Revelation of Jesus' real identity. The climactic statement of Jesus' divine nature comes in Mark 14:62 as Jesus stands before the high priest. The story of the rich young ruler is one in a sequence of stories designed to bring readers ever closer to the recognition of Jesus as the eternal, divine, incarnate Son of God.

Question: What does it mean that Jesus is the Alpha and the Omega?

Answer: Jesus proclaimed Himself to be the "Alpha and the Omega" in Revelation 1:8, 21:6, and 22:13. Alpha and omega are the first and last letters of the Greek alphabet. Among the Jewish rabbis, it was common to use the first and the last letters of the Hebrew alphabet to denote the whole of anything, from beginning to end. Jesus as the beginning and end of all things is a reference to no one but the true God. This concept is seen especially in Revelation 22:13, where Jesus proclaims that He is "the Alpha and the Omega, the First and the Last, the Beginning and the End."

As the Alpha and Omega, Jesus was at the beginning of all things and will be at the close. He always existed and always will exist. It was Christ, as second Person of the Trinity, who brought about creation: "Through him all things were made; without him nothing was made that has been made" (John 1:3), and His second coming will be the beginning of the end of creation as we know it (2 Peter 3:10). As God incarnate, Jesus has no beginning, nor will He have an end, being from everlasting to everlasting.

The phrase "alpha and omega" identifies Jesus as the God of the Old Testament. Isaiah confirms this aspect of Jesus' nature as part of the triune God. "Who has done this and carried it through, calling forth the generations from the beginning? I, the LORD—with the first of them and with the last—I am he" (Isaiah 41:4). "I am the first and I am the last; apart from me there is no God" (44:6). "I am he; I am the first and I am the last" (48:12). These are clear indications of the eternal nature of the Godhead.

Christ, as the Alpha and Omega, is the first and last in so many ways. He is the "author and perfecter" of our faith (Hebrews 12:2), signifying that He begins it and carries it through to completion. He is the sum and substance of the Scriptures, both of the Law and of the Gospel (John 1:1, 14). He is the fulfilling end of the Law (Matthew 5:17), and He is the beginning subject matter of the gospel of grace through faith, not of works (Ephesians 2:8–9). He is found in the first verse of Genesis and in the last verse of Revelation. He is the first and last, the all in all of salvation, from the justification before God to the final sanctification of His people.

Jesus is the Alpha and the Omega, the first and last, the beginning and the end. Only God incarnate could make such a statement. Only Jesus Christ is God incarnate.

Question: Does the Bible support the pre-existence of Jesus?

Answer: The biblical argument for the pre-existence of Jesus is certainly multi-faceted. When we speak of the pre-existence of Jesus Christ, we refer to the fact that, before He became a Man and walked upon the earth, He existed as the second Person of the triune God. The Bible not only explicitly teaches this doctrine but also implies this fact at various points throughout the Gospels and Epistles. In addition, Jesus' own actions reveal His divine identity and, as a consequence, His pre-existence.

We find evidence of Jesus' pre-existence several places in the New Testament. Jesus Himself said, "And now, Father, glorify me in your presence with the glory I had with you before the world began" (John 17:5). This passage alone is sufficient proof of Jesus' pre-existence, but it is just one of many such passages. Jesus often mentioned His own pre-existence (John 3:13; 6:33, 38, 62; 8:23; 16:28). Christ even said that He existed prior to Abraham (John 8:58), even though Abraham's birth preceded Jesus' own by many centuries! Several texts present Jesus as pre-existing with His Father (Romans 8:3; Galatians 4:4; 1 John 1:2). Several passages even identify Jesus as the Creator (John 1:1–3; Colossians 1:16–17; Hebrews 1:2).

Probably the most powerful evidence for the pre-existence of Christ was Jesus' own behavior. He was often doing and saying things that only the God of Israel had the right or power to do. In Mark 2, we see that Jesus healed the paralytic in order to demonstrate His authority over physical ailments and His ability to forgive sins (Mark 2:3–12). Jesus' Jewish audience was well aware that such things were reserved only for Yahweh. Jesus' actions in Luke 7:48–50 drew a similar reaction.

The fact that others often worshipped Jesus is also evidence of His pre-existence. We see this worship occurring repeatedly in the Gospels (Matthew 28:9, 17; Luke 24:52; John 9:38; 20:28). Jesus never rejected such adoration. He saw such worship as entirely appropriate. Jesus stated that He had authority over the Sabbath (Mark 2:28) as well as the authority to fulfill the Law (Matthew 5:17). Such behavior is sheer blasphemy coming from anyone but a divine (pre-existent) Person.

In addition, Jesus identified Himself by the messianic title "Son of Man" (Mark 14:61–64) and claimed to be able to raise Himself from the dead (John 10:17–18)! The resurrection turned out to be the very miracle that He claimed would authenticate His radical claims and ministry (Matthew 12:38–40; 16:1–4). Jesus accomplished this grand miracle and gave convincing proof of it (Luke 24:36–43; John 20:26; 21:1–14; Acts 1:3–5). Jesus' resurrection authenticated His claim to deity and thus provides further confirmation of His pre-existence.

Question: What is the supremacy of Christ, and what are its implications?

Answer: The supremacy of Christ is a doctrine concerning the authority of Jesus and His God-nature. In the simplest of terms, to affirm the supremacy of Christ is to affirm that Jesus is God.

Merriam-Webster's Dictionary defines *supreme* as "highest in rank or authority" or "highest in degree or quality."[14] In essence, there is none better. The supreme of something is its ultimate. Jesus is the ultimate in power, glory, authority, and importance. Jesus' supremacy over all is developed primarily in Hebrews and Colossians. Theologians believe that Colossians was written, in part, to combat heresies rising in Colossae. It seemed fitting to Paul to affirm the supremacy of Christ in order to quash these misled beliefs. He affirmed Christ's supremacy, His lordship, and His sufficiency for us. Hebrews explains the link between the Old Testament covenant and the new covenant of Jesus. Hebrews reveals the old system as a shadow of the ultimate fulfillment in Jesus Christ.

A main purpose of the book of Hebrews is to explain the work of Jesus in the context of the Old Testament system. Jesus was the fulfillment of the Old Testament traditions and roles. Hebrews also shows that Jesus does not simply represent a new way of doing things. Rather, He is supreme. He is the actual fulfillment of the old way of doing things and is therefore greater than those ways. Concerning the temple system under the Mosaic Law, the author of Hebrews writes, "But the ministry Jesus has received is as superior to theirs as the covenant of which he is mediator is superior to the old one, and it is founded on better promises" (Hebrews 8:6). In essence, Jesus is greater than the Old Testament system. He both encompasses and supersedes that system. This is evident in the many comparisons of Jesus to Old Testament roles and rituals. For instance, we are told, "Because Jesus lives forever, he has a permanent priesthood. Therefore he is able to save completely those who come to God through him, because he always lives to intercede for them" (Hebrews 7:24–25). Jesus encompasses the Old Testament priesthood and is supreme over it.

Hebrews explains that Christ is supreme over more than just roles and systems. Hebrews 1:3a says, "The Son is the radiance of God's glory and the exact representation of his being, sustaining all things by his powerful word." Similarly, Colossians 2:9 says, "For in Christ all the fullness of the Deity lives in bodily form." Essentially, Jesus is God.

Colossians 1:15–23 is labeled "The Supremacy of Christ" in some Bibles. In this passage, Paul makes it plain that Jesus is over all things. Christ is called "the image of the invisible God" and "the firstborn over all creation" (verse 15). The word *firstborn* may seem confusing. It does not imply that Christ was created (as in the doctrine of the Jehovah's Witnesses). Instead, the term *firstborn* refers to a position of authority. To be "firstborn" was to hold an honored position. Paul immediately goes on to explain Jesus' role in creation: "For by him all things were created; things in heaven and on earth, visible and invisible, whether thrones or powers or rulers or authorities; all things were created by him

52

and for him" (verse 16). This means that Jesus is not created, but is Creator. He is God.

Paul goes on to say, "He is before all things, and in him all things hold together. And he is the head of the body, the church; he is the beginning and the firstborn from among the dead, so that in everything he might have the supremacy" (Colossians 1:17–18). Paul highlights multiple areas in which Christ holds authority—creation, the church, death, and finally "everything." Christ is before all things and sustains all things ("in Him all things hold together"). Therefore, Christ is supreme.

This doctrine is essential to our view of Christ and worship of Him. The supremacy of Christ affirms that Jesus is fully God. He is not simply a man greater than the rest but is truly above all creation, as only God can be. This truth is essential for our salvation. God is infinite, and, therefore, our sin against Him is an infinite offense. In order to atone for this offense, the sacrifice must be infinite. Jesus, as God, is infinite and thus an able sacrifice.

The fact that Jesus is supreme excludes our saying that He is only one of many to God. He is not just a good moral teacher whom we may choose to follow; rather, He *is* God and He is over all. Jesus' supremacy also makes it evident that the Old Testament sacrificial system has been fulfilled and replaced. And, once we are saved, Jesus' supremacy shows us that we cannot be like Him in our own strength. Christians are called to be like Jesus, but this is only accomplished through the work of the Holy Spirit.

The supremacy of Jesus teaches us that Christ is not simply a spiritual being higher than the rest. Paul tells us that through Him all things visible and invisible and on heaven and on earth (meaning spiritual and physical) were created (see Colossians 1:16). Hebrews 1:4 says Jesus is superior to the angels. This truth negates any tendency toward angel worship. Jesus created the angels and transcends them. Therefore, we need only worship Jesus. Similarly, Jesus created the things of earth, and that means that creation is not worthy of our worship. Jesus is supreme over both the physical and spiritual realms.

When we understand the supremacy of Christ, we have a more accurate view of Him. We more fully understand the depth of His love; we are more able to receive and respond to His love. The supremacy of Christ is central to an accurate view of His Person, His work, our status as believers, and the Kingdom.

Chapter 3

. . . .

QUESTIONS ABOUT JESUS' HUMANITY

Contents

Why is the humanity of Jesus important?

What do John 1:1 and John 1:14 mean when they declare that Jesus is the Word of God?

What does it mean that Jesus is the Son of Man?

What does it mean that Jesus is the Son of David?

What is the kenosis?

Is Jesus was God, how could He pray to God? Was He praying to Himself?

Question: Why is the humanity of Jesus important?

Answer: The humanity of Jesus is as equally important as His deity. The concept of the humanity of Jesus co-existing with His deity is difficult for us to comprehend. Nevertheless, Jesus' nature—wholly man and wholly God—is a biblical fact. Some reject this truth and declare that Jesus was a man, but not God (Ebionism); others believe that Jesus was God, but not human (Docetism). Both views are unbiblical and false.

Jesus had to be born as a human being for several reasons. One is outlined in Galatians 4:4–5: "But when the time had fully come, God sent his Son, born of a woman, born under law, to redeem those under law, that we might receive the full rights of sons." Only a man could be "born under the law." No animal or angelic being is "under the law." Only humans are born under the law, and only a human being could redeem other human beings born under the same law. Born under the law of God, all humans are guilty of transgressing that law. Only a perfect human—Jesus Christ— could perfectly keep the law and perfectly fulfill it, thereby redeeming us from our guilt. He accomplished our redemption on the cross, exchanging our sin for His perfect righteousness (2 Corinthians 5:21).

Another reason Jesus had to be fully human is that God had established the necessity of the shedding of blood for the remission of sins (Leviticus 17:11; Hebrews 9:22). The blood of animals was a temporary foreshadowing of the blood of the perfect God-Man. The Old Testament sacrifices were insufficient for the permanent remission of sin because "it is impossible for the blood of bulls and goats to take away sins" (Hebrews 10:4). Jesus Christ, the perfect Lamb of God, sacrificed His human life and shed His human blood to cover the sins of all who would believe in Him. If He were not human, this would have been impossible.

Furthermore, the humanity of Jesus enables Him to relate to us in an intimate way: "For we do not have a high priest who is unable to sympathize with our weaknesses, but we have one who has been tempted in every way, just as we are—yet was without sin" (Hebrews 4:15). Only a human could sympathize with our weaknesses and temptations. In His humanity, Jesus was subjected to the same kinds of trials that we are, and He is, therefore, able to sympathize with us and aid us. He was tempted, He was persecuted, He was poor, He was despised, He suffered physical pain, and He endured the sorrows of a lingering and most cruel death. Only a human being could experience these things.

Believing that Jesus Christ came in the flesh is a prerequisite for salvation. Declaring that Jesus has come in the flesh is the Mark of a spirit from God; the Antichrist and all who follow him will deny Jesus' humanity (1 John 4:2–3). The biblical teaching is that Jesus has come in the flesh, sympathizes with our human frailties, shed His own blood for our sins, and is fully God and fully Man. These are biblical truths that cannot be denied.

Question: What do John 1:1 and John 1:14 mean when they declare that Jesus is the Word of God?

Answer: The answer to this question is found by first understanding the reason why John wrote his Gospel. We find his purpose clearly stated in John 20:30–31: "Jesus did many other miraculous signs in the presence of his disciples, which are not recorded in this book. But these are written that you may believe that Jesus is the Christ, the Son of God, and that by believing you may have life in his name." John's purpose was to introduce the readers of his Gospel to Jesus Christ, establishing who Jesus is (God in the flesh) and what He did, with the sole aim of leading them to embrace the saving work of Christ in faith. This knowledge helps us better understand why John introduces Jesus as "the Word" in John 1:1.

By starting out his Gospel stating, "In the beginning was the Word, and the Word was with God, and the Word was God," John is introducing Jesus with a term that both Jewish and Gentile readers would have recognized. The Greek word translated "Word" in this passage is *Logos*, and it was common in both Greek philosophy and Jewish thought of that day. For example, in the Old Testament the "word" of God is often personified as an instrument for the execution of God's will (Psalm 33:6; 107:20; 119:89; 147:15–18). So, for his Jewish readers, by introducing Jesus as the "Word," John is in a sense pointing them back to the Old Testament where the *logos* or "word" of God is associated with the personification of God's revelation. And in Greek philosophy, the term *logos* was used to describe the intermediate agency by which God created material things and communicated with them. In the Greek worldview, the *logos* was thought of as a bridge between the transcendent God and the material universe. Therefore, for John's Greek readers, the use of the term *logos* would have likely evoked the idea of a mediating principle between God and the world.

But John goes beyond the familiar concept of *Logos* and presents Jesus Christ as a personal being—fully divine, yet fully human—not as a mere mediating principle as the Greeks supposed. Also, the *Logos* was not simply a personification of God's Revelation as the Jews thought, but was indeed God's perfect Revelation of Himself in the flesh. Later in his Gospel, John records Jesus' words to Philip: "Anyone who has seen me has seen the Father" (John 14:9).

By using the term *Logos* or "Word" in John 1:1, John is applying and amplifying a concept familiar to his audience. Jesus Christ is the true *Logos* of God: the Living Word of God, fully God and fully man, the One who came to reveal God to man and to redeem all who believe in Him from their sin.

Question: What does it mean that Jesus is the Son of Man?

Answer: Jesus is referred to as the "Son of Man" 88 times in the New Testament. This title, "Son of Man," is an obvious reference to the prophecy in Daniel 7:13–14, "In my vision at night I looked, and there before me was one like a son of man, coming with the clouds of heaven. He approached the Ancient of Days and was led into his presence. He was given authority, glory and sovereign power; all peoples, nations and men of every language worshipped him. His dominion is an everlasting dominion that will not pass away, and his kingdom is one that will never be destroyed." "Son of Man" was a Messianic title. Jesus is the One given dominion and glory and a kingdom. When Jesus used this title of Himself, He was applying Daniel's Son of Man prophecy to Himself. The Jews of that era would have been intimately familiar with the phrase and to whom it referred. Jesus was proclaiming Himself as the Messiah.

"Son of Man" also carries the connotation of humanity. The title emphasizes that Jesus was truly human, that He was flesh and blood (Luke 24:39; Hebrews 2:14). God referred to the prophet Ezekiel as "son of man" 93 times. A son of a man is a man. Jesus was fully God (John 1:1), but He was also a human being (John 1:14). The incarnation is one of the basic doctrines of Christianity: "This is how you can recognize the Spirit of God: Every spirit that acknowledges that Jesus Christ has come in the flesh is from God" (1 John 4:2). Yes, Jesus is the Son of God—He is in His essence God. Jesus is also the Son of Man—He is in His essence a human being.

In summary, the title "Son of Man" indicates that Jesus is the Messiah and that He lived among us as a human being.

Question: What does it mean that Jesus is the Son of David?

Answer: Seventeen verses in the New Testament describe Jesus as the "Son of David." But the question arises: how could Jesus be the Son of David if David lived approximately 1,000 years before Jesus? The answer is that Christ (the Messiah) was the fulfillment of the prophecy of the seed of David (2 Samuel 7:16; John 7:42). Matthew chapter 1 gives the genealogical proof that Jesus, in His humanity, was a direct descendant of Abraham and David through Joseph, Jesus' legal father. The genealogy in Luke chapter 3 gives Jesus' lineage through His mother, Mary. Jesus is a descendant of David, by adoption through Joseph and by blood through Mary. Primarily, though, when Christ was referred to as the Son of David in the Gospels, it was meant as His Messianic title, the fulfillment of Old Testament prophecies.

Jesus was addressed as "Lord, Son of David" several times by people who, by faith, were seeking mercy or healing. The woman whose daughter was being tormented by a demon (Matthew 15:22), the two blind men by the wayside (Matthew 20:30), and blind Bartimaeus (Mark 10:47) all cried out to the Son of David for help. The title of honor they gave Him declared their faith in Him. Calling Him "Lord" expressed their sense of His deity, dominion, and power, and by calling Him "Son of David," they were professing Him to be the Messiah.

The Pharisees, too, understood what was meant when they heard the people calling Jesus "Son of David." But unlike those who cried out in faith, they were so blinded by their own pride and lack of understanding of the Scriptures that they couldn't see what the blind beggars could see—that here was the Messiah that the Pharisees had supposedly been waiting for all their lives. They hated Jesus because He would not give them the honor they thought they deserved, so when they heard the people hailing Jesus as the Savior, they became enraged (Matthew 21:15) and plotted to destroy Him (Luke 19:47).

Jesus discussed the title during a confrontation with the scribes and Pharisees. How could it be that the Messiah is the Son of David when David himself refers to Him as "my Lord" (Mark 12:35–37)? The teachers of the Law couldn't answer the question. Jesus thereby proved the pre-existence of the Messiah and exposed the religious leaders' ineptitude as teachers and their ignorance of the Messiah's true nature.

Jesus Christ, the only Son of God and the only means of salvation for the world (Acts 4:12), is also the Son of David, physically, spiritually, and prophetically.

Question: What is the kenosis?

Answer: The term *kenosis* comes from the Greek verb used in Philippians 2 to communicate the fact that Christ "emptied Himself" in His incarnation. The kenosis was a self-renunciation, but it was not an emptying of deity or an exchange of deity for humanity. Philippians 2:7 tells us that Jesus "made himself nothing, taking the very nature of a servant, being made in human likeness." Jesus did not cease to be God during His earthly ministry. But He did set aside His heavenly glory, a face-to-face relationship with the Father, and His independent authority. During His earthly ministry, Christ completely submitted Himself to the will of the Father.

Because of the kenosis, Jesus sometimes operated within the limitations of humanity (John 4:6; 19:28). For instance, Matthew 24:36 tells us, "No one knows about that day or hour, not even the angels in heaven, nor the Son, but only the Father." We might wonder: if Jesus was God, how could He not know everything, as God does (Psalm 139:1–6)? It seems that while Jesus was on earth, He voluntarily and intentionally suspended the use of some of His divine attributes. Jesus was still perfectly holy, just, merciful, gracious, righteous, and loving, but to varying degrees He chose not to exercise His omniscience and omnipotence.

When it comes to the kenosis, we often focus too much on what Jesus gave up. The kenosis also deals with what Christ added to Himself. Jesus took on a human nature and humbled Himself. He went from being the glory of glories in heaven to a human being who was put to death on the cross. Philippians 2:7–8 declares that Jesus took "the very nature of a servant, being made in human likeness. And being found in appearance as a man, he humbled himself and became obedient to death—even death on a cross!" In the ultimate act of humility, the God of the universe became a human and died for His creation. The kenosis, therefore, is Christ taking on a human nature with all of its limitations, except with no sin.

Question: If Jesus was God, how could He pray to God? Was Jesus praying to Himself?

Answer: To understand Jesus as God on earth praying to His Father in heaven, we need to realize that the eternal Father and the eternal Son had an eternal relationship before Jesus took upon Himself the form of a man (see John 5:19–27, particularly verse 21 where Jesus teaches that the Father sent the Son; also see John 15:10). Jesus did not *become* the Son of God when He was born in Bethlehem. He has *always* been the Son of God from eternity past, still *is* the Son of God, and always *will be* the Son of God.

Isaiah 9:6 tells us that the Son was given and the Child was born. Jesus was always part of the tri-unity, along with the Holy Spirit. The tri-unity always existed, the Father God, the Son God, and the Spirit God—not three gods, but one God existing as three Persons. Jesus taught that He and His Father are one (John 10:30), meaning that He and His Father are of the same substance and the same essence. The Father, Son, and Spirit are three co-equal Persons existing as God. These three had, and continue to have, an eternal relationship.

When Jesus, the eternal Son of God, took upon Himself sinless humanity, He also took on the form of a servant, giving up His heavenly glory (Philippians 2:5–11). As the God-man, He had to "learn" obedience (Hebrews 5:8) to His Father as He faced Satan's temptations, men's accusations, Israel's rejection, and eventual crucifixion. He prayed to His heavenly Father to ask for power (John 11:41–42) and wisdom (Mark 1:35; 6:46). His prayers showed His dependence upon His Father as Jesus, in His humanity, carried out His Father's plan of redemption. His prayers demonstrated that He submitted to His Father's will, which was to go to the cross and pay the penalty we deserve for breaking God's law (Matthew 26:31–46).

There is no problem with God the Son praying or talking to God the Father. A relationship must involve communication. The relationship between Father and Son is depicted in the Gospels. Humanly speaking, Christ's prayer life kept Him focused and empowered to continually submit to His heavenly Father. His example of prayer is ours to follow.

Jesus Christ was no less God on earth when praying to His Father in heaven. As the perfect Man, Jesus showed us the necessity of prayer. Doing the Father's will depends on a vital prayer life. If Jesus, the God-man, needed a vibrant prayer life, how much more does the follower of Christ today?

Chapter 4

CHAPTER 4

QUESTIONS ABOUT
JESUS' BIRTH AND LIFE

Contents

What is the meaning of the incarnation of Christ?

Why did God send Jesus to earth when He did? Why not earlier? Why not later?

Why are Jesus' genealogies in Matthew and Luke so different?

What year was Jesus Christ born?

Why is the virgin birth so important?

What happened during Jesus' childhood?

Did Jesus have brothers and sisters (siblings)?

Could Jesus have sinned? If He was not capable of sinning, how could He truly be able to "sympathize with our weaknesses" (Hebrews 4:15)? If He could not sin, what was the point of the temptation?

Was Jesus Christ married? Did Jesus have a wife?

Was Jesus a Jew?

What did Jesus look like?

Was Jesus black?

What was Jesus like as a person?

When did Jesus know that he was God?

What language did Jesus speak?

Was Jesus sinless?

Was Jesus rich/wealthy?

What were the key events in the life of Jesus Christ?

Question: What is the meaning of the incarnation of Christ?

Answer: "Incarnation" is a term used by theologians to indicate that Jesus, the Son of God, took on human flesh. A related topic is the hypostatic union, which explains how Jesus' human and divine natures are joined. The doctrine of the incarnation more specifically affirms His humanity.

The word *incarnation* means "the act of being made flesh." It comes from the Latin version of John 1:14, which in English reads, "The Word became flesh and made His dwelling among us." Because of the near-exclusive use of the Latin Vulgate in the church through the Middle Ages, the Latin term became standard.

Biblical support for Jesus' humanity is extensive. The Gospels report Jesus' human needs, including sleep (Luke 8:23), food (Matthew 4:2; 21:18), and physical protection (Matthew 2:13–15; John 10:39). Other indications of His humanity are that He perspired (Luke 22:43–44) and bled (John 19:34). Jesus also expressed emotions including joy (John 15:11), sorrow (Matthew 26:37), and anger (Mark 3:5). During His life, Jesus referred to Himself as a man (John 8:40), and after His resurrection His humanity was still recognized (Acts 2:22).

But the purpose of the incarnation was not to taste food or to feel sorrow. The Son of God came in the flesh in order to be the Savior of mankind. First, it was necessary to be born "under the law" (Galatians 4:4). All of us have failed to fulfill God's law. Christ came in the flesh, under the law, to fulfill it on our behalf (Matthew 5:17; Galatians 4:5).

Second, it was necessary for the Savior to shed His blood for the forgiveness of sins (Hebrews 9:22). A blood sacrifice, of course, requires a body of flesh and blood. And this was God's plan for the incarnation: "Therefore, when Christ came into the world, he said: 'Sacrifice and offering [under the Old Covenant] you did not desire, but a body you prepared for me'" (Hebrews 10:5). Without the incarnation, Christ could not really die, and the cross would be meaningless.

God did an incredible work in sending His only begotten Son into the world and providing us with a salvation we do not deserve. Praise the Lord for that moment in which "the Word became flesh" (John 1:14). We are now redeemed "with the precious blood of Christ, a lamb without blemish or defect" (1 Peter 1:19).

Question: Why did God send Jesus to earth when He did? Why not earlier? Why not later?

Answer: "But when the time had fully come, God sent his Son, born of a woman, born under law" (Galatians 4:4). This verse declares that God the Father was following His own schedule and that He sent His Son at just the right time. There are several things that, at least by human reasoning, seem to make Christ's advent ideally timed.

1. In the first century AD, there was great anticipation among the Jews that the Messiah would come. The Roman rule over Israel made the Jews hungry for a savior.
2. Rome had united much of the world under its government and provided a relative amount of peace. The Romans had built many roads, aiding early evangelism. Such freedom of travel was nonexistent in earlier eras.
3. While Rome had conquered militarily, Greece had conquered culturally. A "common" form of the Greek language (different from classical Greek) was the trade language and was spoken throughout the empire. This universal language made it possible to communicate the gospel to many different people groups. The entire New Testament was written in common Greek.
4. Many were abandoning idol worship due to the idols' failure to grant victory over the Roman conquerors. At the same time, in the more "cultured" cities, Greek philosophy and the science of the day left others spiritually empty. As a result, the gospel was able to fill a spiritual void.
5. The mystery religions of the time emphasized a savior-god and required worshipers to offer bloody sacrifices, thus

making the gospel of Christ, which involved one ultimate sacrifice, more believable to them.

6. The Roman army recruited soldiers from among the provinces, introducing these men to Roman culture and to ideas (such as the gospel) that had not reached those outlying provinces yet. The earliest introduction of the gospel to Britain was the result of Christian soldiers being stationed there.

The above observations may or may not have been some reasons why God chose to send His Son when He did. From the context of Galatians 3 and 4, it is evident that God sought to lay a foundation through the Jewish Law that would prepare for the coming of the Messiah. The Law was meant to help people understand the depth of their sinfulness (in that they were incapable of keeping the Law), so they might more readily accept the cure for that sin through Jesus, the Messiah (Galatians 3:22–23; Romans 3:19–20). The Law was "put in charge" (Galatians 3:24) to lead people to Christ. It did this through its many prophecies concerning the Messiah, which Jesus fulfilled. The sacrificial system emphasized the need for atonement for sin and, in itself, was a type of Messianic foretelling.

The Old Testament contains numerous pictures of the person and work of Christ: the serpent on the pole, the water from the rock, the manna from heaven, the offering of Isaac, the "resurrection" of Jonah, and the details of the Passover and other religious feasts, just to name a few. Those familiar with the Hebrew Scriptures would be primed for the arrival of the One to fulfill those types.

Finally, Christ came when He did in fulfillment of a specific prophecy. Daniel 9:24–27 speaks of the "seventy weeks" or the seventy "sevens." From the context, these "weeks" or "sevens" refer to groups of seven years, not seven days. As we examine history and line up the details of the first 69 weeks, we see that Jesus came right on schedule. The countdown of the seventy weeks began with "the issuing of the decree to restore and rebuild Jerusalem" (verse 25). Artaxerxes Longimanus gave this command in 445 BC (see Nehemiah 2:5–8). After seven "sevens" plus 62 "sevens" (69 x 7 years), "the Anointed One will be cut off and will have nothing. The people of the ruler who will come will destroy the city and the sanctuary." Then the "end will come like a flood" (meaning major destruction) (v. 26). Here we have an unmistakable reference to the Savior's death on the cross and the destruction of Jerusalem.

A century ago in his book *The Coming Prince*, Sir Robert Anderson gave detailed calculations of the 69 weeks, using "prophetic years," allowing for leap years, errors in the calendar, and the change from BC to AD, and figured that the 69 weeks ended on the very day of Jesus' triumphal entry into Jerusalem, five days before His death.[15] Whether one uses this timetable or not, the point is that the time of Christ's incarnation ties in with this detailed prophecy recorded by Daniel over 500 years beforehand.

The timing of Christ's first advent was such that the people of that generation were prepared for His coming. Every century since, people have had more than sufficient evidence that Jesus was indeed the promised Messiah, the One who came with such impeccable timing and fulfilled the Scriptures in such great detail.

Question: Why are Jesus' genealogies in Matthew and Luke so different?

Answer: Jesus' genealogy is given in two places in Scripture: Matthew 1 and Luke 3:23–38. Matthew traces the genealogy from Jesus to Abraham. Luke traces the genealogy from Jesus to Adam. However, there is good reason to believe that Matthew and Luke are in fact tracing entirely different genealogies. For example, Matthew gives Joseph's father as Jacob (Matthew 1:16), while Luke gives Joseph's father as Heli (Luke 3:23). Matthew traces the line through David's son Solomon (Matthew 1:6), while Luke traces the line through David's son Nathan (Luke 3:31). In fact, between David and Jesus, the only names the genealogies have in common are Shealtiel and Zerubbabel (Matthew 1:12; Luke 3:27).

Some point to these differences as evidence of errors in the Bible. However, the Jews were meticulous record keepers, especially in regard to genealogies. It is inconceivable that Matthew and Luke could build two entirely contradictory genealogies of the same lineage. Again, from David through Jesus, the genealogies are completely different. Even the reference to Shealtiel and Zerubbabel likely refer to different individuals of the same names. Matthew gives Shealtiel's father as Jeconiah while Luke gives Shealtiel's father as Neri. It would be normal for a man named Shealtiel to name his son Zerubbabel in light of the famous individuals of those names (see the books of Ezra and Nehemiah).

One explanation of the differences is that Matthew is tracing the primary lineage while Luke is taking into account the occurrences of "levirate marriage." If a man died without having any sons, it was tradition for the man's brother to marry his wife and have a son who would carry on the man's name. While possible, this view is unlikely as every generation from David to Jesus would have had a "levirate marriage" in order to account for the differences in every generation.

With these concepts in view, most conservative Bible scholars assume Luke is recording Mary's genealogy and Matthew is recording Joseph's. Matthew is following the line of Joseph (Jesus' legal father), through David's son Solomon, while Luke is following the line of Mary (Jesus' blood relative), though David's son Nathan. There was no Greek word for "son-in-law," and Joseph would have been considered a son of Heli through marrying Heli's daughter Mary. Through either line, Jesus is a descendant of David and therefore eligible to be the Messiah. Tracing a genealogy through the mother's side is unusual, but so was the virgin birth. Luke's explanation is that Jesus was the son of Joseph, "so it was thought" (Luke 3:23).

Question: What year was Jesus Christ born?

Answer: The Bible does not provide the exact day or even the exact year in which Jesus was born in Bethlehem. But a close examination of the chronological details of history narrows the possibilities to a reasonable window of time.

The details of Jesus' birth are found in the Gospels. Matthew 2:1 states that Jesus was born during the days of Herod the king. Since Herod died in 4 BC, we have a parameter to work with. Further, after Joseph and Mary fled Bethlehem with Jesus, Herod ordered all the boys two years old and younger in that vicinity killed. This indicates that Jesus could have been as old as two before Herod's death. This places the date of His birth between 6 and 4 BC.

Luke 2:1–2 notes several other facts: "In those days Caesar Augustus issued a decree that a census should be taken of the entire Roman world. (This was the first census that took place while Quirinius was governor of Syria.)" We know that Caesar Augustus reigned from 27 BC to AD 14.

Quirinius governed Syria during this time period, and we have records of a census that included Judea in approximately 6 BC. Some scholars debate whether this is the same census Luke mentions—but it does appear to be the same event. Based on these historical details, the most likely time of Christ's birth in Bethlehem is 6–5 BC.

Luke mentions another detail concerning our timeline: "Jesus, when he began his ministry, was about thirty years of age" (Luke 3:23). Jesus began His ministry during the time John the Baptist ministered in the wilderness, and John's ministry started "in the fifteenth year of the reign of Tiberius Caesar—when Pontius Pilate was governor of Judea, Herod tetrarch of Galilee, his brother Philip tetrarch of Iturea and Traconitis, and Lysanias tetrarch of Abilene—during the high priesthood of Annas and Caiaphas" (Luke 3:1–2).

The only time period that fits all of these facts is AD 27–29. If Jesus was "about thirty years of age" by AD 27, a birth sometime between 6 and 4 BC would fit the chronology. More specifically, Jesus would have been approximately 32 years old at the time He began His ministry (still "about" thirty years old).

What about the day of Christ's birth? The tradition of December 25 was developed long after the New Testament period. It's the day Christians have agreed on to celebrate the birth of Jesus, but the exact day of His birth is unknown.

What is known is that biblical and historical details point to an approximate year of birth. Jesus was born in Bethlehem of Judea approximately 6–5 BC. His birth changed history forever, along with the lives of countless people around the world.

Question: Why is the virgin birth so important?

Answer: The doctrine of the virgin birth is crucially important (Isaiah 7:14; Matthew 1:23; Luke 1:27, 34). First, let's look at how Scripture describes the event. In response to Mary's question, "How will this be?" (Luke 1:34), Gabriel says, "The Holy Spirit will come upon you, and the power of the Most High will overshadow you" (Luke 1:35). The angel encourages Joseph not to fear marrying Mary with these words: "What is conceived in her is from the Holy Spirit" (Matthew 1:20). Matthew states that the virgin "was found to be with child through the Holy Spirit" (Matthew 1:18). Galatians 4:4 also teaches the virgin birth: "God sent His Son, born of a woman."

From these passages, it is certainly clear that Jesus' birth was the result of the Holy Spirit working within Mary's body. The immaterial (the Spirit) and the material (Mary's womb) were both involved. Mary, of course, could not impregnate herself, and in that sense she was simply a "vessel." Only God could perform the miracle of the incarnation.

However, denying a physical connection between Mary and Jesus would imply that Jesus was not truly human. Scripture teaches that Jesus was fully human, with a physical body like ours. This He received from Mary. At the same time, Jesus was fully God, with an eternal, sinless nature (John 1:14; 1 Timothy 3:16; Hebrews 2:14–17.)

Jesus was not born in sin; that is, He had no sin nature (Hebrews 7:26). It would seem that the sin nature is passed down from generation to generation through the father (Romans 5:12, 17, 19). The virgin birth circumvented the transmission of the sin nature and allowed the eternal God to become a perfect man.

Question: What happened during Jesus' childhood?

Answer: Other than Luke 2:41–52, the Bible does not tell us anything about Jesus' youth. But we do know certain things about Jesus' childhood from this passage. First, He was the son of parents who were devout in their religious observances. As required by their faith, Joseph and Mary made the yearly pilgrimage to Jerusalem for the Feast of the Passover. In addition, they brought their 12-year-old son to celebrate His first feast in preparation for His bar mitzvah at age 13, when Jewish boys commemorate their passage into adulthood. Here we see a typical boy in a typical family of that day.

We see also in this story that Jesus' lingering in the temple was neither mischievous nor disobedient, but a natural result of His knowledge that He must be about His Father's business. That He was astonishing the temple teachers with His wisdom and knowledge speaks to His extraordinary abilities, while His listening and asking questions of His elders shows that He was utterly respectful, taking the role of a student as was fitting for a child of His age.

From this incident to His baptism around age 30, all we know of Jesus' youth was that He left Jerusalem and returned to Nazareth with His parents and "was obedient to them" (Luke 2:51). He fulfilled His duty to His earthly parents in submission to the fifth commandment, an essential part of the perfect obedience to the Law of Moses that He rendered on our behalf. Beyond that, all we know is that "Jesus grew in wisdom and stature, and in favor with God and men" (Luke 2:52).

Evidently, this is all God determined that we need to know. There are some extra-biblical writings that contain stories of Jesus' youth (the Gospel of Thomas, for example), but we have no way of knowing whether any of these stories are true and reliable. God chose not to tell us much about Jesus' childhood, and we trust Him that nothing else occurred that we need to know about.

Question: Did Jesus have brothers and sisters (siblings)?

Answer: Jesus' brothers are mentioned in several Bible verses. Matthew 12:46, Luke 8:19, and Mark 3:31 say that Jesus' mother and brothers came to see Him. The Bible tells us that Jesus had four brothers: James, Joseph, Simon, and Judas (Matthew 13:55). The Bible also says that Jesus had sisters, but they are not named or numbered (Matthew 13:56). In John 7:1–10, His brothers go on to the festival while Jesus stays behind. In Acts 1:14, His brothers and mother are described as praying with the disciples. Galatians 1:19 mentions that James was Jesus' brother. The most natural meaning of these passages is that Jesus had actual half-siblings, related by blood.

Some Roman Catholics claim that these "brothers" were actually Jesus' cousins. However, in each instance, the specific Greek word for "brother" is used. While the word can refer to other relatives, its normal and literal meaning is a physical brother. There was a Greek word for "cousin," but it was not used. Further, if they were Jesus' cousins, why would they so often be described as being with Mary, Jesus' mother? There is nothing in the context of His mother and brothers coming to see Him that even hints that they were anyone other than His literal, blood-related, half-brothers.

A second Roman Catholic argument is that Jesus' brothers and sisters were the children of Joseph from a previous marriage. The Catholic Church has created an entire backstory concerning Joseph—that he was significantly older than Mary and that he was a widower with multiple children from his first marriage. The story is made of whole cloth. The Bible does not even hint that Joseph was married or had children before he married Mary. If Joseph had at least six children before he married Mary, why are they not mentioned in Joseph and Mary's trip to Bethlehem (Luke 2:4–7) or their trip to Egypt (Matthew 2:13–15) or their trip back to Nazareth (Matthew 2:20–21)?

There is no biblical reason to believe that Jesus' brothers and sisters mentioned in the Gospels are anything other than the actual children of Joseph and Mary. Those who oppose the idea that Jesus had siblings do so not from a reading of Scripture, but from a desire to uphold the notion of Mary's perpetual virginity. Such a concept of Mary is itself clearly unbiblical: "But he (Joseph) had no union with her (Mary) until she gave birth to a son" (Matthew 1:25). The undeniable implication of this verse is that, after the birth of Jesus, Joseph and Mary engaged in normative marital relations. Jesus had half-siblings, half-brothers and half-sisters, who were the children of Joseph and Mary. That is the unambiguous teaching of God's Word.

Question: Could Jesus have sinned? If He was not capable of sinning, how could He truly be able to "sympathize with our weaknesses" (Hebrews 4:15)? If He could not sin, what was the point of the temptation?

Answer: There are two sides to this interesting question. It is important to remember that this is not a question of whether Jesus sinned. Both sides agree, as the Bible clearly says, that Jesus did not sin (2 Corinthians 5:21; 1 Peter 2:22). The question is whether Jesus *could have* sinned. Those who hold to "impeccability" believe that Jesus could not have sinned. Those who hold to "peccability" believe that Jesus could have sinned, but did not. Which view is correct? The clear teaching of Scripture is that Jesus was impeccable—Jesus could not have sinned. If He could have sinned, He would still be able to sin today because He retains the same essence He did while living on earth. He is the God-Man and will forever remain so, having full deity and full humanity so united in one person as to be indivisible. To believe that Jesus could sin is to believe that God could sin. "For God was pleased to have all his fullness dwell in him" (Colossians 1:19). Colossians 2:9 adds, "For in Christ all the fullness of the Deity lives in bodily form."

Although Jesus is fully human, He was not born with the same sinful nature that we are born with. He certainly was tempted in the same way we are, in that Satan put temptations before Him (Matthew 4:1; Hebrews 2:18), yet He remained sinless because God is incapable of sinning. It is against His very nature (Hebrews 4:15; James 1:13). Sin is by definition a trespass of the Law. God spoke the Law as an expression of His holiness, and the Law is by nature what God would or would not do; therefore, sin is anything that God would not do by His very nature.

To be tempted is not necessarily sinful. For example, a person could tempt you to commit murder or participate in sexual perversions. You probably have no desire whatsoever to take part in those actions, but you were still "tempted" because someone placed the possibility before you. Thus, there are at least two definitions for the word *tempted*: 1) To have a sinful action suggested to you by someone or something outside yourself or by your own sin nature, and 2) To consider actually participating in a sinful act and the possible pleasures and consequences of such an act to the degree that the act is already taking place in your mind.

The first definition does not describe a sinful act/thought; the second does. When you dwell upon a sinful act and consider how you might be able to bring it to pass, you have crossed the line of sin (see Matthew 5:28). Jesus was tempted in the fashion of the first definition except that He was never tempted by a sin nature because it did not exist within Him. Satan proposed certain sinful Acts to Jesus, but Jesus had no inner desire to participate in the sin. Therefore, He was tempted (externally) like we are, but remained sinless.

Those who hold to peccability believe that, if Jesus could not have sinned, He could not have truly experienced temptation, and therefore could not truly empathize with our struggles against sin. We have to remember that one does not have to experience something in order to understand it. God knows everything about everything. While God has never had the desire to sin, and has most definitely never sinned, He knows and understands what sin is. He knows and understands what it is like to be tempted. Jesus can empathize with our temptations because He knows, not because He has "experienced" all the same things we have.

Jesus knows what it is like to be tempted, but He has not experienced sinning. This does not prevent Him from assisting us. We are tempted with sins that are common to man (1 Corinthians 10:13). These sins fall into three general types:

"the lust of the eyes, the lust of the flesh, and the pride of life" (1 John 2:16, NKJV). Examine the temptation and sin of Eve, as well as the temptation of Jesus, and you will find that the temptations for each came from these three categories.

Jesus was tempted in every way and in every area that we are but remained perfectly holy. Although our corrupt natures have an inner desire to participate in some sins, we have the ability, through Christ, to overcome temptation. We are no longer slaves to sin but rather slaves of God (Romans 6, especially verses 2 and 16–22).

Question: Was Jesus Christ married? Did Jesus have a wife?

Answer: The recent discovery and translation of the fourth-century "Jesus' wife papyrus" has reopened the discussion as to whether Jesus was married. The "Jesus' wife papyrus" says, "Jesus said to them, 'My wife...'" This discovery is interesting in that it is the first Gnostic writing to explicitly state that Jesus had a wife. While a couple of the Gnostic Gospels mention Jesus having a close relationship with Mary Magdalene, none of them specifically state that Jesus was married to her or to anyone else. Ultimately, it does not matter what the "Jesus' wife papyrus" or Gnostic Gospels say. They have no authority. They have all been proven to be forgeries invented to create a Gnostic view of Jesus.

If Jesus had been married, the Bible would have told us so, or there would be some unambiguous statement to that fact. Scripture would not be completely silent on such an important issue. The Bible mentions Jesus' mother, adoptive father, half-brothers, and half-sisters. Why would it neglect to mention the fact that Jesus had a wife? Those who believe/teach that Jesus was married are doing so in an attempt to "humanize" Him, to make Him more ordinary, more like everyone else. People simply do not want to believe that Jesus was God in the flesh (John 1:1, 14; 10:30). So, they invent and believe myths about Jesus being married, having children, and being an ordinary human being.

A secondary question would be, "*Could* Jesus Christ have been married?" There is nothing sinful about being married. There is nothing sinful about having sexual relations in marriage. So, yes, Jesus could have been married and still be the sinless Lamb of God and Savior of the world. At the same time, there is no biblical reason for Jesus to marry. That is not the point in this debate. Those who believe Jesus was married do not believe that He was sinless or that He was the Messiah. Getting married and having children is not why God sent Jesus. Mark 10:45 tells us why Jesus came, "For even the Son of Man did not come to be served, but to serve, and to give his life as a ransom for many."

Question: Was Jesus a Jew?

Answer: One need only search the Internet to determine that there is great disagreement over the question of whether Jesus of Nazareth was actually Jewish. Before we can answer this question adequately, we must first ask another: who (or what) is a Jew? Even this question has its controversial elements, and the answer depends on who is answering. But one definition that each of the major sects of Judaism— Orthodox, Conservative, and Reformed— would probably agree to is, "any person whose mother was a Jew or any person who has gone through the formal process of conversion to Judaism."

Although the Hebrew Bible does not specifically state the condition of matrilineal descent, modern rabbinical Judaism believes that there are several passages in the Torah where this is understood or implied, such as Deuteronomy 7:1–5; Leviticus 24:10; and Ezra 10:2–3. There are also several examples in Scripture of Gentiles converting to Judaism (e.g., Ruth the Moabitess; see Ruth 1:16) who are then considered every bit as Jewish as an ethnic Jew.

So, let's examine these three questions: Was Jesus a Jew ethnically? Was Jesus an observant Jew religiously? And then finally, if Jesus was a Jew, why don't Christians follow Judaism?

Was Jesus a Jew ethnically, or was His mother a Jew? Jesus clearly identified with the Jews of His day, His physical people and tribe, and their religion (although correcting its errors). God purposely sent Him to Judah: "He came to His own [Judah], and His own did not receive Him. But as many [Jews] as received Him, to them He gave the right to become children of God, to those who believe in His name..." (John 1:11–12, NKJV). Jesus also said, "You Samaritans worship what you do not know; we [Jews] know what we worship, for salvation is of the Jews" (John 4:22).

The very first verse of the New Testament clearly proclaims the Jewish ethnicity of Jesus. "The book of the genealogy of Jesus Christ, the son of David, the son of Abraham" (Matthew 1:1). It is evident from Hebrews 7:14 that Jesus descended from the tribe of Judah, from which we get the name "Jew." And what about Mary, the mother of Jesus? In the genealogy in Luke chapter 3, we find that Mary was a direct descendant of King David, which gave Jesus the legal right to ascend the Jewish throne as well as establishing, without any doubt, that Jesus was a Jew ethnically.

Was Jesus an observant Jew religiously? Both of Jesus' parents had "done everything required by the Law of the Lord" (Luke 2:39). His aunt and uncle, Zechariah and Elizabeth, were also Torah-observant Jews (Luke 1:5–6), so we can see that probably the whole family took their Jewish faith very seriously.

In the Sermon on the Mount (Matthew 5—7), Jesus continually affirmed the authority of the Torah and the Prophets (Matthew 5:17), even in the kingdom of heaven (Matthew 5:19–20). He regularly attended synagogue (Luke 4:16), and His teaching was respected by the other Jews of His day (Luke 4:15). He taught in the Jewish temple in Jerusalem (Luke 21:37); if He were not a Jew, His going into that part of the temple would not have been allowed.

Jesus also displayed the outward signs of being an observant Jew. He wore *tzitzit* (tassles) on His clothing (Luke 8:43; Matthew 14:36) to serve as a reminder of the commandments (Numbers 15:37–39). He observed Passover (John 2:13) and went up to Jerusalem on this important Jewish pilgrimage feast day (Deuteronomy 16:16). He observed Succoth, or the Feast of Tabernacles, and went up to Jerusalem as required in the Torah (John 7:2, 10). He also observed Hanukkah, the Festival of Lights (John 10:22) and probably Rosh

Hashanah, the Feast of Trumpets (John 5:1), going up to Jerusalem on both those occasions as well. Clearly, Jesus identified Himself as a Jew (John 4:22) and as King of the Jews (Mark 15:2). From His birth to His last Seder (Luke 22:14–15), Jesus lived as an observant Jew.

So, if Jesus was a Jew, why is it that Christians don't follow Judaism? The Laws of Judaism were given to Moses for the children of Israel in a sacred covenant at Mount Sinai and recorded for us in the book of Exodus. In this covenant, God wrote His laws on tablets of stone, and Israel was commanded to be obedient to all that was revealed to them. But this wonderful covenant was only a picture of a new and better covenant that God would one day give to His people, both Jew and Gentile.

This new covenant was predicted in Jeremiah 31:31–34, "'The time is coming,' declares the LORD, 'when I will make a new covenant with the house of Israel and with the house of Judah. It will not be like the covenant I made with their forefathers when I took them by the hand to lead them out of Egypt, because they broke my covenant, though I was a husband to them,' declares the LORD. 'This is the covenant I will make with the house of Israel after that time,' declares the LORD. 'I will put my law in their minds and write it on their hearts. I will be their God, and they will be my people. No longer will a man teach his neighbor, or a man his brother, saying, "Know the LORD," because they will all know me, from the least of them to the greatest,' declares the LORD. 'For I will forgive their wickedness and will remember their sins no more.'"

Christians don't follow Judaism today because the Mosaic Covenant has been fulfilled in Jesus Christ. Jesus said, "Do not think that I have come to abolish the Law or the Prophets; I have not come to abolish them but to fulfill them" (Matthew 5:17). And the writer of Hebrews wrote, "By calling this covenant 'new,' he has made the first one obsolete; and what is obsolete and aging will soon disappear" (Hebrews 8:13).

As Christians we don't need to follow the old covenant any longer because that old covenant has been replaced. We now have a better covenant, with a better sacrifice, administered by a better high priest (Hebrews 8:6)! "Therefore, brothers, since we have confidence to enter the Most Holy Place by the blood of Jesus, by a new and living way opened for us through the curtain, that is, his body, and since we have a great priest over the house of God, let us draw near to God with a sincere heart in full assurance of faith, having our hearts sprinkled to cleanse us from a guilty conscience and having our bodies washed with pure water. Let us hold unswervingly to the hope we profess, for he who promised is faithful" (Hebrews 10:19–23).

Question: What did Jesus look like?

Answer: The Bible never gives any physical description of Christ. The closest thing to a description is in Isaiah 53:2b, "He had no beauty or majesty to attract us to him, nothing in his appearance that we should desire him." All this tells us is that Jesus' appearance was like any other man's—He was ordinary-looking. Isaiah was prophesying that the Suffering Servant would arise in lowly conditions and wear none of the usual emblems of royalty, making His true identity visible only to the discerning eye of faith.

Isaiah further describes the appearance of Christ as He would appear after His scourging: "His appearance was so disfigured beyond that of any man and his form marred beyond human likeness" (Isaiah 52:14). These words describe the inhuman cruelty He suffered to the point that He no longer looked like a human being (Matthew 26:67; 27:30; John 19:3). His appearance was so awful that people looked at Him in astonishment.

Most of the images we have of Jesus today are probably not accurate. Jesus was a Jew, so He likely had dark skin, dark eyes, and dark hair. This is a far cry from the blue-eyed, fair-skinned Jesus in many modern pictures. One thing is clear: if it were important for us to know what He looked like, Matthew, Peter, and John, who spent three years with Him, would have given us a description. Yet these New Testament writers offer no details of His physical attributes.

Question: Was Jesus black?

Answer: There are some groups, usually affiliated with some form of the "Black Hebrew" movement, who vehemently argue that Jesus was black/African in skin color/appearance. This view goes directly against the fact that the Bible declares Jesus' Jewishness, meaning He likely had light to dark brown skin. Ultimately, however, the argument misses the point. Does it really matter that we know the color of Jesus' skin—whether He was black, brown, or white? Though this may be a controversial issue for some, the truth is that we simply don't know what color Jesus' skin was. The Bible provides little, if any, description of what Jesus might have looked like.

It is the prophet Isaiah who gives us the best "description" of the physical appearance of Jesus, but it's more of a non-description: "He grew up before him like a tender shoot, and like a root out of dry ground. He had no beauty or majesty to attract us to him, nothing in his appearance that we should desire him" (Isaiah 53:2). If Jesus' skin color were important, then God would have told us about it. Furthermore, to wrangle over Jesus' skin color is to speculate on information not found in Scripture. As such, it is useless speculation at best (1 Timothy 1:4; Titus 3:9). In the whole scheme of redemption, it does not matter what color of skin Jesus had (Ephesians 1:7; Colossians 1:14).

So, what should we concern ourselves with when it comes to Jesus? Peter tells us: "His divine power has given us everything we need for life and godliness through our knowledge of him who called us by his own glory and goodness" (2 Peter 1:3). In other words, Christ has called us to a life of glory and moral excellence. We are to live pure and righteous lives for His glory. It is His glory and goodness that attract us to seek life and godliness in Him. It has absolutely nothing to do with the way He looks or the color of His skin.

Peter also tells us that God "does not show favoritism but accepts men from every nation who fear him and do what is right" (Acts 10:34–35). When Jesus calls for us to go into all the world and teach the gospel (Acts 1:8), He is telling us that there are no cultural or racial barriers, and that we are all one in Christ Jesus. Paul echoes this in his letter to the churches in Galatia: "There is neither Jew nor Greek, slave nor free, male nor female, for you are all one in Christ Jesus" (Galatians 3:28). The color of our Savior's skin has no bearing on our sharing the gospel. Nor should our neighbor's skin color have any bearing on our imparting the gospel message to him (Romans 1:16).

Paul may have changed his method of teaching whenever he entered a new culture or foreign land, but he never changed his message. He kept preaching the same things he had always taught, regardless of the color of his listeners' skin. What mattered was that they received the good news of Christ. The truth is that the message of the gospel of Christ worked then and still works today! It still reaches into the hearts of those who yearn to know God, no matter their skin color. It's not the color of Jesus' skin or the color of our neighbor's skin that matters in our eternal destiny. But what does matter is this: "Salvation is found in no one else, for there is no other name under heaven given to men by which we must be saved" (Acts 4:12).

Question: What was Jesus like as a person?

Answer: Although He had "nothing in his appearance that we should desire him" (Isaiah 53:2), Jesus still attracted large crowds when He spoke, at least in the beginning of His ministry (Luke 5:1). Part of the reason for His early popularity must have been His compelling personality.

Jesus had a compassionate nature. He had compassion on the crowds "because they were harassed and helpless, like sheep without a shepherd" (Matthew 9:36). He compassionately healed their diseases (Matthew 14:14; 20:34), taught them God's Word (Luke 5:3), blessed their children (Mark 10:16), and provided for their needs (Matthew 15:32).

Jesus was also serious and focused. He had a mission in life and never got sidetracked from it. He knew the importance of His work and the shortness of the time. His attitude was that of a servant. He "did not come to be served, but to serve" (Mark 10:45). Kindness and selflessness characterized His personality.

Jesus was submissive to His Father's will, even to the point of dying on the cross (Philippians 2:8; Hebrews 5:8). He prayed the night of His betrayal, "My Father, if it is possible, may this cup be taken from me. Yet not as I will, but as you will" (Matthew 26:39). He was a submissive Son to Mary and Joseph as well. He grew up in a normal (sinful) household, yet He "was obedient to them" (Luke 2:51).

Jesus was kind and had a heart of mercy and forgiveness: "Father, forgive them, for they do not know what they are doing" (Luke 23:34). He was also loving in His relationships: "Now Jesus loved Martha and her sister and Lazarus" (John 11:5). John was known as the disciple "whom Jesus loved" (John 13:23). Jesus sympathized with the pain of His friends (John 11:35).

Jesus was a man of integrity. He never violated His own word. He spoke truth wherever He went. He lived a life we could follow explicitly: "I am the way and the truth and the life" (John 14:6). At the same time, He was peaceable. He did not argue His case, nor try to bully His way into people's hearts.

Jesus was intimate with His followers. He spent quality and quantity time with them. He coveted their fellowship, taught them, and helped them focus on what was eternal. He was also intimate with His Heavenly Father. He prayed to Him regularly, listened, obeyed, and cared about God's reputation. He spoke with authority and boldly stood for righteousness (Mark 1:22; Luke 19:46). He was obviously a strong leader. At the same time, He was exceedingly meek and humble (Matthew 11:29).

Another quality of Jesus was His patience—He knew and understood our frailties. How often He showed patience with His disciples, even when they were fighting among themselves and acting rashly! Jesus was and is "patient with you, not wanting anyone to perish, but everyone to come to repentance" (2 Peter 3:9).

These are traits that all believers should desire to become a part of their own personality and character. The things that drew people to Jesus should be the very things that draw people to us. Jesus has given those who believe in Him His Holy Spirit, who enables us to be progressively changing into His image (Romans 8:29). This will only come about as we yield to Him and acknowledge who He truly is—Lord of the universe! We must not resist His will for us. Jesus never drew attention to Himself, but rather to His Father; even so, we ought to say as John the Baptist did, "He must become greater; I must become less" (John 3:30).

Question: When did Jesus know that He was God?

Answer: The Bible never states that there was a point at which Jesus knew that He is the second Person of the Trinity. At some point, Jesus fully realized who He was from eternity past, expressing it this way: "Most assuredly, I say to you, before Abraham was, I AM" (John 8:58, NKJV). "And now, O Father, glorify Me together with Yourself, with the glory which I had with You before the world was" (John 17:5, NKJV). But the preincarnate Christ always knew He is the second Person of the Trinity. He made the universe: "But in these last days he [God] has spoken to us by his Son, whom he appointed heir of all things, and through whom he made the universe" (Hebrews 1:2). Jesus knew from the foundation of the world that He would die for our sins: "And I will put enmity between you and the woman, and between your offspring and hers; he will crush your head and you will strike his heel" (Genesis 3:15), and "...the Lamb that was slain from the creation of the world" (Revelation 13:8).

We do not have a clear Scripture revealing the thoughts of Jesus as a baby, but Scripture does tell us that as a young child He was well aware of His work. Jesus was preparing even as a boy to finish the work His Father sent Him to do. When His parents were concerned about His absence on a trip back home from Jerusalem, they found Him in the temple "sitting among the teachers, listening to them and asking them questions" (Luke 2:46). Joseph and Mary asked Jesus why He would disappear and worry them so, and He responded, "'Why were you searching for me?...Didn't you know I had to be in my Father's house?' But they did not understand what he was saying to them" (Luke 2:49–50). Joseph and Mary may not have understood, but Jesus certainly did understand, at the age of 12, that He is the Son of God and that the Father had foreordained the work He was to do.

Back in Nazareth, Jesus "grew in wisdom and stature, and in favor with God and men" (Luke 2:52). If at this point in Jesus' experience He knew *everything*, it would not follow logically that He would need to "increase in wisdom." We know He had to grow physically (in stature), but we must also believe the Scripture where our understanding fails us, that is, that Jesus put Himself in a position where He needed to assimilate knowledge as a man. He needed to be truly man. He was always God, but when He took on human nature, He became like us in all ways, except for sin. This included a need to learn and increase in wisdom. The theological term for the relationship between Jesus' human and divine natures is the hypostatic union.

We can conclude that, although the preincarnate Jesus knew from eternity past who He was and what His work in the world was to be, the incarnate Jesus came to that realization at some point in His earthly life. Just when that point was, we cannot know for sure.

Question: What language did Jesus speak?

Answer: While Jesus likely knew Hebrew and Greek, Aramaic was probably the language He spoke the most. The Gospels record Jesus speaking numerous Aramaic words: *talitha koum* (Mark 5:41); *ephphatha* (Mark 7:34); *Eloi Eloi lama sabachthani* (Matthew 27:46; Mark 15:34); and *Abba* (Mark 14:36). Historians, archaeologists, and cultural anthropologists are almost in universal agreement that Aramaic was the common or colloquial language in Israel during Jesus' time. Aramaic was very similar to Hebrew, but with many words and phrases that were borrowed from other languages and cultures—particularly Babylonian.

The scribes, Pharisees, and Sadducees—the "religious elite"—spoke Hebrew primarily. Hebrew was likely often read in the synagogues, so most Jews were probably able to speak and understand some Hebrew. Greek was the universal trade language at that time, so the ability to speak Greek was a highly desirable skill, and many Romans learned Greek side by side with Latin. Some Jews, however, refused to speak Greek out of resentment toward their Roman oppressors. When Jesus spoke with Pontius Pilate, it is possible that He spoke to him in Greek, although it is also probable that Pilate, as the governor, would have been able to speak Aramaic as well.

Jesus, as God incarnate, could have spoken any language He chose. In His humanity, Jesus probably limited Himself to the languages common to His culture: Aramaic, Hebrew, and Greek. Jesus likely spoke whichever of the three languages was most appropriate for the audience He was addressing.

Question: Was Jesus sinless?

Answer: Yes, Jesus was sinless, and it is because Jesus was sinless that we have hope of an eternity in heaven. If Jesus were not sinless, there would be no sacrifice for sin. Adam and Eve's disobedience to God in the Garden of Eden ushered sin into this world (Genesis 3:6). And with this sin came death, just as God had warned (Genesis 2:17). As a result, mankind is now born with a sin nature (Romans 5:12–14), which is with us from the time we are conceived (Psalm 51:5). The Bible makes it clear, however, that Jesus Christ, though tempted in every way just as we are (Hebrews 4:15), never committed a sin (2 Corinthians 5:21; 1 John 3:5). "He committed no sin, and no deceit was found in his mouth" (1 Peter 2:22). Indeed, as Jesus Christ is God, He has no capacity to sin.

In addition to putting a barrier between us and our Creator, our inherited sinful nature subjects all of us to physical and eternal death because "the wages of sin is death" (Romans 6:23). To be reconciled with God there needs to be forgiveness, and "without the shedding of blood there is no forgiveness" (Hebrews 9:22). After Adam and Eve sinned, God clothed them with "garments of skin" (Genesis 3:21), which required the shedding of the blood of an animal. The many subsequent animal sacrifices illustrated that sin brings death, but they could provide only a temporary covering of sins. The blood of those animals could never completely take away sin (Hebrews 10:4, 11).

These sacrifices, however, were a foreshadowing of the perfect, "once-for-all" sacrifice of Jesus Christ (Hebrews 7:27; 10:10). The only way for us to be reconciled to a holy and perfect God was to have a holy and perfect offering, which required Jesus Christ to be sinless. As Peter declared, "For you know that it is not with perishable things such as silver or gold that you were redeemed... but with the precious blood of Jesus Christ, a lamb without blemish or defect" (1 Peter 1:18–19). Indeed, it was the blood of the sinless Christ alone that was able to bring peace between God and mankind (Colossians 1:20). And, with this reconciliation, we can be "holy in [God's] sight, without blemish and free from accusation" (Colossians 1:22).

The sinless Christ's death on the cross paid the full penalty for the sin of all who believe in Him. Thus, what was lost at the fall was given back at the cross. Just as sin entered the world through one man (Adam), God was able to redeem the world through one man—the sinless Jesus Christ (Romans 5:12–21).

Question: Was Jesus rich/wealthy?

Answer: As the second Person of the Trinity, Jesus is as rich as God. Indeed, our Lord owns everything and possesses all power, authority, sovereignty, glory, honor, and majesty (Isaiah 9:6; Micah 5:2; John 1:1; 8:58; 10:30; 17:5; Colossians 1:15–18; 2:9–10; Hebrews 1:3). Yet during the time Jesus was here on earth, He willingly relinquished His eternal riches and most of the privileges of His deity. Becoming poor, our Lord took on the nature of a lowly and humble servant (2 Corinthians 8:9; Philippians 2:6–8). By the time our Savior endured the tortures of the cross for us, His earthly possessions amounted to no more than the clothes on His back, which were divided up by the soldiers who crucified Him.

Sadly, however, there are many prosperity preachers today who would like you to believe that Jesus was rich while here on earth and that God wants nothing more than to lavish His children with an abundance of material blessings. However, a materially rich Jesus is utterly incompatible with biblical truth. Even a cursory examination of the Bible should dispel any notion of our Savior being wealthy in an earthly sense. During His public ministry, Christ and His disciples depended entirely on the hospitality of others as they ministered from town to town (Matthew 10:9–10). As Jesus told a would-be follower, "Foxes have holes and birds of the air have nests, but the Son of Man has no place to lay His head" (Luke 9:58).

It is unfortunate, then, that this false teaching about Christ's wealth and a "gospel of greed" has gained a foothold in churches today. But "there is nothing new under the sun" (Ecclesiastes 1:9), and Paul addressed similar matters in his own churches: "Watch out for those who cause divisions and put obstacles in your way that are contrary to the teaching you have learned. Keep away from them. For such people are not serving our Lord Christ, but their own appetites. By smooth talk and flattery they deceive the minds of naive people" (Romans 16:17–18).

Paul's terse commentary in his first letter to Timothy captures the essence of Christ's numerous teachings on the dangers that accompany a heart bent on the accumulation of earthly treasure: "People who want to get rich fall into temptation and a trap and into many foolish and harmful desires that plunge men into ruin and destruction. For the love of money is a root of all kinds of evil. Some people, eager for money, have wandered from the faith and pierced themselves with many griefs" (1 Timothy 6:9–10).

Jesus taught, "Be on your guard against all kinds of greed; a man's life does not consist in the abundance of his possessions" (Luke 12:15). He also cautioned us not to "store up for [ourselves] treasures on earth, where moths and vermin destroy, and where thieves break in and steal. But store up...treasures in heaven, where moths and vermin do not destroy, and where thieves do not break in and steal" (Matthew 6:19–20). Our Lord, who knows the hearts of men, is aware of the deceitfulness of riches and what a considerable stumbling block wealth can be (Mark 4:19; 10:25). Thus, it would be a strange paradox indeed—and one that would certainly dilute the gospel message—if Jesus Christ were a member of the rich class of people who, as He declared, would find it difficult "to enter the kingdom of heaven" (Matthew 19:23).

Question: What were the key events in the life of Jesus Christ?

Answer: The following are the key events in the life of Christ and the Bible books where each is described.

Birth (Luke 2:1–20)

Within this passage are most of the elements of the well-known Christmas story. Mary and Joseph, no room at the inn, the babe in the manger, the shepherds with their flocks, a multitude of angels rejoicing—all these things make up the amazing story of the birth of the Savior 2,000 years ago. But the story of God coming to earth as a man began many years earlier with the prophecies of the coming Messiah. Isaiah foretold of a virgin who would conceive and bear a son and call Him Immanuel, which means "God with us" (Isaiah 7:14). The first of the key events in the life of Christ is His humble beginning in a stable, when God came to be with us. He was born to set His people free and to save us from our sins.

Baptism (Matthew 3:13–17; Mark 1:9–11; Luke 3:21–23)

Jesus' baptism by John at the Jordan River is the first act of His public ministry. John's was a baptism of repentance, and, although Jesus did not need such a baptism, He submitted Himself to it in order to identify Himself with sinners. He would soon bear their sins on the cross where He would exchange His righteousness for their sin (2 Corinthians 5:21). The baptism of Christ symbolized His death and resurrection, prefigured and lent importance to Christian baptism, and publicly identified Christ with those for whom He would die. In addition, God Himself confirmed

Jesus' identity as the long-awaited Messiah when He spoke from heaven: "This is my Son, whom I love; with him I am well pleased" (Matthew 3:17). Finally, Jesus' baptism was the scene of the first recorded appearance of the Trinity to man. The Son was baptized, the Father spoke, and the Holy Spirit descended like a dove. The Father's command, the Son's obedience, and the Holy Spirit's empowerment present a beautiful picture of the life and ministry of Christ.

First Miracle (John 2:1–11)

It is fitting that John's Gospel is the only one that records Jesus' first miracle. The theme and purpose of John's account is the Revelation of the deity of Christ. Surely, this first miracle of creating something from nothing proves that Jesus was God in the flesh, the Creator, through whom all things came to be (John 1:3). Only God could do a miracle of this nature. This event shows Jesus' divine power over the elements of the earth, the same power that would be revealed again in many more miracles. John goes on to tell us that this first miracle had two outcomes—the glory of Christ was manifest and the disciples "put their faith in him" (John 2:11). The divine, glorified nature of Christ was hidden when He assumed human form, but in instances such as this miracle, His true nature was made manifest to all who had eyes to see (Matthew 13:16). The disciples always believed in Jesus, but the miracles helped to strengthen their faith and prepare them for the difficult times that lay ahead.

Sermon on the Mount (Matthew 5:1–7:29)

Jesus preached what is perhaps the most famous sermon of all time to His disciples early in His public ministry. Many memorable phrases come from this sermon, including "blessed are the meek, for they shall inherit the earth," "salt of the earth," "the lilies of the field," "ask and it will be given to you," and "wolves in sheep's clothing," as well as the concepts of going the extra mile, turning the other cheek, etc. Jesus also taught the Lord's Prayer in this sermon. Most importantly, though, the Sermon on the Mount dealt a devastating blow to the Pharisees and their religion of works-based righteousness. By expounding on the spirit of the Law and not just the letter of it, Jesus left no doubt that legalism is of no avail for salvation and that, in fact, the demands of the Law are humanly impossible to meet. He ends the sermon with a call to true faith for salvation and a warning that the way to that salvation is narrow—few find it.

Feeding of the 5,000 (Matthew 14:15–21; Mark 6:34–44; Luke 9:12–17; John 6:5–13)

We learn several important lessons from this miraculous event. As with the miracle of the water and wine at Cana, we see Jesus' absolute power over the elements of nature. Only God could have done this miracle, and from five small loaves and two fish Jesus created enough food to feed many thousands of people. The Gospels tell us there were 5,000 men present, but Matthew adds that there were women and children there besides. Estimates of the crowd are as high as 20,000. Our God is a God of abundant provision, and little is much in the hands of the Lord. We can learn a poignant lesson by seeing that before He multiplied the loaves and fishes, Jesus commanded the multitude to sit down. This is a beautiful picture of the power of God to accomplish what we cannot while we rest in Him. There was nothing the people could do to feed themselves; only Jesus could do that. They had only a pittance, but in God's hands it became a feast that was not only sufficient, it was bountiful.

Transfiguration (Matthew 17:1–8; Mark 9:2–8; Luke 9:28–36)

This event is referred to as the transfiguration— meaning "a change in form"—because Jesus was changed before the eyes of Peter, James, and John into a reflection of His true nature. His divine glory radiated from Him, changing His face and clothing in such a way that the Gospel writers had trouble relating it. Just as the apostle John used many metaphors to describe what he saw in the visions of Revelation, so, too, did Matthew, Mark, and Luke have to resort to images like "lightning," "the sun,"

91

and "light" to describe Jesus' appearance at the transfiguration. Truly, it was otherworldly. The appearance of Moses and Elijah to converse with Jesus shows us two things. First, the two men represent the Law and the Prophets, both of which foretold Jesus' coming and His death. Second, the fact that they talked about Jesus' upcoming death in Jerusalem (Luke 9:31) shows their foreknowledge of these events and the sovereign plan of God that was unfolding just as He had foreordained. God spoke from heaven and commanded the disciples to "Listen to him!" thereby stating that Jesus, not Moses and Elijah, now had the power and authority to command them.

Raising of Lazarus (John 11:1–44)

Lazarus, the brother of Mary and Martha of Bethany, was a personal friend of Jesus. This is why the family sent for Jesus when Lazarus was sick. Jesus delayed several days before going to Bethany, knowing that Lazarus would be dead long enough by then to verify an amazing display of His divine power. Only God has the power over life and death, and by raising Lazarus from the grave, Jesus was reiterating His authority as God and His supremacy over death. Through this incident, the Son of God was glorified in an unmistakable way. As with many other miracles and incidents, one of the goals was that the disciples—and we—"may believe." Jesus is who He said He was and this most astounding of His miracles testifies to that fact. Jesus told Martha, "I am the resurrection and the life" (verse 25) and asked her if she believed what He was saying. This is the basis of the Christian life. We believe that Jesus is the very power of resurrection, and we trust in Him to give us eternal life through that power. We are buried with Him and raised by His authority over death. Only through His power can we be truly saved.

Triumphal Entry (Matthew 21:1–11, 14–17; Mark 11:1–11; Luke 19:29–44; John 12:12–19)

Jesus' triumphal entry into Jerusalem the week before the crucifixion is the basis for what is now called Palm Sunday.

The multitudes that greeted Jesus laid palm branches in the road for Him, but their worship of Him was short-lived. In just a few days, these same crowds would be calling for His death, shouting, "Crucify him!" (Matthew 27:22–23). But as He rode into Jerusalem on the back of a donkey's colt—signifying peace and gentleness—He received the adoration of the crowd and their acknowledgement of His messianic claim. Even the little children welcomed Him, demonstrating that they knew what the Jewish leaders did not—that Jesus was the Messiah. Jesus' entry into Jerusalem fulfilled the Old Testament prophecy of Zechariah, which was repeated in John 12:15: "See, your king is coming, seated on a donkey's colt."

Last Supper (Matthew 26:17–29; Mark 14:12–25; Luke 22:7–20; John 13:1–38)

This poignant last meeting of Jesus and His beloved disciples begins with an object lesson from Jesus. The disciples had been arguing about who among them was the greatest (Luke 22:24) when Jesus quietly rose and began to wash their feet, a task normally performed by the lowest, most menial slave. By this simple act, Jesus reminded them that His followers are those who serve one another, not those who expect to be served. He went on to explain that unless the Lamb of God cleanses a person's sin, that person will never be clean: "Unless I wash you, you have no part with me" (John 13:8). During the Last Supper, Jesus also identified the traitor, Judas, who would betray Him to the authorities and bring about His arrest, and instructed Judas to leave and do quickly what he had to do. After Judas' departure, Jesus instituted the new covenant in His blood. He gave a new command that those who follow Him are to love one another and live by the power of the Holy Spirit. Each time we observe the Christian ordinance of communion, we celebrate Christ's body, which was broken for us, and His blood, which was shed for us.

Arrest at Gethsemane (Matthew 26:36–56; Mark 14:32–50; Luke 22:39–54; John 18:1–12)

After the Last Supper, Jesus led the disciples to the garden of Gethsemane, where several things took place. Jesus separated Himself from His disciples in order to pray, asking them to watch and pray as well. But several times He returned to find them sleeping, overcome with fatigue and grief at the prospect of losing Him. As Jesus prayed, He asked the Father to remove the cup of wrath He was about to drink when God poured out on Him the punishment for the sins of the world. But, as in all things, Jesus submitted to the will of His Father and began to prepare for His death, strengthened by an angel sent to minister to Him in His last hours. Judas arrived with a multitude and identified Jesus with a kiss, and Jesus was arrested and taken to Caiaphas for the first of a series of mock trials.

Crucifixion, Burial, and Resurrection (Matthew 27:27—28:7; Mark 15:16—16:7; Luke 23:26—24:8; John 19:17—20:9)

Jesus' death on the cross was the culmination of His ministry on earth. It is the reason He was born as a man—to die for the sins of the world so that those who believe in Him would not perish, but have everlasting life (John 3:16). After being found innocent of all charges against Him, Jesus was nevertheless handed over to the Romans to be crucified. The events of that day include the mocking and taunting of Jesus by the soldiers and the crowd, the casting of lots among the soldiers for Jesus' clothing, and three hours of darkness. When Jesus gave up His spirit, there was an earthquake and the huge, heavy curtain separating the Holy of Holies from the rest of the temple was torn from top to bottom, signifying that access to God was now open to all who believe in Jesus. The body of Jesus was later taken down from the cross, laid in a borrowed tomb, and left until after the Sabbath. When women came to prepare the body for burial, they found the tomb empty. Jesus had risen from the dead in His glorified state and would appear to many to prove that death had no hold over Him.

Post-Resurrection Appearances (Matthew 28:1–20; Mark 16:1–18; Luke 24:1–49; John 20:1—21:25; Acts 1:3; 1 Corinthians 15:6)

During the 40 days between Jesus' crucifixion and ascension, Jesus appeared several times to 500 of His disciples and others. He first appeared to the women near the tomb who came to prepare His body with spices, then to Mary Magdalene, to whom He declared that He had not yet ascended to the Father. Jesus appeared also to two men on the road to Emmaus and, as He ate with them and talked with them, they recognized Him. The men returned to Jerusalem, found the disciples, and testified of their encounter with Jesus. He appeared to the disciples in Jerusalem, then a second time where "doubting Thomas" was given proof, and then again in Galilee where the disciples saw another miracle: though they had fished all night and caught nothing, Jesus told them to lower their nets one more time, and their nets were filled with fish. Jesus cooked breakfast for them and taught them many important truths. Peter was told to feed the Lord's sheep. At this time, they also received the Great Commission.

Ascension (Mark 16:19–20; Luke 24:50–53; Acts 1:9–11)

Jesus' final act on earth was His return to heaven in the presence of the disciples. He was taken up in a cloud that hid Him from their view, and two angels came to tell them that Jesus would return one day in a similar manner. For now, Jesus sits at the right hand of His Father in heaven. The act of sitting down signifies that His work is done, as He affirmed on the cross when He said, "It is finished." There is nothing more to be done to secure the salvation of those who believe in Him. His life on earth is over, the price is paid, the victory is won and death itself has been defeated. Hallelujah!

"Jesus did many other things as well. If every one of them were written down, I suppose that even the whole world would not have room for the books that would be written" (John 21:25).

Chapter 5

······································

QUESTIONS ABOUT
JESUS' MINISTRY

Contents

Why was Jesus baptized? Why was Jesus' baptism important?

Why did Jesus teach in parables?

Why did Jesus command people not to tell others of the miracles He performed?

What was the meaning and purpose of Jesus' temptations?

What was the meaning and importance of the transfiguration?

Was Jesus ever angry?

How many times did Jesus cleanse the temple? Why did He cleanse the temple?

Why did Jesus curse the fig tree?

Did Jesus ever travel to India?

Was Jesus a pacifist?

Does the bible describe Jesus being worshipped?

What is the significance of the triumphal entry?

How long was Jesus' ministry?

Question: Why was Jesus baptized? Why was Jesus' baptism important?

Answer: At first glance, it seems that Jesus' baptism has no purpose at all. The baptism John the Baptist performed was the baptism of repentance (Matthew 3:11), but Jesus was sinless and had no need of repentance. Even John was taken aback at Jesus' coming to him. John recognized his own sin and was aware that he, a sinful man in need of repentance himself, was unfit to baptize the spotless Lamb of God: "I need to be baptized by you, and do you come to me?" (Matthew 3:14). Jesus replied that it should be done because "it is proper for us to do this to fulfill all righteousness" (Matthew 3:15).

There are several reasons why it was fitting for John to baptize Jesus at the beginning of His public ministry. Jesus was about to embark on His great work, and it was appropriate that His forerunner recognize Him publicly. John was the "voice of one crying in the wilderness" prophesied by Isaiah, calling people to repentance in preparation for their Messiah (Isaiah 40:3, NKJV). By baptizing Him, John was declaring to all that here was the One they had been waiting for, the Son of God, the One he had predicted would baptize "with the Holy Spirit and with fire" (Matthew 3:11).

Jesus' baptism also showed that He identified with sinners. His baptism symbolized the sinners' baptism into the righteousness of Christ, dying with Him and rising free from sin and able to walk in the newness of life. His perfect righteousness would fulfill all the requirements of the Law for sinners who could never hope to do so on their own. When John hesitated to baptize the sinless Son of God, Jesus replied that it was proper to "fulfill all righteousness" (Matthew 3:15). By this He alluded to the righteousness that He provides to all who come to Him to exchange their sin for His perfection (2 Corinthians 5:21).

In addition, Jesus came to John to show His approval of John's baptism, bearing witness that it was from heaven and approved by God. This would be important later, when others began to doubt John's authority, particularly after his arrest by Herod (Matthew 14:3–5).

98

Perhaps most importantly, the occasion of Jesus' public baptism recorded for all generations to come the Revelation of the triune God revealed in glory from heaven. The voice of the Father, the presence of the Son, and the descent of the Holy Spirit combine for a beautiful picture of the trinitarian nature of God (Matthew 3:16–17). The scene also depicts the work of the Father, Son, and Spirit in the salvation of those Jesus came to save. The Father loves the elect from before the foundation of the world (Ephesians 1:4–5); He sends His Son to seek and save the lost (Luke 19:10); and the Spirit convicts of sin (John 16:8) and draws the believer to the Father through the Son. God displays the glorious truth of His mercy through Jesus Christ at Jesus' baptism.

Question: Why did Jesus teach in parables?

Answer: It has been said that a parable is an earthly story with a heavenly meaning. The Lord Jesus frequently used parables as a means of illustrating profound, divine truths. Stories such as these are easily remembered, the characters bold, and the symbolism rich in meaning. Parables were a common form of teaching in Judaism. Before a certain point in His ministry, Jesus had employed many graphic analogies using common things that would be familiar to everyone (salt, bread, sheep, etc.), and their meaning was fairly clear in the context of His teaching. Parables required more explanation, and at one point in His ministry, Jesus taught using parables exclusively (Matthew 13:34).

The question is why Jesus would let most people wonder about the meaning of His parables. The first instance of this is in His telling the parable of the seed and the soils. Before He interpreted this parable, Jesus drew His disciples away from the crowd. They said to Him, "'Why do you speak to the people in parables?' He replied, 'The knowledge of the secrets of the kingdom of heaven has been given to you, but not to them. Whoever has will be given more, and he will have an abundance. Whoever does not have, even what he has will be taken from him. This is why I speak to them in parables: Though seeing, they do not see; though hearing, they do not hear or understand. In them is fulfilled the prophecy of Isaiah: "You will be ever hearing but never understanding; you will be ever seeing but never perceiving. For this people's heart has become calloused; they hardly hear with their ears, and they have closed their eyes. Otherwise they might see with their eyes, hear with their ears, understand with their hearts

and turn, and I would heal them." But blessed are your eyes because they see, and your ears because they hear. For I tell you the truth, many prophets and righteous men longed to see what you see but did not see it, and to hear what you hear but did not hear it'" (Matthew 13:10–17).

From this point on in Jesus' ministry, when He spoke in parables, He explained them only to His disciples. Those who had continually rejected His message were left in their spiritual blindness to wonder as to His meaning. Jesus made a clear distinction between those who had been given "ears to hear" and those who persisted in unbelief—ever hearing, but never actually perceiving and "always learning but never able to acknowledge the truth" (2 Timothy 3:7). The disciples had been given the gift of spiritual discernment by which things of the Holy Spirit were made clear to them. Because they accepted truth from Jesus, they were given more and more truth. The same is true today of believers who have been given the gift of the Holy Spirit, who guides us "into all truth" (John 16:13). He has opened our eyes to the light of truth and our ears to the sweet words of eternal life.

Our Lord Jesus understood that truth is not sweet music to all ears. Simply put, there are those who have neither interest in nor regard for the deep things of God. So why, then, did He speak in parables? To those with a genuine hunger for God, the parable is an effective and memorable vehicle for the conveyance of divine truths. Our Lord's parables contain great volumes of truth in very few words—and His parables, rich in imagery, are not easily forgotten. So, then, the parable is a blessing to those with willing ears. But to those with dull hearts and ears that are slow to hear, the parable is an instrument of judgment. Rejecting the truth leads to the withholding of truth.

Question: Why did Jesus command people not to tell others of the miracles He performed?

Answer: After healing a man of leprosy (Mark 1:41–42), "Jesus sent him away at once with a strong warning: 'See that you don't tell this to anyone...'" (verses 43–44). To our way of thinking, it would seem that Jesus would want everyone to know about the miracle. But Jesus knew that publicity over such miracles might hinder His mission and divert attention from His message. Mark records that this is exactly what happened. In his excitement over being healed, the man disobeyed. "As a result, Jesus could no longer enter a town openly but stayed outside in lonely places. Yet the people still came to Him from everywhere" (Mark 1:45).

Another reason for commanding the leper not to tell of the healing was so that the man could go immediately to the priest. Jesus required the leper to obey the law in having his cleansing confirmed (Leviticus 14). It was possible that, if the leper did not go at once, evil-minded men would go before him and prejudice the priest, preventing the former leper from declaring the truth of his healing. It was important that the priest pronounce the man genuinely cured so there might be no misunderstanding among the Jews that this was a real miracle.

Finally, Jesus did not want people to focus on the miracles He performed, but rather on the message He proclaimed and the death He was going to die. Yes, Jesus could heal the body, but the more important miracle was that of a healed and forgiven heart. The same is true today. God wants us to focus on the miracle of salvation through Jesus Christ instead of focusing on physical healings and/or miracles.

Question: What was the meaning and purpose of Jesus' temptations?

Answer: The three temptations in the wilderness were not the only temptations our Lord ever suffered on Earth. We read in Luke 4:2 that He was tempted by the devil for 40 days, but He was undoubtedly tempted at other times (Luke 4:13; Matthew 16:21–23; Luke 22:42), yet in all this He was without sin or compromise. Although some have suggested that the Lord's period of fasting compares with that of Moses (Exodus 34:28) and Elijah (1 Kings 19:8), an application point from Jesus' wilderness experience is how the Lord deals with temptation in the light of His humanity.

It is because He *was* human, and made like us in every way, that Jesus could do three crucial things: 1) destroy the devil's power and free those who were "held in slavery by their fear of death" (Hebrews 2:15); 2) "become a merciful and faithful high priest in service to God" and atone for our sins (Hebrews 2:17); and 3) be the One who is able to sympathize with us in all our weaknesses and infirmities (Hebrews 4:15). In Jesus, we have a high priest who is able to intercede on our behalf and provide the grace of forgiveness.

Temptation is never as great as when one has made a public declaration of faith, as did our Lord when He was baptized in the Jordan (Matthew 3:13–17). However, we also note that during this time of testing, angels ministered to our Lord—a mystery indeed that the omnipotent One should condescend to receive help from lesser beings! Here is a beautiful picture of the ministry that Christ's people also benefit from. We, too, are aided by angels—ministering spirits sent to believers—during times of testing and trial (Hebrews 1:14).

Jesus' temptations follow a pattern common to what all men face (1 John 2:16). The first temptation concerns the lusts of the flesh (Matthew 4:3–4). Our Lord is hungry, and the devil tempts Him to convert stones into bread, but He replies with Scripture, quoting Deuteronomy 8:3. The second temptation concerns the pride of life (Matthew 4:5–7), and here the devil uses (or misuses) a passage of Scripture (Psalm 91:11–12). If Jesus wanted the quick route to notoriety and the Messiahship, bypassing the passion and crucifixion, this was the way! But the Lord again replies with Scripture to the contrary (Deuteronomy 6:16), stating that it would be wrong for Him to show a lack of faith by putting God to the test. The third temptation concerns the lusts of the eyes (Matthew 4:8–10); the devil had control over the kingdoms of the world (Ephesians 2:2), and he was now showing everything to

Christ, offering it to Him in return for His allegiance. But the mere thought of giving worship to the evil one is anathema to the Lord, and He replies sharply, "You shall worship the Lord your God and serve Him only" (Deuteronomy 6:13).

Sadly, there are many temptations we fall into because our flesh is naturally weak. But we have a God who will not let us be tempted beyond what we can bear; He will provide a way out (1 Corinthians 10:13). We can therefore be victorious and thank the Lord for deliverance from temptation. Jesus' experience in the desert helps us recognize the common temptations that keep us from serving God effectively.

Furthermore, we learn from Jesus exactly how we are to respond to temptation—with Scripture. The forces of evil come to us with a myriad of temptations, but all are similar at their core: the lust of the eyes, the lust of the flesh, and the pride of life. We can only combat these temptations by saturating our hearts and minds with the Truth. The armor of a Christian soldier in the spiritual battle includes only one offensive weapon, the sword of the Spirit—the Word of God (Ephesians 6:17). Knowing the Bible intimately will put the Sword in our hands and enable us to be victorious over temptations.

Question: What was the meaning and importance of the transfiguration?

Answer: About a week after Jesus told His disciples that He would suffer, be killed, and be raised to life (Luke 9:22), He led Peter, James, and John up a mountain to pray. As He prayed, His appearance was changed into a glorified form, and His clothing became dazzling white. Moses and Elijah appeared and talked with Jesus about His imminent death on the cross. In fear and confusion, Peter offered to put up three shelters for them [most likely a reference to the booths used to celebrate the Feast of Tabernacles (Leviticus 23:34–42)]. Then a cloud enveloped the men, and a voice said, "This is my Son, whom I love; with him I am well pleased. Listen to him!" The cloud lifted, Moses and

Elijah had disappeared, and Jesus was alone with His frightened disciples. Jesus warned them not to tell anyone what they had seen until after His resurrection. The three accounts of this event are found in Matthew 17:1–9, Mark 9:2–9, and Luke 9:28–36.

Undoubtedly, the purpose of Christ's transfiguration was so that the "inner circle" of His disciples could gain a greater understanding of who He was. Christ underwent a dramatic change in appearance so that the disciples could behold Him in His glory—if only in part. After this incident, the disciples had a greater realization of the deity of Christ, though they still did not fully comprehend it. The disciples probably needed a little reassurance after hearing the shocking prediction of Jesus' death.

The appearance of Moses and Elijah is significant in that the two of them represented the Law and the Prophets. But God's voice from heaven—"Listen to Him!"—showed that the Law and the Prophets must yield to Jesus. He is the living Word of God (John 1:1). The One who is the new and living way was to replace the old; He was the fulfillment of the Law and all the prophecies of the Old Testament (Matthew 5:17). Jesus' glorified form also gave a preview of His coming glorification and His enthronement as King of kings and Lord of lords.

Question: Was Jesus ever angry?

Answer: When Jesus cleared the temple of the moneychangers and animal-sellers, He showed great emotion and anger (Matthew 21:12–13; Mark 11:15–17; John 2:13–17). Jesus' emotion was described as "zeal" for God's house (John 2:17). His anger was pure and completely justified because at its root was concern for God's holiness and worship. Because of what was at stake, Jesus took quick and decisive action. Another time Jesus showed anger was in the synagogue of Capernaum. When the Pharisees refused to answer Jesus' questions, "He looked around at them in anger, deeply distressed at their stubborn hearts" (Mark 3:5).

Many times, we think of anger as a selfish, destructive emotion that we should eradicate from our lives altogether. However, the fact that Jesus sometimes did become angry indicates that anger itself, as an emotion, is amoral. This is borne out elsewhere in the New Testament. Ephesians 4:26 instructs us "in your anger do not sin" and not to let the sun go down on our anger. The command is not to "avoid anger" (or suppress it or ignore it) but to deal with it properly, in a timely manner. We note the following facts about Jesus' displays of anger:

1. His anger had the proper motivation. In other words, He was angry for the right reasons. Jesus' anger did not arise from petty arguments or personal slights against Him. There was no selfishness involved.

2. His anger had the proper focus. He was not angry at God or at the "weaknesses" of others. His anger targeted sinful behavior and true injustice.

3. His anger had the proper supplement. Mark 3:5 says that His anger was attended by grief over the Pharisees' lack of faith. Jesus' anger stemmed from love for the Pharisees and concern for their spiritual condition. It had nothing to do with hatred or ill will.

4. His anger had the proper control. Jesus was never out of control, even in His wrath. The temple leaders did not like His cleansing of the temple (Mark 11:18), but He had done nothing sinful. He controlled His emotions; His emotions did not control Him.

5. His anger had the proper duration. He did not allow His anger to turn into bitterness; He did not hold grudges. He dealt with each situation properly, and He handled anger in good time.

6. His anger had the proper result. Jesus' anger had the inevitable consequence of godly action. The Word of God held in check Jesus' anger, as it did with all His emotions; thus, Jesus' response was always to accomplish God's will.

When we get angry, too often we have improper control or an improper focus. We fail in one or more of the above points. This is the wrath of man, which we are told "does not bring about the righteous life that God desires" (James 1:19–20). Jesus did not exhibit man's anger but the righteous indignation of God.

Question: How many times did Jesus cleanse the temple? Why did He cleanse the temple?

Answer: Twice, Jesus cleansed the temple of the moneychangers and sellers of merchandise. He did so because of how they were corrupting God's house of prayer. His actions proved His authority as the Son of God and His zeal for holiness in worship.

The official currency in Judea at the time of Christ was of Roman mintage. However, Jewish law required that every man should pay a "temple tax" of half a shekel, a Jewish coin, equal to two Greek drachmas (see Matthew 17:24–26). As a matter of convenience, money exchanges were located in the temple area so travelers could exchange the Roman coin for the Jewish half shekel. The moneychangers provided this service but would demand a fee for the exchange. Because so many thousands of worshipers came to the great feasts, changing money was a profitable business—and one that came to be associated with fraud and oppression of the poor.

The Law required animals for sacrifice (Leviticus 14:22; Luke 2:24). Because it was difficult to bring them from the more distant parts of Israel, a lucrative business selling sacrificial animals sprang up, with the sellers gouging the faithful. When Jesus saw these animal sellers and moneychangers preying on the poor, He was filled with righteous indignation. He overturned their tables and drove them out of the temple. His actions were a condemnation of their greed, dishonesty, and exploitation of the poor. Jesus said they had turned God's house of prayer into "a den of thieves" (Matthew 21:13). His disciples watched in amazement and remembered Psalm 69:9, "Zeal for your house consumes me."

Jesus' first cleansing of the temple is described in John 2:11–12. It occurred early in Jesus' public ministry, just after His first

106

miracle. This first of two temple cleansings is not mentioned in the Synoptic Gospels.

The second cleansing of the temple occurred just after Jesus' triumphal entry into Jerusalem in the last week of His life. This event is recorded in Matthew, Mark, and Luke, but not in John.

There are differences in the two events, aside from their being nearly three years apart. In the first cleansing, temple officials confronted Jesus immediately (John 2:18), whereas in the second cleansing, the chief priests and scribes confronted Him the following day (Matthew 21:17–23). In the first event, Jesus made a whip of cords with which to drive out the sellers, but there is no mention of a whip in the second cleansing.

The two occasions when Jesus cleansed the temple serve as bookends to His public ministry—from beginning to end, Jesus pointed to the need to worship God in spirit and in truth (John 4:23).

Question: Why did Jesus curse the fig tree?

Answer: The narrative of Jesus cursing the barren fig tree is found in two different Gospel accounts: Matthew 21:18–22 and Mark 11:12–14. While there are slight differences, the two accounts are easily reconciled. The key to understanding any passage is seeing it in context.

The chronological setting of the event is the week before Jesus' crucifixion. He had entered Jerusalem a day earlier amid the praise and worship of the Jewish people, who looked to Him to deliver them from Roman occupation (Matthew 21:1–11; Mark 11:1–11). The next day, Jesus was again on His way to Jerusalem from where He was staying in Bethany. Both Matthew and Mark record that He was hungry and saw in the distance a fig tree with leaves (Mark 11:13). Jesus came to the tree expecting to find something to eat but discovered that it had no fruit. He then cursed the tree, saying, "May you never bear fruit again!" (Matthew 21:19). In response to Jesus' curse, the fig tree withered. The following day, the disciples expressed their amazement that the tree had shriveled from the roots up (Mark 11:19–20). Jesus gently reproved them for their lack of faith—after all, He had cursed the tree, and doesn't His word have power (Mark 11:22)?

An obvious question is, why did Jesus curse the fig tree if it was not the season for figs? The answer is found in the characteristics of fig trees. The fruit of a fig tree generally appears *before* the leaves, but because the fruit is green, it can blend in with the leaves until almost ripe. Leaves on a fig tree are a sign of fruit. Also, fig trees can produce two or three crops of figs each season—usually an early crop in the spring followed by one or two later crops. Depending on conditions, it was possible for a fig tree in Israel to produce fruit ten months of the year. The fact that this particular tree already had leaves would have been a good indication that it had some early fruit, in spite of the fact that the normal growing season had not yet arrived.

The significance of this miracle is found in the setting. Jesus had just arrived at Jerusalem amid great fanfare and high expectations, but then He proceeded to cleanse the temple and curse the barren fig tree. Both actions were a condemnation of Israel's spiritual condition. With Jesus' cleansing of the temple (Matthew 21:13; Mark 11:17), He effectively denounced the corruption in Israel's worship practices. With the cursing of the fig tree, He symbolically called to task Israel as a nation. Outwardly, they made a show of spiritual life, blessing, and prosperity, but there was no spiritual fruit to be found, and they incurred the judgment of God. The fig tree represented the spiritual deadness of the Israelites who were outwardly religious but inwardly barren because of their sins.

Religious profession and observance of ritual do not guarantee salvation. There must be the fruit of genuine conversion evidenced in a person's life. As John the Baptist had told the Pharisees, "Produce fruit in keeping with repentance" (Luke 3:8). James later echoed this truth when he wrote, "Faith without works is dead" (James 2:26, NKJV). God wants no "unfruitful" followers—those who profess faith but show no evidence of a relationship with God.

The lesson of the fig tree is that God's followers should bear spiritual fruit (Galatians 5:22–23), not just give an appearance of religiosity. God judges fruitlessness and expects those who have a relationship with Him to "bear much fruit" (John 15:5–8).

Question: Did Jesus ever travel to India?

Answer: There is no biblical support for the idea that Jesus ever left the land of His birth to go to India or anywhere else. Of the four Gospel accounts, only two mention the birth of Jesus (Matthew and Luke), and only one (Luke) mentions anything about Jesus' life prior to the beginning of His public ministry. So, from about age two until 12 years of age and from 12 until 30, the Bible doesn't tell us anything about the life of Jesus. This has led some to speculate about what Jesus did during those years. One theory is that He meditated in India before beginning His ministry in Israel.

The orthodox position is that Jesus grew up in Nazareth with His family until it was time to begin His ministry. While the Bible doesn't explicitly say this, it is implied by Luke: "He went to Nazareth, where he had been brought up, and on the Sabbath day he went into the synagogue, as was his custom. And he stood up to read...All spoke well of him and were amazed at the gracious words that came from his lips. 'Isn't this Joseph's son?' they asked. Jesus said to them, 'Surely you will quote this proverb to me: "Physician, heal yourself! Do here in your hometown what we have heard that you did in Capernaum." I tell you the truth,' he continued, 'no prophet is accepted in his hometown'" (Luke 4:16, 22–24). Notice that Luke says that Jesus was "brought up" in Nazareth, and he also mentions twice that Nazareth was Jesus' hometown. Furthermore, the people in the synagogue knew Jesus and knew that He was Joseph's son. All of this leads to the conclusion that Jesus lived in Nazareth until His baptism.

Despite Luke's account, there are those who want to fill in the gaps in Jesus' life with extraordinary tales of adventure and mystery. From apocryphal tales of Jesus' infancy in which He Acts more like a malevolent trickster than the very Son of God, to the supposed tales of Jesus' journey to India to learn the secrets of

Hinduism and Buddhism from Eastern gurus, there is no shortage of theories claiming the "truth" of Jesus' "lost" years. Depending on the source, Jesus either spent 17 years in India before His ministry in Palestine, or He spent the remainder of His life in India after surviving the crucifixion—dying at the age of 120. These theories stem from the identification of Jesus with the Kashmiri saint, Issa Yuz Asaf ("Jesus Son of Joseph").

One recent author to promote this view is Holger Kersten, whose book *Jesus Lived in India: His Unknown Life Before and After the Crucifixion* supposedly presents "irrefutable evidence that Jesus did indeed live in India."[16]

A precursor to Kersten is Nicolas Notovitch, a Russian war correspondent who visited India and Tibet in the late 19th century. While there, Mr. Notovitch learned of the life of Saint Issa. Mr. Notovitch chronicles the life of Saint Issa, whom he identifies as Jesus, and told how Saint Issa grew in wisdom and knowledge while attending the ancient Indian university at Nalanda.[17] However, a Professor named J. Archibald Douglas visited the monastery of Hemis (where Notovitch purportedly learned of Saint Issa) to ask about Notovich. He afterward discredited Mr. Notovitch's work, claiming that Mr. Notovitch never even visited the monastery.

We can speculate on why such theories regarding Jesus exist, but the main thing to take away is that their ultimate source is the father of lies, Satan (John 8:44). We heard the truth at the baptism of Jesus, when God the Father proclaimed, "This is my Son, whom I love; with him I am well pleased" (Matthew 3:17). The theories of Jesus in India attempt to divert us from God's declaration that Jesus is His Son. They do so by denying the deity of Jesus Christ, reducing Jesus to just another rabbi, prophet, or sage.

Despite the claims of Kersten and others, the four Gospels still provide the most accurate and compelling account of the life of Jesus. If Jesus went to India prior to His three-year ministry, then one would expect there to be a distinct Indian influence in His teaching. Such an influence is missing. Rather, His teaching style was consistent with the Jewish itinerant teachers of His day. And how would one explain Jesus' knowledge of the Torah? Jesus quotes the Hebrew Scriptures throughout His ministry, to the point even of correcting the learned scholars of His day. Scholars would study most of their lives to have the same encyclopedic knowledge of Hebrew law and customs that Jesus had. Are we to believe that Jesus took the Old Testament with Him to India and studied the Scriptures between lessons on transcendental meditation?

Of course, there are those who simply deny the authenticity of the four Gospels. How are we to respond? With the exception of John, all the apostles (including Paul and Matthias in the place of Judas) died martyrs' deaths. Why would they do that for a lie? More importantly, why would they do that for something they *knew* to be a lie? The four Gospels have been under attack for nearly 2,000 years; in fact, no book has undergone as much scrutiny as the Bible or endured so many attempts to extinguish it. Yet it is still here, still changing lives and still attesting to the truth of the good news of Jesus Christ. "The grass withers and the flowers fall, but the word of our God stands forever" (Isaiah 40:8).

Question: Was Jesus a pacifist?

Answer: According to Webster's dictionary, a pacifist is someone who is opposed to violence, especially war, for any purpose, often accompanied by the refusal to bear arms by reason of conscience or religious conviction.

While Jesus is the "Prince of Peace" (Isaiah 9:6), He was not, and is not, a pacifist. Revelation 19:15 declares of Jesus, "Out of His mouth comes a sharp sword with which to strike down the nations. He will rule them with an iron scepter. He treads the winepress of the fury of the wrath of God Almighty." Ecclesiastes 3:1, 3, and 8 say, "There is a time for everything, and a season for every activity under heaven...a time to kill and a time to heal, a time to tear down and a time to build...a time to love and a time to hate, a time for war and a time for peace." Daniel 9:26 says that "war will continue until the end, and desolations have been decreed." Matthew 24:6–8 says, "You will hear of wars and rumors of wars, but see to it that you are not alarmed. Such things must happen, but the end is still to come. Nation will rise against nation, and kingdom against kingdom. There will be famines and earthquakes in various places. All these are the beginning of birth pains."

Jesus Himself said, "Do not suppose that I have come to bring peace to the earth. I did not come to bring peace, but a sword. For I have come to turn 'a man against his father, a daughter against her mother, a daughter-in-law against her mother-in-law—a man's enemies will be the members of his own household'" (Matthew 10:34–36). He also said, "From the days of John the Baptist until now, the kingdom of heaven has been forcefully advancing, and forceful men lay hold of it" (Matthew 11:12).

We are commanded to hate evil and cling to good things (Romans 12:9). In doing so, we must take a stand against what is evil in this world and pursue righteousness (2 Timothy 2:22). Jesus did this and, in so doing, spoke openly against the religious and political rulers of His time (Luke 20:1–8; Romans 9:31–33). Zeal for God's righteousness consumed Jesus, and He was not afraid to stand up against those who opposed and dishonored His Father (John 2:15–17). "Those who hate him he will repay to their face by destruction; he will not be slow to repay to their face those who hate Him" (Deuteronomy 7:10). "While people are saying, 'Peace and safety,' destruction will come on them suddenly, as labor pains on a pregnant woman, and they will not escape" (1 Thessalonians 5:3).

The Old Testament is full of examples of how God used His people to bring judgment upon nations whose sin had reached its full measure (e.g., Genesis 15:16; Numbers 21:3; 31:1–7; 32:20–21; Deuteronomy 7:1–2; Joshua 6:20–21; 8:1–8; 10:29–32; 11:7–20). We can be assured that it is always with justice that God judges and makes war (Revelation 19:11). "For we know Him who said, 'It is mine to avenge; I will repay,' and again, 'The Lord will judge his people.' It is a dreadful thing to fall into the hands of the living God" (Hebrews 10:30–31). We learn from these passages that we are only to wage war when it is the will of God and not at our own discretion (John 18:11; Numbers 14:41–45). It is God's choice as to how and when He brings judgment of sin upon this world and its inhabitants. We are simply called to follow Him (Matthew 16:24–25).

All of this may sound contradictory to the teachings of Jesus—who was God incarnate—in which He instructs us to "love your neighbor as yourself" (Matthew 19:19) and turn the other cheek (Matthew 5:39). He also taught, "Blessed are the peacemakers" (Matthew 5:9). Was Jesus teaching pacifism in these verses? No, the Judge of all the earth (John 5:22), the One who will one day "strike the earth with the rod of his mouth" (Isaiah 11:4) knows that sometimes war is inevitable.

Question: Does the Bible describe Jesus being worshipped?

Answer: Worship is reverence paid to a person, object, or divine being. From the beginning of Jesus' life we see examples of His being worshipped. As soon as the magi laid eyes on the infant Christ, "they bowed down and worshipped him" (Matthew 2:11). When Jesus made His triumphal entry into Jerusalem the Bible records the response He received: "They took palm branches and went out to meet him, shouting, 'Hosanna! Blessed is he who comes in the name of the Lord! Blessed is the King of Israel!'" (John 12:13). The behavior exhibited by the crowd was definitely a form of worship, as the Pharisees recognized (Luke 19:39–40).

Just after Jesus amazed the disciples by walking on water, He climbed into a boat where "those who were in the boat worshipped him, saying, 'Truly you are the Son of God'" (Matthew 14:33). Two more memorable examples of Jesus accepting worship occurred just after His resurrection. Mary Magdalene and some other women (Matthew 28:1; Mark 16:1; Luke 24:10) were on their way to tell the disciples of the resurrection when Jesus met them. When they recognized Him, they "came to him, clasped his feet and worshipped him" (Matthew 28:9).

Then there is the case of Thomas, who didn't believe Jesus had risen from the dead despite the other disciples testifying to that fact. It had been about a week since the resurrection, but Thomas still doubted because he had not seen the risen Lord. Jesus, knowing Thomas doubted, appeared to him and showed him the nail marks and the wound on His side. How did Thomas respond? "Thomas said to him, 'My Lord and my God!'" (John 20:28). In none of these instances do we see Jesus telling those worshipping Him to stop, as did mere men, and even angels, who were being worshipped wrongly by others (Acts 10:25–26; Revelation 19:9–10).

We continue to offer worship to Jesus today by offering ourselves to Him as a living sacrifice—offering ourselves to God, through faith in Jesus Christ, to do with as He sees fit (Romans 12:1). Jesus said, "God is spirit, and his worshipers must worship in spirit and in truth" (John 4:24). We worship God in spirit and truth by obedience to His commands. Worship is not just about bowing before Jesus, throwing palm branches at His feet or singing and shouting about our love for Him. It's about giving ourselves to Him.

Question: What is the significance of the triumphal entry?

Answer: The story of the triumphal entry is one of the few events in the life of Jesus that appears in all four Gospel accounts (Matthew 21:1–17; Mark 11:1–11; Luke 19:29–40; John 12:12–19). It concerns Jesus' entrance to Jerusalem on the Sunday before His crucifixion (John 12:1, 12). The triumphal entry was a significant event, not only to the people of Jesus' day, but also to Christians throughout history. We celebrate Palm Sunday to remember that momentous occasion.

On that day, Jesus rode into Jerusalem on the back of a borrowed donkey's colt, one that had never before carried a rider. The disciples spread their cloaks on the donkey for Jesus to sit on, and the multitudes came out to welcome Him, laying in His path their cloaks and the branches of palm trees—symbols of victory in that day. The people hailed Jesus as the "king who comes in the name of the Lord" (Luke 19:38) as He rode to the temple (see Malachi 3:1).

Jesus' purpose in riding into Jerusalem was to make public His claim to be the Messiah and King of Israel in fulfillment of Old Testament prophecy. Matthew tells us that the King coming on the foal of a donkey was an exact fulfillment of Zechariah 9:9, "Rejoice greatly, O Daughter of Zion! Shout, Daughter of Jerusalem! See, your king comes to you, righteous and having salvation, gentle and riding on a donkey, on a colt, the foal of a donkey." Jesus rides into His capital city as a conquering King and is praised by the people in the manner of the day. He receives the worship and adoration because He is truly worthy of it. No longer does He tell His disciples to be quiet about Him (Matthew 12:15–16; 16:20), but instead allows them to shout His praises and worship Him openly. The spreading of cloaks on the road was an act of paying homage to royalty (see 2 Kings 9:13). Jesus was openly declaring to the people that He was their King and the Messiah they had been waiting for.

The people welcomed Jesus that day because they desired a deliverer, someone who would overturn Roman rule in Palestine. There were many who, though they did not believe in Christ with a spiritual faith, hoped that perhaps He might be to them a great temporal deliverer. These hailed Him as King with their many *hosannas*, recognizing Him as the Son of David who came in the name of the Lord (Psalm 118:26). But when Jesus fell short of their expectations by refusing to lead them in a revolt against the Roman occupiers, the crowds quickly turned on Him. Within just a few days, their *hosannas* would change to cries of "Crucify him!" (Luke 23:20–21). Those who hailed Jesus as a hero would soon reject and abandon Him.

The story of the triumphal entry is one of contrasts, and those contrasts provide the application to believers. It is the story of the King who came as a lowly servant on a donkey, not on a prancing steed and not in royal robes. Jesus Christ came not to conquer by force, but by love, grace, mercy, and His own sacrifice for His people. His is not a kingdom of armies and splendor, but of lowliness and servanthood. He conquers not nations, but hearts and minds. His message is not of temporal peace but of peace with

God. If Jesus has made a triumphal entry into our hearts, He reigns there in peace and love. As His followers, we should exhibit those same qualities, and the world should see the true King living and reigning triumphantly in us.

Question: How long was Jesus' ministry?

Answer: According to Luke 3:1, John the Baptist began his ministry in the 15th year of Tiberius Caesar's reign. Tiberius was appointed as co-regent with Augustus in AD 11, and 15 years later would be AD 26. Jesus began His ministry shortly thereafter, at approximately the age of thirty (Luke 3:23). This gives us a basis upon which we can approximate what year Jesus began His public ministry: around AD 26. As for the end of His ministry, we know that it culminated with His crucifixion, resurrection, and ascension.

According to John's Gospel, Jesus attended at least three annual Feasts of Passover through the course of His ministry: one in John 2:13, another in 6:4, and then the Passover of His crucifixion in 11:55–57. Just based on that information, Jesus' ministry lasted two years, at the very least.

Because of the amount of things that Jesus accomplished and the places He traveled during His ministry, many scholars believe there was another Passover, not mentioned in the Gospels, which fell between the Passovers of John 2 and John 6. This would lengthen Jesus' ministry to at least three years.

We can add more time because of all that took place before the first Passover of Jesus' ministry in John 2. By the time of that first Passover (in the spring of 27), Jesus had already traveled from the area of the Jordan to Cana to Capernaum to Jerusalem. He had been baptized by John the Baptist (Matthew 3:13–17), been tempted in the wilderness (Matthew 4:1–2), began His preaching ministry (Matthew 4:17), called His first disciples (John 1:35–51), performed His first miracle (John 2:1–11), and made a trip to Capernaum with His family (John 2:12). All this would have taken several months, at least.

Add to that the 40 days between Jesus' resurrection and His ascension (Acts 1:3) and we have a total length of Jesus' earthly ministry. From His baptism to His ascension, the late summer of 26 to the spring of 30, we have approximately three and a half years.

Chapter 6

....

QUESTIONS ABOUT JESUS' CRUCIFIXION

Contents

What happened during Jesus' last hours before His death?

What trials did Jesus face before His crucifixion?

On what day was Jesus crucified?

Why did Jesus have to experience so much suffering?

What is the meaning and significance of the crown of thorns?

Was Jesus crucified on a cross, pole, or stake?

Did the nails go through Jesus' hands or wrists when He was nailed to the cross?

What does INRI stand for? What was written on the sign nailed to the cross above Jesus' head?

What were the seven last statements of Jesus Christ on the cross, and what do they mean?

What are the Stations of the Cross and what can we learn from them?

119

Who was responsible for Christ's death?

What is the meaning of the "blood of Christ"?

Why did blood and water come out of Jesus' side when He was pierced?

What is the meaning of the cross?

What is the meaning of the resurrection of the Jerusalem saints at Jesus' death? (Matthew 27:52–53)?

Did Jesus go to hell between His death and resurrection?

Question: What happened during Jesus' last hours before His death?

Answer: The night before Jesus' death, He washed the feet of His disciples, and then shared the Passover meal with them. During this time Judas was revealed as the one who would betray His master (John 13:1–30). At the conclusion of the meal, Jesus instituted the Lord's Supper (Matthew 26:26–29; 1 Corinthians 11:23–26). Then the group sang a hymn and left for the Mount of Olives, a place where Jesus often spent time with His disciples (Mark 14:26). That same night, He spoke many things to His disciples concerning the Holy Spirit, His soon departure, and their responsibility to love one another and abide in Christ (John 14–16). He also prayed for His disciples and for everyone who would someday believe in Him (John 17).

When they came to the garden of Gethsemane, Jesus pulled Peter, John, and James away, told them to pray so they wouldn't fall into temptation, and went off a short distance by Himself to pray. The disciples promptly fell asleep.

Jesus was grieved and depressed as He approached death. He was so anguished that His sweat fell like drops of blood (Luke 22:44). He asked God to take the coming torment from Him, but only if it was the Father's will (Luke 22:42). It wasn't only the anticipation of scourging or the horrible hours on the cross that caused Jesus' sorrow. Adding to His distress in the garden was the knowledge that He would be separated from God and bear the sin of the world (Matthew 27:46; Isaiah 53).

God sent an angel to strengthen Jesus. The Lord again asked Peter, James, and John to pray, but again they fell asleep. Their spirits may have been willing to pray, but their flesh was weak (Matthew 26:41). As Jesus was speaking to them, Judas approached with an armed mob. Judas greeted Jesus as a friend and then turned Him over to the mob. At this time, Jesus performed two miracles: at His word, the entire mob was prostrated (John 18:6), and He healed a wounded man (Luke 22:51). The disciples made a brief show of defending Jesus, but they all forsook Him and fled

(Mark 14:50). Peter and John followed at a distance to see what would happen (John 18:15).

The next few hours included several mock trials before Annas (John 18:13), Caiaphas and the Sanhedrin (Matthew 26:57–68), Herod, and Pontius Pilate (Luke 23:1–25). Jesus endured beatings and a scourging. He was forced to wear a crown of thorns and mocked as a pretender to royalty. Pilate, who knew Jesus was innocent and publicly proclaimed Him so, finally bent to the will of the crowd that was shouting, "Crucify him!" Washing his hands of the matter, Pilate sent Jesus to the cross (Luke 23:1–25).

On the cross, Jesus hung between two thieves. People passed by. Those who had celebrated Him a week earlier now taunted Him. Roman soldiers divided Jesus' meager possessions among themselves. Jesus prayed, "Father, forgive them" (Luke 23:34). This prayer showed Jesus' humility and the whole of the reason He was there—to provide redemption and the forgiveness of sins.

His mother Mary stood nearby, as did John. Jesus committed Mary to John's care. He also spoke to one of the thieves hanging next to Him, forgiving his sin and promising him paradise.

For three hours, darkness covered the earth. Jesus cried out, "My God, my God, why have you forsaken me?" (Matthew 27:46). At the end of His life, Jesus said in a loud voice, "It is finished" (John 19:30). At that moment, the temple veil tore, and there was a violent earthquake (Matthew 27:51). A Roman centurion, after all he had heard and seen, "praised God and said, 'Surely this was a righteous man'" (Luke 23:47).

Question: What trials did Jesus face before His crucifixion?

Answer: The night of Jesus' arrest, He was brought before Annas, Caiaphas, and an assembly of religious leaders called the Sanhedrin (John 18:19–24; Matthew 26:57). After this, He was taken before Pilate, the Roman Governor (John 18:28), sent off to Herod (Luke 23:7), and returned to Pilate (Luke 23:11), who finally sentenced Him to death.

There were six parts to Jesus' trial: three stages in a religious court and three stages before a Roman court. Jesus was tried before Annas, the former high priest; Caiaphas, the current high priest; and the Sanhedrin. He was charged with blasphemy in these "ecclesiastical" trials, since He claimed to be the Son of God, the Messiah.

The trials before Jewish authorities, the religious trials, showed the degree to which the Jewish leaders hated Him as they carelessly disregarded many of their own laws. There were several illegalities involved in these trials from the perspective of Jewish law: 1) no trial was to be held during feast time; 2) each member of the court was to vote individually to convict or acquit, but Jesus was convicted by acclamation; 3) if the death penalty was given, a night must pass before the sentence was carried out. However, only a few hours passed before Jesus was placed on the cross; 4) the Jews had no authority to execute anyone; 5) no trial was to be held at night, but this trial was held before dawn; 6) the accused was to be given counsel or representation, but Jesus had none; and 7) the accused was not to be asked self-incriminating questions, but Jesus was asked the outrageous question, "What is this testimony that these men are bringing against you?" (Matthew 26:62).

The trials before the Roman authorities started with Pilate (John 18:28) after Jesus was beaten. The charges brought against Him in the secular court were very different from the charges in His religious trials. He was charged with inciting people to riot, forbidding people to pay their taxes, and claiming to be king. Pilate found no reason to kill Jesus, so he sent Him to Herod (Luke 23:7). Herod had Jesus ridiculed but, wanting to avoid a political liability, sent Jesus back to Pilate (Luke 23:11). This was the last trial, as Pilate tried to appease the animosity of the Jews by having Jesus scourged. The Roman scourge is a terrible whipping of 39 lashes. In a final effort to have Jesus released, Pilate offered the prisoner Barabbas to be crucified and Jesus released, but to no avail. The crowds called for Barabbas to be released and Jesus to be crucified. Pilate granted their demand and gave up Jesus to the people's will (Luke 23:25).

The trials of Jesus represent the ultimate mockery of justice. Jesus, the only truly innocent man in the history of the world, was found guilty of crimes and sentenced to death by crucifixion.

Question: On what day was Jesus crucified?

Answer: The Bible does not explicitly state on which day of the week Jesus was crucified. The two most widely held views are Friday and Wednesday. Some, however, using a synthesis of both the Friday and Wednesday arguments, argue for Thursday as the day.

Jesus said in Matthew 12:40, "For as Jonah was three days and three nights in the belly of a huge fish, so the Son of Man will be three days and three nights in the heart of the earth." Those who argue for a Friday crucifixion say that there is still a valid way in which He could have been considered in the grave for three days. In first-century Jewish thinking, part of a day was considered a full day. Since Jesus was in the grave for part of Friday, all of Saturday, and part of Sunday, He could be considered to have been in the grave for three days. One of the principal arguments for Friday is found in Mark 15:42, which notes that Jesus was crucified "the day before the Sabbath." If that was the weekly Sabbath, i.e., Saturday, then that fact leads to a Friday crucifixion. Another argument for Friday says that verses such as Matthew 16:21 and Luke 9:22 teach that Jesus would rise *on* the third day; therefore, He would not need to be in the grave a full three days and nights. But not everyone agrees that "on the third day" is the best way to translate these verses. Furthermore, Mark 8:31 says that Jesus will be raised "after" three days.

The Thursday argument expands on the Friday view and argues mainly that there are too many events (some count as many as twenty) happening between Christ's burial and Sunday morning to fit between Friday evening and Sunday morning. Proponents of the Thursday view point out that this is especially a problem when the only full day between Friday and Sunday is Saturday, the Jewish Sabbath. An extra day or two eliminates that problem.

The Thursday advocates could reason thus: suppose you haven't seen a friend since Monday evening. The next time you see him is Thursday morning, and you say, "I haven't seen you in three days," even though it had technically only been 60 hours (2.5 days). If Jesus was crucified on Thursday, this example shows how it could be considered three days.

The Wednesday opinion states that there were two Sabbaths that week. After the first one (the one that occurred on the evening of the crucifixion [Mark 15:42; Luke 23:52–54]), the women purchased spices—note that they made their purchase "after" the Sabbath (Mark 16:1). The Wednesday view holds that this "Sabbath" was the Passover (see Leviticus 16:29–31; 23:24–32, 39, where high holy days that are not necessarily the seventh day of the week are referred to as the Sabbath). The second Sabbath that week was Saturday, the normal weekly Sabbath. Note that in Luke 23:56, the women who had purchased spices after the first Sabbath returned and prepared the spices, then "rested on the Sabbath." The argument states that they could not purchase the spices after the Sabbath, yet prepare those spices before the Sabbath—unless there were two Sabbaths. With the two-Sabbath view, if Christ was crucified on Thursday, then the high holy Sabbath (the Passover) would have begun Thursday at sundown and ended at Friday sundown—at the beginning of the weekly Sabbath or Saturday. Purchasing the spices after the first Sabbath (Passover) would have meant they purchased them on Saturday and were breaking the Sabbath.

Therefore, according to the Wednesday viewpoint, the only explanation that does not violate the biblical account of the women and the spices and holds to a literal understanding of Matthew 12:40 is that Christ was crucified on Wednesday. The Sabbath that was a high holy day (Passover) occurred on Thursday, the women purchased spices (after that) on Friday and returned and prepared the spices on the same day. They rested on Saturday (which was the weekly Sabbath), then brought the spices to the tomb early Sunday. Jesus was buried near sundown on Wednesday, which began Thursday in the Jewish calendar.

Using a Jewish calendar, you have Thursday night (night one), Thursday day (day one), Friday night (night two), Friday day (day two), Saturday night (night three), Saturday day (day three). We do not know exactly when He rose, but we do know that it was before sunrise on Sunday (John 20:1, Mary Magdalene came "while it was still dark"), so He could have risen as early as just after sunset Saturday evening, which began the first day of the week to the Jews.

A possible problem with the Wednesday view is that the disciples who walked with Jesus on the road to Emmaus did so on "the same day" of His resurrection (Luke 24:13). The disciples, who do not recognize Jesus, tell Him of Jesus' crucifixion (24:20) and say, "it is the third day since all this took place" (24:21). Wednesday to Sunday is four days. A possible explanation is that they were counting from Wednesday evening (Christ's burial), which begins the Jewish Thursday. Thursday to Sunday could be counted as three days.

In the grand scheme of things, it is not all that important to know what day of the week Christ was crucified. If it were very important, then God's Word would have clearly communicated the day and timeframe. What is important is that He did die and that He physically, bodily rose from the dead. What is equally important is the reason He died—to take the punishment all sinners deserve. John 3:16 and 3:36 both proclaim that putting your trust in Him results in eternal life! This is true whether He was crucified on a Wednesday, Thursday, or Friday.

Question: Why did Jesus have to experience so much suffering?

Answer: Isaiah 52:14 declares, "There were many who were appalled at him—his appearance was so disfigured beyond that of any man and his form marred beyond human likeness." Jesus suffered most severely throughout the trials, torture, and crucifixion (Matthew 27; Mark 15; Luke 23; John 19). As horrible as His physical suffering was, it was nothing compared to the spiritual suffering He went through. Second Corinthians 5:21 says, "God made him who had no sin to be sin for us, so that in him we might become the righteousness of God." Jesus had the weight of the sins of the entire world on Him (1 John 2:2). It was the guilt of these sins that caused Jesus to cry out, "My God, my God, why have you forsaken me?" (Matthew 27:46). So, as brutal as Jesus' physical suffering was, it was just a small part of His overall suffering as He, in His innocence, bore our sins (Romans 5:8).

Isaiah predicts Jesus' suffering in no uncertain terms: "He was despised and rejected by men, a man of sorrows, and familiar with suffering. Like one from whom men hide their faces he was despised, and we esteemed him not. But he was pierced for our transgressions, he was crushed for our iniquities; the punishment that brought us peace was upon him, and by his wounds we are healed" (Isaiah 53:3, 5). Psalm 22:14–18 is another powerful passage predicting the Messiah's suffering, written from a first-person perspective: "I am poured out like water, and all my bones are out of joint. My heart has turned to wax; it has melted away within me. My strength is dried up like a potsherd, and my tongue sticks to the roof of my mouth; you lay me in the dust of death. Dogs have surrounded me; a band of evil men has encircled me, they have pierced my hands and my feet. I can count all my bones; people stare and gloat over me. They divide my garments among them and cast lots for my clothing."

Why did Jesus have to suffer so badly? Some think that Jesus' physical torture was part of His punishment for our sins. To some extent, this is true. At the same time, the torture Jesus underwent speaks more of the hatred and cruelty of humanity than it does of God's punishment for sin. Satan's absolute hatred of God and Jesus was surely a part of the motivation behind the relentless torture and abuse. The suffering heaped on Jesus is the ultimate example of the hatred and rage sinful man feels toward a holy God (Romans 3:10–18).

Question: What is the meaning and significance of the crown of thorns?

Answer: After Jesus' sham trials and subsequent flogging, and before He was crucified, the Roman soldiers "twisted together a crown of thorns and set it on his head. They put a staff in his right hand and knelt in front of him and mocked him. 'Hail, king of the Jews!' they said" (Matthew 27:29; see also John 19:2–3). While a crown of thorns would be exceedingly painful, Jesus' crown of thorns was more about mockery than pain. Here was the "King of the Jews" being beaten, spit upon, and insulted by presumably low-level Roman soldiers. The crown of thorns was their highest mockery—taking a symbol of royalty and majesty and turning it into something painful and degrading.

When Adam and Eve sinned, bringing evil and a curse upon the world, God said, "Cursed is the ground because of you; through painful toil you will eat of it all the days of your life. It will produce *thorns* and thistles for you, and you will eat the plants of the field." (Genesis 3:17–18, emphasis added). The Roman soldiers unknowingly took an object of the curse and fashioned it into a crown for the one who would deliver us from that curse. "Christ redeemed us from the curse of the law by becoming a curse for us, for it is written: 'Cursed is everyone who is hung on a tree'" (Galatians 3:13). Christ, in His perfect atoning sacrifice, has delivered us from the curse of sin, of which thorns are a symbol. Though the crown of thorns was intended to be a mockery, it was in fact an excellent symbol of who Jesus is and what He came to accomplish.

For Christians, the crown of thorns is a reminder of two things: 1) Jesus was, and is, indeed a king. One day, the entire universe will bow to Jesus as the King of kings and Lord of lords (Revelation 19:16). What the Roman soldiers meant as a mockery was in fact a picture of Christ's two roles: the Suffering Servant (Isaiah 53) and the conquering Messiah-King (Revelation 19). 2) Jesus was willing to endure the pain, the insults, and the shame, all on our account. The crown of thorns and the suffering it caused are long gone, and Jesus has now received the crown of which

He is worthy. "But we see Jesus, who was made a little lower than the angels, now crowned with glory and honor because he suffered death, so that by the grace of God he might taste death for everyone" (Hebrews 2:9).

Question: Was Jesus crucified on a cross, pole, or stake?

Answer: The cross is arguably the most beloved symbol in all of Christianity. It adorns our churches and cathedrals, our jewelry, and our books, and it is used in numerous marketing logos. The empty cross symbolizes the work performed there by our Savior, who went to death willingly to pay the penalty for our sins. Jesus' last words before He died were, "It is finished" (John 19:30). The Law was fulfilled, the Messianic prophecies were accomplished, and redemption was complete. It is no wonder that the cross has come to symbolize the greatest story ever told—the story of the sacrificial death of Christ.

In spite of the overwhelming symbolism of the cross, its precise shape cannot be proven explicitly from the Bible. The Greek word translated "cross" is *stauros*, meaning "a pole or a cross used as an instrument of capital punishment." The Greek word *stauroo*, which is translated "crucify," means "to be attached to a pole or cross." Though the Greek words can refer to a pole or stake, many scholars argue that Jesus most likely died on a cross in which the upright beam projected above the shorter crosspiece. Biblically, though, no one can make an airtight case for either a cross or a pole/stake. The Romans were not picky in regard to how they crucified people. The Romans used crosses, poles, stakes, upside-down crosses, x-shaped crosses, walls, roofs, trees, etc. Jesus could have been crucified on any of these objects and it would not have affected the perfection or sufficiency of His sacrifice.

Certain cults, notably the Jehovah's Witnesses, are adamant that Jesus did not die on a cross and that the cross is, in fact, a pagan symbol. Equally adamant are Christians who, in an effort to refute the Witnesses' doctrine, cling to the idea of the cross and deny the pole/stake theory. Even if the Jehovah's Witnesses are correct that Jesus was not crucified on a cross, it would *not* give any credence to their other beliefs, such as their denial of the deity of Christ. The truth is that we cannot definitively—from the Scriptures—make the case that Jesus died on a cross or a pole/stake. In the end, such arguments only serve to get us off message. What's important is that Jesus shed His blood and died (on *something*) and that His death is the sole atoning sacrifice for our sins (1 John 2:2).

Crucifixion was probably the most horrible form of capital punishment ever devised by man. It was designed to be a lingering death. First, the victim was usually subjected to flagellation; that is, a beating with a three-thong whip (fashioned of plaited leather and studded with bone and metal). After the beating, the soldiers would escort the prisoner through the crowds to the place of crucifixion.

At the crucifixion site, the victim was stripped naked and fastened to the cross. The soldiers would place a placard bearing the prisoner's indictment around his neck. Here we see the picture of Christ carrying the charge of "sinner" for us, which we ourselves would have to carry if it were not for Him. He took the death sentence we rightly deserve so that we could go free. "He himself bore our sins in his body on the tree, so that we might die to sins and live for righteousness; by his wounds you have been healed" (1 Peter 2:24).

As the victim was being crucified, the Roman executioners would subject him to slow torture. Some victims lingered until they were eaten alive by birds of prey or wild beasts. Most hung on the cross for days before dying. When the legs could no longer support the weight of the body, the diaphragm was constricted in a way that made breathing impossible. That is why breaking the legs hastened death (John 19:31–33). However Jesus' legs were not broken, in fulfillment of prophecy (John 19:36). He, not the Romans, chose the moment of His death (John 19:30).

The significance of Jesus' crucifixion is completely lost in arguments over the *shape* of the cross. Jesus said, "If anyone would come after me, he must deny himself and take up his cross and follow me. For whoever wants to save his life will lose it, but whoever loses his life for me will find it" (Matthew 16:24–25). The cross/stake/pole was an instrument of death, and by telling us to take up our cross, Jesus reveals that, in order to be His true followers, we must die to self. If we call ourselves Christians, we must deny ourselves and give up our lives for His sake. This may take the extreme form of being martyred for our faith; but even in the most peaceful political settings, we must be willing to lose the self—crucifying self-righteousness, self-promotion, selfish ambitions—in order to be His followers. Those who are not willing to do this are "not worthy" of Him (Matthew 10:38).

Did Jesus die on a traditionally shaped cross? Probably. Could it have been a pole or stake? Possibly. Frankly, the shape of the implement on which Jesus died is peripheral. What matters is that Jesus died for our sins and that His death purchased for us eternal life.

Question: Did the nails go through Jesus' hands or wrists when He was nailed to the cross?

Answer: The question of where the nails were placed leads to the question of whether Jesus was crucified on a cross, pole, or stake. Some scientists have suggested that if He was crucified on a cross, as tradition states, the hands would not have been strong enough to hold His weight. Therefore, they suggest that the nails were actually in His wrists, which are stronger and more capable of holding weight. Others have posited that Jesus' hands would have been strong enough, considering that His feet were also nailed and helped support some weight. There is also some historical evidence that sometimes a cross would have a sort of seat to help support the crucified person's weight.

While historical scholars are uncertain of the nail placement in Jesus' crucifixion, or anyone else's for that matter, the Bible states that Jesus had wounds in His hands (John 20:25–27). The Greek word translated "hands" is *cheir*, which literally means "hands." There is no Greek word for "wrists" in the New Testament. Some versions translate Acts 12:7 to say that the chains fell off Peter's "wrists"; however, the Greek word in this verse is also *cheir*.

It's possible that the nails may have been angled to enter through the hand and exit through the wrist, but it's just as likely that the nails were driven straight through the hand somewhere near the base of the thumb. Experiments have shown that both ways do work and either method could have been used in the crucifixion of Jesus.

The wounds of Christ hold infinite spiritual significance to us and are a part of Christ's glory; their exact physical location is a minor issue. We know that Jesus has five wounds—in His hands, side, and feet. Although we don't know exactly where on His hands, side, or feet, we do know that the wounds on Jesus' body allowed His blood to be shed for the forgiveness of sin for all who would ever believe in Him (Isaiah 53:5; 1 Peter 2:24).

Question: What does INRI stand for? What was written on the sign nailed to the cross above Jesus' head?

Answer: John 19:19 records, "Pilate had a notice prepared and fastened to the cross. It read: JESUS OF NAZARETH, THE KING OF THE JEWS." Verse 20 says that the sign was written in Aramaic, Latin, and Greek. Today, many displays of the crucifixion include the letters *INRI* on the sign above the cross. In Latin, the text "JESUS OF NAZARETH, THE KING OF THE JEWS" would have been written, "*Iesus Nazarenus Rex Iudaeorum*." Abbreviated, this phrase becomes "INRI." It is unlikely that the letters *INRI* were truly on the sign that Pilate placed over Jesus' head, as John 19:20 specifically states that the sign was written out in Aramaic, Greek, and Latin.

Mark and Matthew both refer to the writing as an "accusation." It was customary to set up over the heads of persons crucified the crime for which they suffered, and the name of the sufferer. According to the sign, Pilate's condemnation of Jesus was His claim to be the King of the Jews. Ironically, the "crime" for which Jesus was crucified was not a crime at all, but a truth. Not only is Jesus King of the Jews, but He is the King of all—the King of

132

kings and the Lord of lords (Revelation 17:14; 19:16). He is King over the entire universe and all its inhabitants. He is a King who was rejected by His subjects (John 1:11).

The real reason Jesus was nailed to the cross was to bear the crimes (sins) of everyone who would ever put his or her faith in Him for salvation. "When you were dead in your sins and in the uncircumcision of your sinful nature, God made you alive with Christ. He forgave us all our sins, having canceled the written code, with its regulations, that was against us and that stood opposed to us; he took it away, nailing it to the cross" (Colossians 2:13–14).

Question: What were the seven last statements of Jesus Christ on the cross, and what do they mean?

Answer: The seven statements that Jesus Christ made on the cross were (not in any particular order):

1. *"Eloi, Eloi, lama sabachthani?"* This phrase, a mixture of Hebrew and Aramaic, means "my God, my God, why have you forsaken me?" (Matthew 27:46). Here, Jesus was expressing His feelings of abandonment as God placed the sins of the world on Him. Because Jesus was the sin-bearer, God had to "turn away" from His Son. As Jesus was feeling the weight of sin, He experienced a separation from God for the only time in all of eternity. His statement was also a fulfillment of the prophecy in Psalm 22:1.

2. "Father, forgive them, for they do not know what they are doing" (Luke 23:34). Those who crucified Jesus were not aware of the full scope of what they were doing because they did not recognize Him as the Messiah. While their ignorance of divine truth did not mean they deserved forgiveness, Christ's prayer in the midst of their mocking Him is an expression of the limitless compassion of divine grace.

3. "I tell you the truth, today you will be with me in paradise" (Luke 23:43). With these words, Jesus assured one of the criminals on a nearby cross that when he died, he would be

with Jesus in heaven. This salvation was granted because the criminal had expressed his faith in Jesus, recognizing Him for who He was (Luke 23:42).

4. "Father, into your hands I commit my spirit" (Luke 23:46). In saying this, Jesus willingly gave His soul into the Father's hands, indicating that He had full control over His death (John 10:18)—and that God had accepted His sacrifice. He "offered himself unblemished to God" (Hebrews 9:14).

5. "Dear woman, here is your son," and "Here is your mother." When Jesus saw His mother standing near the cross with the apostle John, He committed His mother's care into John's hands. And from that hour John took her into his own home (John 19:26–27). In these verses Jesus, ever the compassionate Son, is making sure His earthly mother is cared for after His death.

6. "I am thirsty" (John 19:28). Here, Jesus was fulfilling the Messianic prophecy from Psalm 69:21: "They put gall in my food and gave me vinegar for my thirst." By proclaiming His thirst, Jesus prompted the Roman guards to give Him vinegar, which was customary at a crucifixion, and the prophecy was fulfilled.

7. "It is finished" (John 19:30). Jesus' last words meant that His suffering was over and the whole work His Father had given Him to do—preaching the gospel, working miracles, and obtaining eternal salvation for His people—was done, accomplished, fulfilled. The debt of sin was fully paid.

Question: What are the Stations of the Cross and what can we learn from them?

Answer: The Stations of the Cross, along what is known as the *Via Dolorosa*, is a narration of the final hours before Jesus died. The Stations of the Cross serve as a stark reminder of the humble manner in which Jesus set aside the privileges of deity so He could provide salvation (Philippians 2:6–8).

There are several widely accepted versions describing those final hours, one being biblical and the others being more traditional accounts. The traditional form of the Stations of the Cross is as follows:

1. Jesus is condemned to death.
2. Jesus is given His cross.
3. Jesus falls down for the first time.
4. Jesus meets His mother Mary.
5. Simon of Cyrene is forced to carry the cross.
6. Veronica wipes blood off Jesus' face.
7. Jesus falls down for the second time.
8. Jesus meets the women of Jerusalem.
9. Jesus falls down for the third time.
10. Jesus is stripped of His clothing.
11. Jesus is nailed to the cross—the Crucifixion.
12. Jesus dies on the cross.
13. Jesus' body is removed from the cross—the Deposition or Lamentation.
14. Jesus' body is placed in the tomb.

In this traditional form, stations 3, 4, 6, 7, and 9 are not explicitly biblical. As a result, a "Scriptural Way of the Cross" has been developed. Below are the biblical descriptions of the 14 Stations of the Cross and the life application of each:

First Station of the Cross: Jesus on the Mount of Olives (Luke 22:39–46)

Jesus prayed on the Mount of Olives for His Father to take the "cup" of His suffering from His hand. This prayer demonstrated Jesus' humanity. It is not difficult to imagine His great concern over the events He was about to face. There comes a time in the life of all Christians when they must also choose between God's will and their own. That choice, like Jesus' choice, displays the level of a believer's commitment and obedience to God, as well as the true condition of the believer's heart. Jesus was aware of what

He was about to face when He prayed on the Mount of Olives, and His prayer was that the Father's will be done regardless of what the future held for Him.

Second Station of the Cross: Jesus is betrayed by Judas and arrested (Luke 22:47–48)

Judas not only became one of the most despised characters in history when he betrayed Jesus, but he also became a haunting reminder to every Christian that there have been times we have fallen into sin. For the Christian, choosing to sin is like betraying the One who gave His life for us. Judas lived with Jesus, sat at His feet, and learned from Him for years. But because his heart was not truly transformed by the power of the Holy Spirit, he fell away when tempted by Satan.

Third Station of the Cross: Jesus is condemned by the Sanhedrin (Luke 22:66–71)

The Sanhedrin council, made up of 70 priests and scribes and one high priest, demanded that the Roman government execute Jesus. This incident serves as a warning for all Christians to be careful not to exalt ourselves by self-righteously judging others. Biblical knowledge and exalted positions still fall pitifully short of holy perfection, and even the most pious among men can be overtaken by pride. The Bible teaches us to respect positions of authority, but ultimately it is God's will and God's Word that should reign supreme in our lives.

Fourth Station of the Cross: Peter denies Jesus (Luke 22:54–62)

When Jesus was arrested, a number of those present accused Peter of being one of Jesus' followers. Peter denied knowing Jesus three times, just as Jesus had predicted earlier (Luke 22:34). Peter was Jesus' beloved and trusted disciple who witnessed many miracles firsthand and even walked on water with Jesus (Matthew 14:29–31). Even so, Peter demonstrated the weakness of humanity by denying Jesus for fear of also being arrested. Christians all over the world still face persecution and humiliation, from verbal abuse to beatings and death. We might self-righteously judge Peter for his denial of Jesus, but how many Bible-believing Christians can say they have never remained silent about their faith in the face of discrimination, public or private? Such silence demonstrates the frailty of humanity. Peter's faith was imperfect, primarily because the Holy Spirit did not indwell him at that time. After the Spirit came at Pentecost (Acts 2), Peter was a valiant lion of faith, never again fearing to proclaim His Lord.

Fifth Station of the Cross: Jesus is judged by Pontius Pilate (Luke 23:13–25)

By today's legal standards, it is unlikely that Jesus would have been convicted in any court, especially since none of His accusers could produce any real evidence against Him. Pontius Pilate could find no fault in Jesus and wanted to release Him, but the Sanhedrin demanded that Pilate order His execution. The Sanhedrin considered Jesus a major threat to their authority over the Jews. Jesus taught that salvation was by the grace of God and not by adherence to the Sanhedrin's many precepts. Such teaching not only undermined the authority of the religious leaders, but it also posed a serious threat to the livelihood they enjoyed as a result of their control over the Jewish people. Even today, the message of salvation by grace through faith, apart from our own efforts, is unpopular. Because of their fallen nature, human beings naturally want to achieve their own salvation—or at least have a part in it—so they can claim some of the glory. But salvation is of the Lord, who shares His glory with no one (Isaiah 42:8).

Sixth Station of the Cross: Jesus is scourged and crowned with thorns (John 19:1–3)

Over 500 years before Mary gave birth to Jesus, Isaiah prophesied that Jesus would be wounded for our transgressions and bruised for our iniquities and that by His stripes we would be healed (Isaiah 53:3–6). The healing referred to in this passage is not physical healing, but spiritual. Pardon of sin and restoration to God's favor are Acts of spiritual healing, and they are why Jesus died.

Seventh Station of the Cross: Jesus takes up His cross (John 19:17)

When Jesus took up His cross, He was carrying more than wood. Unknown to the many spectators that day, Jesus was carrying the sins of mankind, facing the punishment those sins deserved. Having been saved by Jesus' work on the cross, we serve Him. Jesus exhorts us in Matthew 16:24, "If anyone would come after me, he must deny himself and take up his cross and follow me." He also reveals that this is not optional: "And anyone who does not take his cross and follow me is not worthy of me" (Matthew 10:38). Taking up our cross, an instrument of death, means dying to self in order to live as completely new creations (2 Corinthians 5:17) in obedience to Christ. This means surrendering to God our will, our affections, our ambitions, and our desires. We are not to seek our own happiness as the supreme object. Instead, we should be willing to renounce all and lay down our lives for Christ, if required.

Eighth Station of the Cross: Simon of Cyrene helps Jesus carry His cross (Luke 23:26)

Simon of Cyrene might be considered a victim of circumstance. We do not know much about Simon, but he had most likely come to Jerusalem for the Passover festivities and probably knew little about the proceedings at hand. The Roman soldiers ordered Simon to help, and he did not resist—most likely fearing for his own life. Unlike Jesus, who carried His cross willingly, Simon of Cyrene was forced to carry it. As Christians, we are to willingly join Jesus in His suffering. As Paul exhorts us, "So do not be ashamed to testify about our Lord, or ashamed of me his prisoner. But join with me in suffering for the gospel, by the power of God" (2 Timothy 1:8).

Ninth Station of the Cross: Jesus meets the women of Jerusalem (Luke 23:27–31)

When Jesus encountered the mourning women on His way to His crucifixion, He told them not to weep for Him. Instead, their concern should be for themselves and their children because of the rising evil throughout Jerusalem. Even while suffering great pain and personal humiliation, Jesus' concern was not for Himself, but for the souls of those who faced the danger of eternal damnation due to sin. The same caution is relevant for Christians today. We should be careful not to allow our concern for this world to come before our devotion and obedience to God. Jesus said, "My kingdom is not of this world" (John 18:36), and as citizens of heaven, our focus and attention should be there.

Tenth Station of the Cross: Jesus is crucified (Luke 23:33–38)

We cannot imagine the horror of the moment as those closest to Jesus were forced to watch the spikes being driven through His hands and feet. Jesus' loved ones were not yet able to understand that this evil deed was the result of divine purpose and planning for the salvation of all who would believe in the Christ. For us today: "How shall we escape if we ignore such a great salvation?" (Hebrews 2:3). "Salvation is found in no one else, for there is no other name under heaven given to men by which we must be saved" (Acts 4:12).

Eleventh Station of the Cross: Jesus promises His kingdom to the believing thief (Luke 23:39–43)

It is possible that the thief being crucified next to Jesus was able to grasp the concept that life was not ending for Jesus, but that He was transcending the physical world into eternal promise. The thief would become one of the first to enter paradise by grace through faith in Jesus Christ (Ephesians 2:8–9). Jesus told the thief that he would be in paradise with Him that day because he believed in the Son of God. The thief had done nothing to earn his salvation but was accepted into paradise on the basis of his faith.

Clearly, this shows that a person is saved by grace through faith rather than by works.

Twelfth Station of the Cross: Jesus speaks with His mother and disciples (John 19:26–27)

In His dying moment, Jesus was still putting the needs of others before His own as He selflessly committed the care of His mother to His beloved disciple, John. Jesus' entire life—and even His death—taught by example that we are to put the needs of others before our own, subjecting everything to God's perfect will. Jesus' willingness to abide by God's Word and make the ultimate sacrifice for others is an example for all Christians.

Thirteenth Station of the Cross: Jesus dies on the cross (Luke 23:44–46)

At the moment of Jesus' death, the curtain in the temple, which separated men from the holy of holies, tore from top to bottom. This was terrifying for all the Jews who witnessed it and who did not realize it signified the end to the old covenant and the beginning of the new covenant. No longer would man have to suffer separation from God because of sin—we would now be able to approach the throne of grace for forgiveness. The life and sacrificial death of Jesus removed the barrier of sin, making it possible for man to obtain salvation by grace.

Fourteenth Station of the Cross: Jesus is laid in the tomb (Luke 23:50–54)

After Jesus died and was taken down from the cross, He was laid to rest in a tomb provided by a man named Joseph, from the town of Arimathea. Christian baptism is a picture of being "buried" with Christ (Romans 6:4); that is, our old life has been put to death, and Christ gives us a brand-new life of godliness (Ephesians 4:22–24).

Jesus' great sacrifice was the atonement for man's sins, and it also became the victory that would overcome the fate of all men born under the curse of sin—death. Our God is just and fair and so demanded that the penalty for sin be paid. But because He is loving and merciful as well as just, He sent His only Son to pay that penalty for us (John 3:16).

Question: Who was responsible for Christ's death?

Answer: The answer to this question has many facets. First, there is no doubt the religious leaders of Israel were responsible for Jesus' death. Matthew 26:3–4 tells us, "The chief priests and the elders of the people assembled in the palace of the high priest, whose name was Caiaphas, and they plotted to arrest Jesus in some sly way and kill him." The Jewish leaders demanded of the Romans that Jesus be put to death (Matthew 27:22–25). They couldn't continue to allow Him to work signs and wonders because it threatened their position in the religious society they dominated (John 11:47–50). Therefore, "they plotted to take his life" (John 11:53).

The Romans were the ones who actually crucified Jesus (Matthew 27:27–37). Crucifixion was a Roman method of execution, authorized and carried out by the Romans under the authority of the Roman governor, Pontius Pilate. Roman soldiers drove the nails into Jesus' hands and feet, Roman troops erected the cross, and a Roman solider pierced His side (Matthew 27:27–35).

The people of Israel were also complicit in the death of Jesus. They were the ones who shouted, "Crucify him! Crucify him!" as He stood on trial before Pilate (Luke 23:21). They also cried for the thief Barabbas to be released instead of Jesus (Matthew 27:21). Peter confirmed this in Acts 2:22–23 when he told the men of Israel, "You, with the help of wicked men, put him to death by nailing him to the cross."

From a historical perspective, then, Pontius Pilate, Roman soldiers, King Herod, the Jewish leaders, and the people of Israel were all involved in the murder of Jesus. This was a diverse group of people who never worked together on anything before or since, but who came together this one time to carry out the unthinkable— the murder of the Son of God.

Ultimately, and perhaps amazingly, it was God Himself who put Jesus to death. This was the greatest act of divine justice ever carried out, done "by God's set purpose and foreknowledge" (Acts 2:23) and for the highest purpose. Jesus' death on the cross secured the salvation of countless millions and provided the only way God could forgive sin without compromising His holiness and perfect righteousness. Christ's death was God's perfect plan for the eternal redemption of His children. That is why "it was the Lord's will to crush him and cause him to suffer" (Isaiah 53:10).

Far from being a victory for Satan, as some have suggested, or an unnecessary tragedy, the death of Christ was the most gracious act of God's goodness and mercy, the ultimate expression of the Father's love for sinners (1 John 4:9–10). God put Jesus to death for our sin so that we could live in righteousness before Him. "God made him who had no sin to be sin for us, so that in him we might become the righteousness of God" (2 Corinthians 5:21).

So now we see that everyone on earth is guilty of Jesus' blood, shed on the cross for us. He died to pay the penalty for our sins (Romans 5:8; 6:23). It is you and I who are responsible for Christ's death.

Question: What is the meaning of the "blood of Christ"?

Answer: The phrase "blood of Christ" is used several times in the New Testament and is the expression of the sacrificial death and full atoning work of Jesus on our behalf. References to the Savior's blood include the reality that He literally bled on the cross, but more significantly that He bled and died for sinners. The blood of Christ has the power to atone for an infinite number of sins committed by an infinite number of people throughout the ages, and all whose faith rests in that blood will be saved.

The reality of the blood of Christ as the means of atonement for sin has its origin in the Mosaic Law. Once a year, the high priest was to make an offering of the blood of animals on the altar of the temple for the sins of the people. "In fact, the law requires that nearly everything be cleansed with blood, and without the shedding of blood there is no forgiveness" (Hebrews 9:22). But this was a blood offering that was limited in its effectiveness, which is why it had to be offered again and again. This was a foreshadowing of the "once for all" sacrifice which Jesus offered on the cross (Hebrews 7:27). When that sacrifice was made, there was no longer a need for the blood of bulls and goats.

The blood of Christ is the basis of the new covenant. On the night before He went to the cross, Jesus offered a Passover cup of wine to His disciples and said, "This cup is the new covenant in my blood, which is poured out for you" (Luke 22:20). The pouring of the wine in the cup symbolized the blood of Christ, which would be poured out for all who would ever believe in Him. When He shed His blood on the cross, He did away with the old covenant requirement for the continual sacrifices of animals. Their blood was not sufficient to cover the sins of the people on a long-term basis, because sin against a holy and infinite God requires a holy and infinite sacrifice. "But those sacrifices are an annual reminder of sins, because it is impossible for the blood of bulls and goats to take away sins" (Hebrews 10:3–4). While the blood of bulls and goats was a "reminder" of sin, "the precious blood of Christ, a lamb without blemish or defect" (1 Peter 1:19) paid in full the debt of sin we owed to God, and we need no further sacrifices for sin. Jesus said, "It is finished" as He was dying (John 19:30), and He meant just that—the entire work of redemption was completed forever, "having obtained eternal redemption" for us (Hebrews 9:12).

Not only does the blood of Christ redeem believers from sin and eternal punishment, but His blood will also "cleanse your conscience from dead works to serve the living God" (Hebrews 9:14, NKJV). This means that we are now free from having to rely on worthless and unproductive works of the flesh to please God. Because the blood of Christ has redeemed us, we are new creations in Christ (2 Corinthians 5:17), and by His blood we are freed from sin to serve the living God, to glorify Him, and to enjoy Him forever.

Question: Why did blood and water come out of Jesus' side when He was pierced?

Answer: The Roman flogging, or scourging, that Jesus endured prior to being crucified normally consisted of 39 lashes (Mark 15:15; John 19:1). The whip that was used, called a *flagrum*, consisted of braided leather thongs with metal balls and pieces of sharp bone intertwined with the braids. The balls added weight to the whip, causing deep bruising as the victim was struck. The pieces of bone served to cut into the flesh. As this severe beating continued, the resulting cuts exposed the skeletal muscles, underlying veins, sinews, and bowels of victims. This beating was so brutal that, at times, victims would not survive it.

Those who were flogged would often go into hypovolemic shock, caused by a high loss of blood. The results of hypovolemic shock would be 1) the heart would race to pump blood that was not there, 2) the victim would collapse or faint due to low blood pressure, 3) the kidneys would shut down to preserve body fluids, and 4) the victim would experience extreme thirst as the body tried to replenish lost fluids.

There is evidence from Scripture that Jesus experienced hypovolemic shock as a result of being flogged. As Jesus carried His cross to Golgotha (John 19:17), He collapsed, and a man named Simon was forced to carry the cross the rest of way (Matthew 27:32–33; Mark 15:21–22; Luke 23:26). This collapse indicates Jesus had low blood pressure. Another sign was His declaration of thirst as He hung on the cross (John 19:28), indicating His body's desire to replenish fluids.

Prior to death, the sustained rapid heartbeat caused by hypovolemic shock also causes fluid to gather in the sacks around the heart (pericardial effusion) and the lungs (pleural effusion). This explains why, after Jesus died and a Roman soldier thrust a spear through Jesus' side (probably His right side, piercing both the lungs and the heart), blood and water came forth (John 19:34).

Question: What is the meaning of the cross?

Answer: Simply put, the meaning of the cross is death. In ancient times (i.e., from about the 6th century BC until the 4th century AD), the cross was an instrument of death in the most torturous and painful of ways. Crucifixion involved either tying or nailing a person to a wooden cross and leaving him to hang until dead. Death would be slow and excruciatingly painful (the word *excruciating* comes from the Latin word for "cross"). However, because of Christ and the work He accomplished, the cross took on new meaning.

The cross is the intersection of God's love and His justice. Jesus Christ is the Lamb of God who took the sin of the world on Himself. The reference to Jesus as the Lamb of God points back to the institution of the Jewish Passover in Exodus 12. The Israelites were commanded to sacrifice an unblemished lamb and smear the blood of that lamb on the doorposts of their homes. The blood would be the sign for the Angel of the Lord to "pass over" that house, leaving those covered by blood in safety. When Jesus came to John to be baptized, John recognized Him and cried, "Look, the Lamb of God, who takes away the sin of the world!" (John 1:29), thereby identifying Him and God's plan for Him to be sacrificed for sin. It is significant that Jesus was crucified at Passover time (John 13:1).

One might ask why Jesus had to die in the first place. This is the overarching message of the Bible—the story of redemption. God created the heavens and the earth, and He created man and woman in His image and placed them in the garden of Eden to be stewards of the earth. However, due to the temptations of Satan (the serpent), Adam and Eve sinned and fell from God's grace. Furthermore, they passed the curse of sin on to their children so that every generation inherits their sin and guilt. God the Father sent His one and only Son, Jesus, into the world to take on human flesh and to be the Savior of His people. Born of a virgin, Jesus avoided the curse of the fall that infects all other human beings. As the sinless Son of God, He provided the unblemished sacrifice that God requires. God's justice demanded judgment and punishment for sin; God's love moved Him to send His Son to be the propitiation for sin.

Because of Jesus' atoning sacrifice on the cross, those who place their faith and trust in Him alone for salvation are guaranteed eternal life (John 3:16). However, Jesus called His followers to take up their cross and follow Him (Matthew 16:24). This concept of "cross-bearing" today has lost much of its original meaning. Typically, we use "cross-bearing" to denote an inconvenient or bothersome circumstance (e.g., "my troubled teen is my cross to bear"). However, we must keep in mind that Jesus is calling His disciples to engage in radical self-denial. Remember, the cross meant only one thing to a first-century person—death. "For whoever wants to save his life will lose it, but whoever loses his life for me will find it" (Matthew 16:25). Galatians reiterates this theme of death of the sinful self and rising to walk in new life through Christ: "I have been crucified with Christ and I no longer live, but Christ lives in me. The life I live in the body, I live by faith in the Son of God, who loved me and gave himself for me" (Galatians 2:20).

Those who live in the 21st century, particularly in North America and Europe, may not face severe persecution for being a Christian. Yet there are places in the world where Christians are being persecuted, even to the point of death, for their faith. They know what it means to carry their cross and follow Jesus. The job of every believer is to remain faithful to Christ. We may never be called upon to give the ultimate sacrifice, but we must be willing to do so out of love for the One who saved us and gave His life for us.

Question: What is the meaning of the resurrection of the Jerusalem saints at Jesus' death? (Matthew 27:52–53)?

Answer: Matthew 27:50–53 records, "And when Jesus had cried out again in a loud voice, he gave up his spirit. At that moment the curtain of the temple was torn in two from top to bottom. The earth shook and the rocks split. The tombs broke open and the

146

bodies of many holy people who had died were raised to life. They came out of the tombs, and after Jesus' resurrection they went into the holy city and appeared to many people."

This event occurred as a testimony to the immortal power ascribed to Jesus Christ alone (1 Timothy 6:14–16). Only God has power over life and death (1 Samuel 2:6; Deuteronomy 32:29). Therefore, the resurrection of Christ is the cornerstone of our faith. No other religion serves a risen Lord. By overcoming death, Jesus Christ immediately receives preeminence; no other founder of a religion ever came back to life. The resurrection has given us a reason to tell others about Him and place our trust in God (1 Corinthians 15:14). The resurrection has given us assurance that our sins are forgiven (1 Corinthians 15:17). And, finally, the resurrection has given us a reason to have hope today (1 Corinthians 15:20–28). If Christ were not raised from the dead, then Christians would be no better off spiritually than non-Christians. But the fact is that God did raise "Jesus our Lord from the dead. He was delivered over to death for our sins and was raised to life for our justification" (Romans 4:24–25).

Matthew's inclusion of the account of the saints near Jerusalem rising from the dead fits the overall strategy of his Gospel. Matthew was intent on presenting Jesus as the Messiah who fulfilled Old Testament prophecy. The Old Testament connection to this story is Ezekiel 37, in which the dry bones are raised to life. Additionally, the raising of the saints relates directly to the future kingdom. The raising of a few and not all of the saints indicates there is another resurrection to come. Jesus will return, and there will be a permanent resurrection of all the "dead in Christ" (1 Thessalonians 4:16).

Knowing that Jesus has conquered death through His resurrection ought to hasten our desire to repent and trust Him alone for salvation, so we, too, can one day be resurrected (Revelation 20:6).

Question: Did Jesus go to hell between His death and resurrection?

Answer: There is a great deal of confusion in regard to this question. The idea that Jesus went to hell comes primarily from the Apostles' Creed, which states, "He descended into hell." There are also a few Scriptures that, depending on how they are translated, describe Jesus going to "hell." In studying this issue, it is important to first understand what the Bible teaches about the realm of the dead.

In the Hebrew Scriptures, the word used to describe the realm of the dead is *sheol*. It simply means the "place of the dead" or the "place of departed souls/spirits." The New Testament Greek word that is used for hell is *hades*, which also refers to "the place of the dead." Other Scriptures in the New Testament indicate that sheol/hades is a temporary place, where souls are kept as they await the final resurrection and judgment. Revelation 20:11–15 gives a clear distinction between the two. Hell (the lake of fire) is the permanent and final place of judgment for the lost. Hades is a temporary place. So, no, Jesus did not go to hell because hell is a future realm, only put into effect after the Great White Throne Judgment.

Sheol/hades is a realm with two divisions (Matthew 11:23; 16:18; Luke 10:15; 16:23; Acts 2:27–31), the abodes of the saved and the lost. The abode of the saved was called "paradise" and "Abraham's bosom." The abodes of the saved and the unsaved are separated by a "great chasm" (Luke 16:26). When Jesus ascended to heaven, He took the occupants of paradise (believers) with Him (Ephesians 4:8–10). The unsaved side of sheol/hades has remained unchanged. All unbelieving dead go there, awaiting their final judgment. Did Jesus go to sheol/hades? Yes, according to Ephesians 4:8–10 and 1 Peter 3:18–20.

Some of the confusion has arisen from such passages as Psalm 16:10–11a, as translated in the King James Version, "For thou wilt not leave my soul in hell; neither wilt thou suffer thine Holy One to see corruption. Thou wilt show me the path of life." "Hell" is not a correct translation in this verse. A correct reading would be "the grave" or "sheol." Jesus said to the thief beside Him, "Today you will be with me in paradise" (Luke 23:43). Jesus' body was in the tomb; His soul/spirit went to the "paradise" side of sheol/hades. He then removed all the righteous dead from paradise and took them with Him to heaven. Unfortunately, in many translations of the Bible, translators are not consistent, or correct, in how they translate the Hebrew and Greek words for "sheol," "hades," and "hell."

Some have the viewpoint that Jesus went to "hell" or the suffering side of sheol/hades in order to further be punished for our sins. This idea is completely unbiblical. It was the death of Jesus on the cross that sufficiently provided for our redemption. It was His shed blood that effected our own cleansing from sin (1 John 1:7). As He hung on the cross, He took the sin burden of the whole human race upon Himself. He became sin for us: "God made him who had no sin to be sin for us, so that in him we might become the righteousness of God" (2 Corinthians 5:21).

When Jesus cried upon the cross, "My God, My God, why have you forsaken me?" (Matthew 27:46), it was then that He was separated from the Father because of the sin He bore. When our redemption was complete, He said, "It is finished" (John 19:30). As He gave up His spirit, He said, "Father, into your hands I commit my spirit" (Luke 23:46). Jesus' suffering was completed. His soul/spirit went to the paradise side of hades. The payment for sin was paid. In paradise, He awaited the resurrection of His body and His return to glory in His ascension. Did Jesus go to hell? No. Did Jesus go to sheol/hades? Yes.

Chapter 7

QUESTIONS ABOUT JESUS' RESURRECTION AND ASCENSION

Contents

Is the resurrection of Jesus Christ true?

Why should I believe in Christ's resurrection?

Why is the truth of the bodily resurrection of Jesus Christ so important?

After His resurrection, why did Jesus tell Mary not to touch Him, but then later tell Thomas to touch Him?

Why didn't the disciples always recognize Jesus after His resurrection?

Is it possible to harmonize the various resurrection accounts from the four Gospels?

What is the swoon theory? Did Jesus survive the crucifixion?

What is the meaning and importance of the ascension of Jesus Christ?

Question: Is the resurrection of Jesus Christ true?

Answer: Scripture presents conclusive evidence that Jesus Christ was in fact resurrected from the dead. Christ's resurrection is recorded in Matthew 28:1–20; Mark 16:1–20; Luke 24:1–53; and John 20:1—21:25. The resurrected Christ also appeared in the book of Acts (Acts 1:1–11). In these passages we see several "proofs" of Christ's resurrection. First is the dramatic change the disciples experienced. They went from a group of men frightened and in hiding to bold witnesses sharing the gospel throughout the world. What can explain their remarkable transformation other than the fact that they saw the risen Christ?

Second is the life of the apostle Paul. What changed him from being a persecutor of the church into an apostle for the church? It was when the risen Christ appeared to him on the road to Damascus (Acts 9:1–6). A third convincing proof is the empty tomb. If Christ is not raised, then where is His body? The enemies of the early church could easily have disproved the gospel by producing the dead body of Christ. That no one did argues for the fact that His body was resurrected, just as the angels had said and Jesus Himself had predicted (Matthew 28:5–7). Fourth is the number of witnesses who saw Him after His resurrection (Matthew 28:5, 9, 16–17; Mark 16:9; Luke 24:13–35; John 20:19, 24–29; 21:1–14; Acts 1:6–8; 1 Corinthians 15:5–7).

Another proof of the resurrection of Jesus is the great amount of weight the apostles gave to Jesus' resurrection. A key passage is 1 Corinthians 15, in which the apostle Paul explains why it is crucial to understand and believe in Christ's resurrection. The resurrection is important for the following reasons: 1) If Christ was not raised from the dead, believers will not be resurrected, either (1 Corinthians 15:12–15). 2) If Christ was not raised from the dead, His sacrifice for sin was not sufficient. Jesus' resurrection proved that God accepted Jesus' death as the atonement for our sins. If He had simply died and stayed dead, that would indicate His sacrifice was not sufficient. 3) If Christ was not raised from the dead, believers would not be forgiven of their sins (1 Corinthians 15:16–19). There would be no such thing as eternal life (John 3:16). "But

Christ has indeed been raised from the dead, the firstfruits of those who have fallen asleep" (1 Corinthians 15:20).

Scripture is clear that all those who believe in Jesus Christ will be raised to eternal life just as He was (1 Corinthians 15:20–23). Christ's resurrection proves His victory over sin and provides us the power to live victoriously (1 Corinthians 15:24–34). As a result of Christ's resurrection, all who believe in Him will ultimately triumph over death (1 Corinthians 15:50–58).

What a glorious truth the resurrection of Christ is! "Therefore, my dear brothers, stand firm. Let nothing move you. Always give yourselves fully to the work of the Lord, because you know that your labor in the Lord is not in vain" (1 Corinthians 15:58). The resurrection of Jesus Christ is most definitely true, and our faith in the Lord will be rewarded.

Question: Why should I believe in Christ's resurrection?

Answer: It is a well-established fact that Jesus Christ was publicly executed in Judea in the 1st century AD, under Pontius Pilate, by means of crucifixion, at the behest of the Jewish Sanhedrin. The non-Christian historical accounts of Flavius Josephus, Cornelius Tacitus, Lucian of Samosata, Maimonides, and even the Jewish Sanhedrin corroborate the early Christian eyewitness accounts of these important historical aspects of the death of Jesus Christ.

As for His resurrection, there are several lines of evidence that make for a compelling case. The late jurisprudential prodigy and international statesman Sir Lionel Luckhoo (of *The Guinness Book of World Records* fame for his unprecedented 245 consecutive defense murder trial acquittals) epitomized Christian confidence in the strength of the case for the resurrection. Luckhoo wrote, "I have spent more than 42 years as a defense trial lawyer appearing in many parts of the world and am still in active practice. I have been fortunate to secure a number of successes in jury trials and I say unequivocally the evidence for the Resurrection of Jesus Christ is so overwhelming that it compels acceptance by proof which leaves absolutely no room for doubt."[18]

The secular community's response to the evidence for Christ's resurrection has been predictably apathetic in accordance with their steadfast commitment to methodological naturalism (the endeavor to explain everything solely in terms of natural causes). If an alleged historical event defies natural explanation (e.g., a miraculous resurrection), secular scholars generally treat it with overwhelming skepticism, no matter how favorable and compelling the evidence may be.

Such unwavering allegiance to natural causes regardless of substantive evidence to the contrary is not conducive to an impartial (and therefore adequate) investigation of the evidence. Forcing a popular philosophical predisposition upon the evidence hinders objectivity.

Let us now examine the several lines of evidence in favor of the resurrection.

The First Line of Evidence for Christ's Resurrection

To begin with, we have demonstrably sincere eyewitness testimony. Early Christian apologists cited hundreds of eyewitnesses, some of whom documented their own alleged experiences. Many of these eyewitnesses willfully and resolutely endured prolonged torture and death rather than repudiate their testimony. Such resolve attests to their sincerity, ruling out deception on their part. According to the historical record (Acts 4:1–17, Pliny's *Letters to Trajan*, etc.) most Christians could have ended their suffering simply by renouncing the faith. Instead, it seems that most opted to endure the suffering and steadfastly proclaim Christ's resurrection.

Granted, while martyrdom is remarkable, it is not necessarily compelling. It does not validate a belief so much as it authenticates a believer (by demonstrating his or her sincerity in a tangible way). What makes the earliest Christian martyrs remarkable is that they knew whether or not what they were professing was true. They either saw Jesus Christ alive and well after His death or they did not. This is extraordinary. If it were all just a lie, why would so many perpetuate it given their circumstances? Why would

154

they all knowingly cling to such an unprofitable lie in the face of persecution, imprisonment, torture, and death?

While the September 11, 2001, suicide hijackers undoubtedly believed what they professed (as evidenced by their willingness to die for it), they could not and did not know if it was true. They put their faith in traditions passed down to them over many generations. In contrast, the early Christian martyrs were the first generation. The fact that they endured martyrdom suggests they actually saw what they claimed to have seen.

Among the most illustrious of the professed eyewitnesses were the apostles. They collectively underwent an undeniable change following the alleged post-resurrection appearances of Christ. Immediately following His crucifixion, they hid in fear for their lives. After the resurrection they took to the streets, boldly proclaiming the resurrection despite intensifying persecution. What accounts for their sudden and dramatic change? It certainly was not financial gain. The apostles gave up everything they had to preach the resurrection, including their lives in most cases.

The Second Line of Evidence for Christ's Resurrection

A second line of evidence concerns the conversion of certain key skeptics, most notably Paul and James. Paul was, of his own admission, a violent persecutor of the early church. After what he described as an encounter with the resurrected Christ, Paul underwent an immediate and drastic change from a vicious persecutor of the church to one of its most prolific and selfless defenders. Like many early Christians, Paul suffered impoverishment, persecution, beatings, imprisonment, and execution for his steadfast commitment to Christ's resurrection.

James was skeptical, though not as hostile as Paul. A purported post-resurrection encounter with Christ turned him into an inimitable believer and leader of the Church in Jerusalem. We still have one of his letters to the early church. Like Paul, James willingly suffered and died for his testimony, a fact that attests to the sincerity of his belief (see Josephus' *Antiquities of the Jews*).

The Third and Fourth Lines of Evidence for Christ's Resurrection

A third line and fourth line of evidence concern enemy attestation to the empty tomb and the fact that faith in the resurrection took root in Jerusalem. Jesus was publicly executed and buried in Jerusalem. It would have been impossible for faith in His resurrection to take root in Jerusalem while His body was still in the tomb—the Sanhedrin could easily exhume the body, put it on public display, and thereby expose the hoax. Instead, the Sanhedrin accused the disciples of stealing the body, apparently in an effort to explain its disappearance (and therefore an empty tomb). How do we explain the fact of the empty tomb? Here are the two most common explanations:

First, the disciples stole the body. If this were the case, they would have known the resurrection was a hoax. They would not, therefore, have been so willing to suffer and die for it. (See the first line of evidence concerning demonstrably sincere eyewitness testimony.) All of the professed eyewitnesses would have known that they hadn't really seen Christ and were therefore lying. With so many conspirators, surely someone would have confessed—if not to end his own suffering then at least to end the suffering of his friends and family. The first generation of Christians was absolutely brutalized, especially following the conflagration in Rome in AD 64. As the Roman historian Cornelius Tacitus recounted in his *Annals of Imperial Rome* (published just a generation after the fire):

"Nero fastened the guilt [for the fire] and inflicted the most exquisite tortures on a class hated for their abominations, called Christians by the populace. Christus, from whom the name had its origin, suffered the extreme penalty during the reign of Tiberius at the hands of one of our procurators, Pontius Pilatus, and a most mischievous superstition, thus checked for the moment, again broke out not only in Judaea, the first source of the evil, but even in Rome, where all things hideous and shameful from every part of the world find their centre and become popular. Accordingly, an arrest was first made of all who pleaded guilty; then, upon their information, an immense multitude was convicted, not so much of

156

the crime of firing the city, as of hatred against mankind. Mockery of every sort was added to their deaths. Covered with the skins of beasts, they were torn by dogs and perished, or were nailed to crosses, or were doomed to the flames and burnt, to serve as a nightly illumination, when daylight had expired."[19]

Nero illuminated his garden parties with Christians whom he burnt alive. Surely, if Jesus' resurrection were a hoax, someone would have confessed the truth under the threat of such terrible pain. The fact is, however, we have no record of any early Christian renouncing the faith to end his suffering. Instead, we have multiple accounts of Jesus' post-resurrection appearances and hundreds of eyewitnesses willing to suffer and die for it.

A second suggestion to explain the empty tomb is that Christ faked His death and later escaped from the tomb. This is patently absurd. According to the eyewitness testimony, Christ was beaten, tortured, lacerated, and stabbed. He suffered internal damage, massive blood loss, asphyxiation, and a spear through His heart. There is no good reason to believe that Jesus Christ (or any other man for that matter) could survive such an ordeal; fake His death; sit in a tomb for three days and nights without medical attention, food, or water; remove the massive stone which sealed His tomb; escape undetected (without leaving behind a trail of blood); convince hundreds of eyewitnesses that He was resurrected from the death and in good health; and then disappear without a trace. Such a notion is ridiculous.

The Fifth Line of Evidence for Christ's Resurrection

A fifth line of evidence concerns a peculiarity of the eyewitness testimony. In all of the major resurrection narratives, women are credited as the first and primary eyewitnesses. This would be an odd invention since in both the ancient Jewish and Roman cultures women were severely disesteemed. Women's testimony was regarded as insubstantial and dismissible. Given this fact, it is highly unlikely that any perpetrators of a hoax in first-century Judea would elect women to be their primary witnesses. There were many male disciples who claimed to see Jesus resurrected; if they all were lying and the resurrection was a scam, why did they pick the most distrusted witnesses they could find?

Dr. William Lane Craig explains, "When you understand the role of women in first-century Jewish society, what's really extraordinary is that this empty tomb story should feature women as the discoverers of the empty tomb in the first place. Women were on a very low rung of the social ladder in first-century Palestine. There are old rabbinical sayings that said, 'Let the words of Law be burned rather than delivered to women' and 'blessed is he whose children are male, but woe to him whose children are female.' Women's testimony was regarded as so worthless that they weren't even allowed to serve as legal witnesses in a Jewish court of Law. In light of this, it's absolutely remarkable that the chief witnesses to the empty tomb are these women...Any later legendary account would have certainly portrayed male disciples as discovering the tomb—Peter or John, for example. The fact that women are the first witnesses to the empty tomb is most plausibly explained by the reality that—like it or not—they were the discoverers of the empty tomb! This shows that the Gospel writers faithfully recorded what happened, even if it was embarrassing. This bespeaks the historicity of this tradition rather than its legendary status."[20]

In Summary

These lines of evidence—the demonstrable sincerity of the eyewitnesses (and in the apostles' case, compelling, inexplicable change), the conversion and demonstrable sincerity of key antagonists- and skeptics-turned-martyrs, the fact of the empty tomb, enemy attestation to the empty tomb, the fact that all of this took place in Jerusalem where faith in the resurrection began and thrived, the testimony of the women, the significance of such testimony given the historical context—all strongly attest to the historicity of the resurrection. We encourage our readers to thoughtfully consider these evidences. What do they suggest to you? Having pondered them ourselves, we resolutely affirm Sir Lionel's declaration:

"The evidence for the Resurrection of Jesus Christ is so overwhelming that it compels acceptance by proof which leaves absolutely no room for doubt."[21]

Question: Why is the truth of the bodily resurrection of Jesus Christ so important?

Answer: The bodily resurrection of Jesus Christ is the most important event in history and provides irrefutable evidence that Jesus is who He claimed to be—the Son of God. The resurrection proved His deity and validated Scripture, which made it clear that Christ's body would see no decay (Psalm 16:10; Acts 2:27), a promise that would make no sense if His body were not resurrected. Moreover, the resurrection authenticated Christ's claims that He would be raised on the third day (John 2:19–21; Mark 8:31; 9:31; 10:32–34). After the resurrection, Christ emphatically told His disciples that it was His body that was resurrected: "A spirit does not have flesh and bones as you see I have" (Luke 24:39, NKJV).

If Christ's body was not resurrected, then we have no hope that ours will be (1 Corinthians 15:13, 16). In fact, apart from Christ's bodily resurrection, we have no Savior, no salvation, and no hope of eternal life. As the apostle Paul lamented, our faith would be "useless" and the life-giving power of the gospel would be altogether eliminated.

Because our eternal destiny rides on the truth of this event, the resurrection has been the target of Satan's greatest attacks. Accordingly, the historicity of Christ's bodily resurrection has been investigated from every angle and studied by countless scholars, theologians, professors, and others over the centuries. A number of theories have been postulated that attempt to disprove this momentous event, but no credible evidence exists which would validate anything other than His literal, corporeal resurrection. In fact, the clear and convincing evidence of the bodily resurrection of Jesus Christ is overwhelming.

Nonetheless, misunderstandings persist relative to certain aspects of our Savior's resurrection. Why, some ask, is it important that Christ's *body* was resurrected? Couldn't His resurrection have been spiritual? How does the resurrection of Jesus Christ guarantee the bodily resurrection of believers? Will our resurrected bodies be the same as our earthly bodies? If not, what will they be like? The answers to these questions are found in the fifteenth chapter of Paul's first letter to the church in Corinth, a church he established several years earlier during his second missionary journey.

In the young Corinthian church, there were misunderstandings of some key Christian doctrines, including the resurrection. Although many of the Corinthians accepted that Christ has been resurrected (1 Corinthians 15:1, 11), they had difficulty believing others could or would be resurrected. The influence of Gnosticism, which held that everything spiritual was good and everything physical (such as the human body) was evil, was responsible for their confusion regarding resurrection. The idea that an evil, detestable body would be resurrected to live in heaven was strongly opposed by the Greek philosophers of the day (Acts 17:32), and that philosophy had found its way into the church.

Yet, most of the Corinthians understood that Christ's resurrection was corporeal and not simply spiritual. After all, "resurrection" means that something comes back to life. They understood that all souls are immortal and, at death, immediately go to be with the Lord (2 Corinthians 5:8). Thus, a "spiritual" resurrection would make no sense, as the spirit doesn't die and therefore cannot be resurrected.

Again, however, the Corinthians' concern was regarding their personal resurrection. Paul worked to convince the Corinthians that, because Christ rose from the dead, they also would rise from the dead someday. The doctrine of the two resurrections—Christ's and ours—must stand or fall together, for "if there is no resurrection of the dead, then not even Christ has been raised" (1 Corinthians 15:13).

"But Christ has indeed been raised from the dead, the firstfruits of those who have fallen asleep. For since death came through a man, the resurrection of the dead comes also through

160

a man. For as in Adam all die, so in Christ all will be made alive" (1 Corinthians 15:20–22).

God had commanded the Israelites to bring a representative sampling (firstfruits) of their crops to the tabernacle as an offering to the Lord (Leviticus 23:10). This is what Paul refers to when he says that Christ's resurrection was the "firstfruits" of the resurrection "harvest" of the believing dead. "Firstfruits" indicates something to follow, and that something would be us—we are the rest of the "crop." Christ's resurrection guarantees ours; in fact, it *requires* ours. (See also Colossians 1:18.)

The Corinthians were concerned about connecting the spirit to what was deemed an undesirable body. To allay their fears, Paul explained the nature of the resurrected body and how it would differ from the earthly body. Paul likened the deceased earthly body to a "seed" planted in the ground to one day bring forth a new body (1 Corinthians 15:37–38) like Christ's glorious, resurrected body (1 Corinthians 15:49; Philippians 4:21). Our bodies that are now perishable, weak, and natural will one day be raised as bodies that are imperishable, glorious, and heavenly (1 Corinthians 15:42–44). Our resurrected bodies will be perfectly equipped for heavenly, supernatural living.

Question: After His resurrection, why did Jesus tell Mary not to touch Him, but then later tell Thomas to touch Him?

Answer: Jesus tells Mary, "Touch me not" (John 20:17, KJV); but then later, speaking to Thomas, He says, "Reach hither thy finger and behold my hands; and reach hither thy hand, and thrust it into my side" (verse 27). Thomas can touch, but Mary cannot. The seeming incongruity of Jesus' statements is resolved when we examine the language Jesus employed and consider the basic difference between the two situations.

In John 20:17, the word translated "touch" is a Greek word which means "to cling to, to lay hold of." This wasn't just a touch; it was a grip. Obviously, when Mary recognized Jesus, she immediately clung to Him. Matthew 28:9 records the other women doing the same thing when they saw the resurrected Christ.

Several things may have motivated Mary's reaction. One is simply her loving devotion to the Lord. Mary is overwhelmed by the events of the morning, and as her grief turns to joy, she naturally embraces Jesus. Another motivation may have been a desire to restore the fellowship that death had broken. She had lost Him once, and she was going to make sure she didn't lose Him again—she wanted to keep Jesus with her always. Also, Mary may have thought that this was the fulfillment of Jesus' promise to return (John 14:3), in which case He would take her (and all believers) with Him to heaven.

However, it was not Jesus' plan to stay in this world always, and His resurrection was not to be seen as His promised return. That is why He tells Mary of the ascension. His plan was to ascend to the Father and then send the Holy Spirit (John 16:7; 20:22; Acts 2:1–4). Fellowship with Jesus would continue, but it would be a spiritual communion, not a physical presence.

Mary desired to keep Jesus always present with her. Such a desire is natural. Jesus lovingly informed her that their relationship was about to change. He was going to heaven, and He would send the Comforter in His place. In loosening Mary's hold on Him, Jesus was, in effect, telling her that she needed to start walking by faith, not by sight.

When Jesus spoke to Thomas, it was not to counter a misplaced desire but to rebuke a lack of faith. Thomas had said he would not believe that Jesus was alive until he had touched His living body (John 20:25). Jesus, knowing all about Thomas's declaration, offered His body as living proof of His resurrection. Jesus offered the same proof to all the disciples on another occasion as well (Luke 24:39–40).

So, both Mary and Thomas needed more faith. Mary needed faith enough to let Jesus go. Thomas needed faith enough to believe without empirical proof. Mary needed to loosen her grip; Thomas needed to strengthen his. The resurrected Christ gave both of them the faith they needed.

Question: Why didn't the disciples always recognize Jesus after His resurrection?

Answer: The Bible does not specifically tell us why the followers of Christ did not always recognize Him after His resurrection. As a result, we can only speculate. Keeping this in mind, there are a few things that might have contributed to the disciples' not recognizing Jesus immediately in His post-resurrection appearances. First, even though Jesus had predicted that He would rise again on the third day, the disciples did not fully understand (Mark 9:30–32). So they clearly were not looking for Him to be resurrected. This can account for some of their surprise and shock at seeing Him. He was the last person they expected to see.

Mary Magdalene was the first to see the risen Lord, but she did not immediately recognize Him. Mary came to the tomb early in the morning (John 20:1). When she first saw Jesus, she mistook Him for the gardener. It is important to remember that we do not know how far Mary was from Jesus when she misidentified Him. It could be that she was simply too far to clearly recognize who He was. It was also very early in the morning. John says it was "still dark," possibly making it difficult for her to see Jesus clearly. Also, Mary was crying (verses 13 and 15). Add to all this the fact that she was not expecting to see Jesus alive, and we have some logical reasons why she did not recognize Him until He spoke to her.

Another instance of Jesus not being immediately recognized occurred at the Sea of Galilee. Jesus stood on the shore as the disciples were out fishing (John 21:4). This also happened "early in the morning" and involved distance.

A third instance is when the two disciples on the road to Emmaus walked and talked with the Lord but did not recognize Him until He broke the bread during their meal (Luke 24:13–35). How could these two disciples have walked, talked, and eaten with Jesus without recognizing Him? In this instance, it seems that they were supernaturally prevented from recognizing Jesus. Perhaps Jesus had taken on a different appearance to keep Himself from being recognized. The Bible does not say why He did this. Perhaps Jesus veiled His identity so the two disciples would truly think through the things He was saying, rather than accepting the teaching blindly—as they may have done had they known it was Jesus.

What we can know for certain is that it was Jesus Himself who appeared to these people. Their unanimous testimony was that they saw the resurrected Christ. In addition, there was a remarkable change in the lives of the disciples after Jesus' resurrection. Immediately before and after the crucifixion, the eleven disciples were hiding in fear; yet after spending considerable time with the resurrected Christ, they became fearless evangelists who proclaimed the gospel boldly, no matter how strong the opposition. All but one of the eleven eventually gave their lives for the sake of the gospel. Only meeting the resurrected Jesus Christ can account for such a radical change.

Question: Is it possible to harmonize the various resurrection accounts from the four Gospels?

Answer: The events surrounding Jesus' resurrection can be difficult to piece together. But we must remember two things: First, the news of Jesus' resurrection produced much excitement in Jerusalem, and in the ensuing chaos many people were going many different directions. People were separated, and several different groups paid visits to the tomb, possibly more than once. Second, the writers of the Gospels did not attempt an exhaustive narrative; in other words, Matthew, Mark, Luke, and John had no intention of telling us every detail of the resurrection or every event in the order that it happened.

In the battle with skeptics regarding Jesus' resurrection, Christians are in a "no-win" situation. If the resurrection accounts harmonize perfectly, skeptics will claim that the writers of the Gospels conspired together. If the resurrection accounts have some differences, skeptics will claim that the Gospels contradict each other and therefore cannot be trusted. It is our contention that the resurrection accounts are accurate, can be harmonized, and do not contradict each other.

However, even if the resurrection accounts cannot be perfectly harmonized, that does not make them untrustworthy. By any reasonable evaluation, the resurrection accounts from the four Gospels are superbly consistent eyewitness testimonies. The central truths—that Jesus was resurrected from the dead and that the resurrected Jesus appeared to many people—are taught clearly in each of the four Gospels. The apparent inconsistencies are in "side issues." How many angels did they see in the tomb—one or two? (Perhaps one person only saw one angel, while the other person saw two angels.) To how many women did Jesus appear, and to whom did He appear first? (While each Gospel has a slightly different sequence to the appearances, none of them claims to be giving the precise chronological order.) So, while the resurrection accounts may seem to be inconsistent, it cannot be proven that the accounts are contradictory.

Here is a possible harmony of the narratives of the resurrection of Christ and His post-resurrection appearances, in chronological order:

1. 1. Jesus is laid in the tomb as several women watch (Matthew 27:57–61; Mark 15:42–47; Luke 23:50–55; John 19:38–42).
2. The tomb is sealed, and a guard is set (Matthew 27:62–66).
3. At least three women, including Mary Magdalene, Mary the mother of James, and Salome, set out for the tomb with spices they had prepared to anoint Jesus' body (Matthew 28:1; Mark 16:1).
4. An angel descends from heaven, rolls the stone away, and sits on it. There is an earthquake, and the guards faint (Matthew 28:2–4).
5. The women arrive at the tomb and find it empty. Mary Magdalene leaves the other women there and runs to tell the disciples (John 20:1–2).
6. The women still at the tomb see two angels who tell them that Jesus is risen and then instruct them to tell the disciples to go to Galilee (Matthew 28:5–7; Mark 16:2–8; Luke 24:1–8).

7. The women leave to bring the news to the disciples (Matthew 28:8). Mark 16:8 says that, out of fear, "they said nothing to anyone," but this must be understood in light of the fact that they *did* eventually tell the disciples. So, Mark's meaning is, "They told no one else until they found the disciples."

8. The guards, having roused themselves, report the empty tomb to the authorities, who bribe the guards to say the body was stolen (Matthew 28:11–15).

9. Mary the mother of James and the other women, on their way to find the disciples, see Jesus (Matthew 28:9–10).

10. The women find the disciples and relate what they had seen and heard (Luke 24:9–11).

11. Peter and John run to the tomb, see that it is empty, and find the grave clothes (Luke 24:12; John 20:2–10).

12. Mary Magdalene returns to the tomb. She sees the angels, and then she sees Jesus (John 20:11–18).

13. Later the same day, Jesus appears to Peter (Luke 24:34; 1 Corinthians 15:5).

14. Still on the same day, Jesus appears to Cleopas and another disciple on their way to Emmaus (Luke 24:13–32).

15. That evening, the two disciples report the event to the Eleven in Jerusalem (Luke 24:32–35).

16. Jesus appears to ten disciples—Thomas is missing (Luke 24:36–43; John 20:19–25).

17. Jesus appears to all eleven disciples—Thomas included (John 20:26–31).

18. Jesus appears to seven disciples by the Sea of Galilee (John 21:1–25).

19. Jesus appears to about 500 disciples in Galilee (1 Corinthians 15:6).

20. Jesus appears to His half-brother James (1 Corinthians 15:7).

21. Jesus commissions His disciples (Matthew 28:16–20).

22. Jesus teaches His disciples the Scriptures and promises to send the Holy Spirit (Luke 24:44–49; Acts 1:4–5).

23. Jesus ascends into heaven (Luke 24:50–53; Acts 1:6–11).

Question: What is the swoon theory? Did Jesus survive the crucifixion?

Answer: The swoon theory is the belief that Jesus didn't really die at His crucifixion but was merely unconscious when He was laid in the tomb, where He recovered. Those who ascribe to the swoon theory believe that Jesus' appearances after three days in the tomb were merely *perceived* to be resurrection appearances. There are several reasons why this theory is invalid and can easily be proven false. There were at least three different persons or groups involved in Jesus' crucifixion who were satisfied that Jesus had died on the cross. They are the Roman guards, Pontius Pilate, and the Sanhedrin.

The Roman Guards

Two separate groups of Roman soldiers had the task of ensuring the death of Jesus: the executioners and the tomb guards. The soldiers in charge of Jesus' execution were specialists in capital punishment, and crucifixion was one of the most brutal forms of execution in history. Jesus was nailed to a cross after enduring horrible beatings at the hands of these professional death merchants. The soldiers' job was to ensure the task was completed. They made certain that Jesus was dead by piercing His side with a spear before they allowed His body to be taken from the cross. The second group of soldiers was given the task of guarding Jesus' tomb due to a request the Sanhedrin made to Pilate. Matthew 27:62–66 tells us, "The chief priests and the Pharisees went to Pilate. 'Sir,' they said, 'we remember that while he was still alive that deceiver said, "After three days I will rise again." So give the order for the tomb to be made secure until the third day. Otherwise, his disciples may come and steal the body and tell the people that he has been raised from the dead. This last deception will be worse than the first.' 'Take a guard,' Pilate answered. 'Go, make the tomb as secure as you know how.' So they went and made the tomb secure by putting a seal on the stone and posting the guard." These guards' lives depended upon completion of their mission. Only the resurrection of the Son of God could have stayed them from their task.

Pontius Pilate

Pilate, the Roman governor of Judea, gave the order for Jesus to be crucified. He entrusted this task to a Roman centurion, a proven commander of 100 Roman soldiers. After the crucifixion, Joseph of Arimathea made a request for the body of Jesus so that it could be placed in a tomb. Only after his centurion gave confirmation of Jesus' death did Pilate release the body into Joseph's care (Mark 15:42–45). Pilate had to be completely satisfied that Jesus was truly dead, or he never would have released the body.

The Sanhedrin

As the ruling council of the Jewish people, the Sanhedrin requested that the dead bodies of those crucified, including Jesus, be taken down from the crosses because of the ensuing Sabbath day. "Now it was the day of Preparation, and the next day was to be a special Sabbath. Because the Jews did not want the bodies left on the crosses during the Sabbath, they asked Pilate to have the legs broken and the bodies taken down. The soldiers therefore came and broke the legs of the first man who had been crucified with Jesus, and then those of the other. But when they came to Jesus and found that he was already dead, they did not break his legs. Instead, one of the soldiers pierced Jesus' side with a spear, bringing a sudden flow of blood and water" (John 19:31–34). The Jewish leaders who demanded that Jesus be crucified would never have allowed His body to be removed from the cross were He not already dead. These men were completely satisfied that Jesus was truly dead.

There is other evidence that the swoon theory is invalid, such as the condition of Jesus' body after the resurrection. At every post-resurrection appearance, Jesus' body was shown to be in a glorified state. The only marks that remained were those that proved His crucifixion (John 20:27). Any surviving victim of crucifixion would have needed months to recover physically. Jesus had no ill effects other than the marks of the nails in His hands and feet and the stab wound in His side.

The purpose of the swoon theory is not to dispute Jesus' death as much as to disprove His resurrection. If Jesus didn't really die, then He didn't really resurrect. And if He did not resurrect, then He is not God. However, if Jesus truly died and rose from the dead, His power over death proves that He is the Son of God. The evidence demands the verdict: Jesus truly died on the cross, and Jesus truly rose from the dead.

Question: What is the meaning and importance of the ascension of Jesus Christ?

Answer: After Jesus rose from the dead, He showed Himself to the women near the tomb (Matthew 28:9–10), to His disciples (Luke 24:36–43), and to more than 500 others (1 Corinthians 15:6). In the days following His resurrection, Jesus taught His disciples about the kingdom of God (Acts 1:3).

Forty days after the resurrection, Jesus and His disciples went to Mount Olivet, near Jerusalem. There, Jesus promised His followers that they would soon receive the Holy Spirit, and He instructed them to remain in Jerusalem until the Spirit had come. Then Jesus blessed them, and as He gave the blessing, He began to ascend into heaven. The account of Jesus' ascension is found in Luke 24:50–51 and Acts 1:9–11.

It is plain from Scripture that Jesus' ascension was a literal, bodily return to heaven. He rose from the ground gradually and visibly, observed by many intent onlookers. As the disciples strained to catch a last glimpse of Jesus, a cloud hid Him from their view, and two angels appeared and promised Christ's return "in the same way you have seen him go into heaven" (Acts 1:11).

The Ascension of Jesus Christ is meaningful for several reasons:

1. It signaled the end of His earthly ministry. God the Father had lovingly sent His Son into the world, and now the Son was returning to the Father. The period of human limitation was at an end.

2. It signified success in His earthly work. All that He had come to do, He had accomplished.
3. It marked the return of His heavenly glory. Jesus' glory had been veiled during His sojourn on earth, with one brief exception at the Transfiguration (Matthew 17:1– 9).
4. It symbolized His exaltation by the Father (Ephesians 1:20–23). The One with whom the Father is well pleased (Matthew 17:5) was received up in honor and given a name above all names (Philippians 2:9).
5. It allowed Him to prepare a place for us (John 14:2).
6. It indicated the beginning of His new work as high priest (Hebrews 4:14–16) and mediator of the new covenant (Hebrews 9:15).
7. It set the pattern for His return. When Jesus comes to set up the Kingdom, He will return just as He left—literally, bodily, and visibly in the clouds (Acts 1:11; Daniel 7:13–14; Matthew 24:30; Revelation 1:7).

Currently, the Lord Jesus is in heaven. The Scriptures frequently picture Him at the right hand of the Father—a position of honor and authority (Psalm 110:1; Ephesians 1:20; Hebrews 8:1). Christ is the head of the church (Colossians 1:18), the giver of spiritual gifts (Ephesians 4:7–8), and the One who fills the universe (Ephesians 4:9–10).

Chapter 8

QUESTIONS ABOUT JESUS IN THE OLD TESTAMENT

Contents

Where does the Old Testament predict the coming of Christ?

Why wasn't Jesus named Immanuel?

Is Isaiah 53, "The Suffering Servant," a prophecy about Jesus?

Where do the Hebrew Scriptures prophesy the death and resurrection of the Messiah?

What does it mean that Jesus is the Prince of Peace (Isaiah 9:6)?

Question: Where does the Old Testament predict the coming of Christ?

Answer: There are many Old Testament prophecies about Jesus Christ. Some interpreters place the number of Messianic prophecies in the hundreds. The following are those that are considered the clearest and most important:

Regarding Jesus' birth—Isaiah 7:14: "Therefore the Lord himself will give you a sign: The virgin will be with child and will give birth to a son, and will call him Immanuel." Isaiah 9:6: "For to us a child is born, to us a son is given, and the government will be on his shoulders. And he will be called Wonderful Counselor, Mighty God, Everlasting Father, Prince of Peace." Micah 5:2: "But you, Bethlehem Ephrathah, though you are small among the clans of Judah, out of you will come for me one who will be ruler over Israel, whose origins are from of old, from ancient times."

Concerning Jesus' ministry and death—Zechariah 9:9: "Rejoice greatly, O Daughter of Zion! Shout, Daughter of Jerusalem! See, your king comes to you, righteous and having salvation, gentle and riding on a donkey, on a colt, the foal of a donkey." Psalm 22:16–18: "Dogs have surrounded me; a band of evil men has encircled me, they have pierced my hands and my feet. I can count all my bones; people stare and gloat over me. They divide my garments among them and cast lots for my clothing."

Likely the clearest prophecy about Jesus is the entire 53rd chapter of Isaiah. Isaiah 53:3–7 is especially definite: "He was despised and rejected by men, a man of sorrows, and familiar with suffering. Like one from whom men hide their faces he was despised, and we esteemed him not. Surely he took up our infirmities and carried our sorrows, yet we considered him stricken by God, smitten by him, and afflicted. But he was pierced for our transgressions, he was crushed for our iniquities; the punishment that brought us peace was upon him, and by his wounds we are healed. We all, like sheep, have gone astray, each of us has turned to his own way; and the LORD has laid on him the iniquity of us all. He was oppressed and afflicted, yet he did not open his mouth;

he was led like a lamb to the slaughter, and as a sheep before her shearers is silent, so he did not open his mouth."

The "seventy sevens" prophecy in Daniel 9 predicted the precise date that Jesus, the Messiah, would be "cut off" (verses 24–27). Isaiah 50:6 accurately describes the beating that Jesus endured. Zechariah 12:10 predicts the "piercing" of the Messiah, which occurred after Jesus died on the cross. Many more examples could be provided. The Old Testament most definitely prophesies the coming of Jesus as the Messiah.

Question: Why wasn't Jesus named Immanuel?

Answer: In Isaiah 7:14, the prophet Isaiah declared, "Therefore the Lord himself will give you a sign: The virgin will be with child and will give birth to a son, and will call him Immanuel." This prophecy refers to the birth of Jesus, according to Matthew 1:22–23, "All this took place to fulfill what the Lord had said through the prophet: 'The virgin will be with child and will give birth to a son, and they will call him Immanuel'—which means, 'God with us.'" This prophecy does not mean, however, that Immanuel would be the Messiah's literal name.

There are many Messianic names that use the phrase "He shall be called," both in the Old and New Testaments. This was a common way of saying that people would refer to Him in these various ways. Isaiah prophesied of the Messiah, "He will be called Wonderful Counselor, Mighty God, Everlasting Father, Prince of Peace" (Isaiah 9:6). None of these titles was Jesus' actual name but were instead descriptions people would use to refer to Him forever. Luke tells us Jesus "will be called the Son of the Most High" (Luke 1:32), "Son of God" (1:35), and "prophet of the Most High" (1:76)—but none of these was His name.

The prophet Jeremiah says in reference to the coming Messiah, "In His days Judah will be saved, And Israel will dwell securely; And this is His name by which He will be called, 'The LORD our righteousness'" (Jeremiah 23:6). Now, we know that God the Father is named Jehovah (or "the LORD"). Jesus was never

173

actually called Jehovah as though it were His name, but His role was that of bringing the righteousness of Jehovah to those who would believe in Him, exchanging that righteousness for our sin (2 Corinthians 5:21). Therefore, "the LORD our righteousness" is one of the many titles or "names" that belong to Him.

In the same way, to say that Jesus would be called "Immanuel" means Jesus is God, that He dwelt among us in His incarnation, and that He will be with us always. Jesus was God making His dwelling among us (John 1:1, 14). No, Jesus' name was not Immanuel, but Jesus embodied the meaning of Immanuel: "God with us."

Question: Is Isaiah 53, "The Suffering Servant," a prophecy about Jesus?

Answer: Perhaps the greatest of all Messianic prophecies in the *Tanakh* (the Hebrew Scriptures/Old Testament) is found in Isaiah 53. This section of the Prophets, also known as the "Suffering Servant," was understood by the rabbis of ancient times to speak of the Redeemer who will one day come to Zion. "The Messiah, what is his name? The Rabbis say, The Leper Scholar, as it is said, 'surely he has borne our griefs and carried our sorrows: yet we did esteem him a leper, smitten of God and afflicted…'"[22]

Unfortunately, modern rabbis believe that the "Suffering Servant" of Isaiah 53 refers perhaps to Israel, to Isaiah himself, or even to Moses or another of the prophets. But Isaiah is clear—he speaks of the Messiah. The second verse of Isaiah 53 confirms this; the figure grows up as "a tender shoot, and like a root out of dry ground." The shoot springing up is a common Messianic reference in Isaiah and elsewhere. As the *Targum Jonathan* says, "Behold my servant Messiah shall prosper; he shall be high and increase and be exceedingly strong."[23] The Davidic dynasty was to be cut down in judgment like a felled tree, but Israel was promised that a new sprout would shoot up from the stump (Isaiah 11:1–2). King Messiah was to be that sprout.

Concerning Isaiah 53, Rabbi Moshe Kohen Ibn Crispin said, "This prophecy was delivered by Isaiah at the divine command for

174

the purpose of making known to us something about the nature of the future Messiah, who is to come and deliver Israel, and his life from the day when he arrives at discretion until his advent as a redeemer, in order that if anyone should arise claiming to be himself the Messiah, we may reflect, and look to see whether we can observe in him any resemblance to the traits described here; if there is any such resemblance, then we may believe that he is the Messiah our righteousness; but if not, we cannot do so."[24]

Beyond doubt, the "Suffering Servant" of Isaiah 53 refers to Jesus, the Messiah. Jesus is the shoot who grew up from the fallen Davidic dynasty (verse 2). He was rejected by men (verse 3). He was pierced as He bore our sin (verses 5–6). He was silent before His accusers (verse 7). He died among the wicked and was buried in a rich man's tomb (verse 9). And having paid for sin, Jesus was exalted by God Himself (verse 12).

Question: Where do the Hebrew Scriptures prophesy the death and resurrection of the Messiah?

Answer: Throughout the Hebrew Scriptures, the promise of a Messiah is clearly given. These Messianic prophecies were made hundreds, sometimes thousands, of years before Jesus Christ was born, and Jesus Christ is the only person who has ever walked this earth that has fulfilled them. In fact, from Genesis to Malachi, there are over 300 specific prophecies detailing the coming of the Anointed One. The Old Testament prophesied His virgin birth (Isaiah 7:14); His natal city, Bethlehem (Micah 5:2); and His lineage, of David's line (2 Samuel 17:12–13). The Messiah's death and resurrection were also foretold. The detailed prophecies concerning His death are amazingly accurate, hundreds of years before crucifixion became a method of execution.

Of the prophecies in the Hebrew Scriptures concerning the death of the Messiah, Psalm 22 and Isaiah 53 certainly stand out. Psalm 22 is particularly remarkable since it predicted numerous elements of Jesus' crucifixion a thousand years before He was crucified. Here are some examples: the Messiah will have His hands and His feet "pierced" (Psalm 22:16; cf. John 20:25), His bones will not be broken (Psalm 22:17; cf. John 19:33), and men will cast lots for His clothing (Psalm 22:18; cf. Matthew 27:35).

Isaiah 53, the classic prophecy of "The Suffering Servant," also details the death of Christ for the sins of His people. More than 700 years before Jesus was born, Isaiah provided details of His life and death: the Messiah will be rejected (Isaiah 53:3; cf. Luke 13:34), He will be killed as a vicarious sacrifice for the sins of His people (Isaiah 53:5–8; cf. 2 Corinthians 5:21), He will be silent in front of His accusers (Isaiah 53:7; cf. 1 Peter 2:23), He will be with criminals in His death (Isaiah 53:12; cf. Mark 15:27), and He will be buried with the rich (Isaiah 53:9; cf. Matthew 27:57–60).

The Messiah's resurrection from the dead is also foretold. One of the clearest of the resurrection prophecies is Psalm 16:10, written a millennium before the birth of Jesus: "You will not abandon me to the grave, nor will you let your Holy One see decay." On the Jewish feast day of Shavuot (Weeks or Pentecost), when Peter preached the first gospel sermon, he boldly asserted that God had raised Jesus, the Jewish Messiah, from the dead (Acts 2:24). He then explained that God had performed this miracle in fulfillment of David's prophecy in Psalm 16. Some years later, Paul used the same passage when he spoke to the Jewish community in Antioch (Acts 13:33–35).

The resurrection of the Messiah is strongly implied in Psalm 22. In verses 19–21, the suffering Savior prays for deliverance "from the lion's mouth" (a metaphor for Satan's wrath). This desperate prayer is then followed immediately by a hymn of praise in which the Messiah thanks God for hearing His prayer and delivering Him (verses 22–24). Between the ending of the prayer in verse 21 and the beginning of the praise song in verse 22, a resurrection is implicit.

In Isaiah 53, the Suffering Servant would endure the punishment for the sins of His people, and He would then be "cut off from the land of the living" (verse 8). In other words, He would die. But Isaiah then stated that He (the Messiah) "will see His offspring" and that God the Father will "prolong His days" (verse 10). Isaiah proceeded to reaffirm the promise in different words:

"After the suffering of his soul, he will see the light of life and be satisfied" (verse 11). The Suffering Servant would rise again.

Every aspect of the birth, life, death, and resurrection of Jesus the Messiah had been prophesied in the Hebrew Scriptures long before the events ever unfolded. No wonder that Jesus the Messiah would say to the religious leaders of His day, "You diligently study the Scriptures because you think that by them you possess eternal life. These are the Scriptures that testify about me" (John 5:39).

Question: What does it mean that Jesus is the Prince of Peace (Isaiah 9:6)?

Answer: In Isaiah's prophecy about the coming Messiah, the prophet says, "For to us a child is born, to us a son is given, and the government will be on his shoulders. And he will be called Wonderful Counselor, Mighty God, Everlasting Father, Prince of Peace" (Isaiah 9:6).

Jesus came 2,000 years ago, but it's hard to see much peace in the world, which is filled with war and violence. It might be difficult to see how Jesus could be the all-powerful God and the embodiment of peace. But physical safety and political harmony don't necessarily reflect the kind of peace He promises (John 14:27).

The Hebrew word for peace, *shalom*, is often used in reference to an appearance of calm and tranquility in individuals, groups, and nations. The Greek word *eirene* means "unity and accord"; Paul uses *eirene* to describe the objective of the New Testament church (1 Corinthians 7:15). But the deeper, more foundational meaning of peace is the spiritual harmony brought about by an individual's restoration with God.

In our sinful state, we are enemies of God (Romans 5:10). "But God demonstrates his own love for us in this: While we were still sinners, Christ died for us" (Romans 5:8). Because of Christ's sacrifice, we are restored to a relationship of peace with God (Romans 5:1). This is the deep, abiding peace between our hearts and our Creator that cannot be taken away (John 10:27–28) and the ultimate fulfillment of Christ's work as "Prince of Peace."

But Christ's sacrifice provides more for us than just eternal peace with God; it also allows us to have a relationship with the Holy Spirit, the Helper who promises to guide us (John 16:7, 13). Further, the Holy Spirit will manifest Himself in us by producing His love, joy, and peace in us (Galatians 5:22–23). This "fruit of the Spirit" can't help but spill over into our relationships with other people.

We desperately need peace with others—especially since God so fervently calls us to live with singleness of purpose with other believers, with humility, gentleness, and patience, and to "make every effort to keep the unity of the Spirit through the bond of peace" (Ephesians 4:1–3). This unity in purpose would be impossible without the Prince of Peace and the work of the Holy Spirit in us.

"Peace" doesn't mean "easy." Jesus never promised life would be easy; He only promised help. In fact, He told us to expect tribulation (John 16:33) and trials (James 1:2). But He also said that, if we call on Him, He will give us the "peace of God, which transcends all understanding" (Philippians 4:7). No matter what hardships face us, we can ask for the peace that comes from the powerful love of God and is not dependent on our own strength or situations. When we surrender to the Prince of Peace, He will rule our lives.

Chapter 9

MISCELLANEOUS QUESTIONS ABOUT JESUS

Contents

What is the love of Christ?

What does it mean that Jesus is the Lamb of God?

What does it mean that Jesus is our high priest?

What does it mean that Jesus is our mediator?

What is the purpose of Jesus interceding for us in heaven?

How is Jesus our Sabbath rest?

What does it mean that Jesus is the second Adam?

If His name was Yeshua, why do we call Him Jesus?

Is it wrong to have pictures of Jesus?

Question: What is the love of Christ?

Answer: The phrase "love of Christ," as opposed to "love *for* Christ," refers to the love that Jesus has toward mankind. His love can be briefly stated as His willingness to act in our best interest, especially in meeting our greatest need—even though it cost Him everything and even though we were the least worthy of such love.

Though Christ Jesus, being God in nature, existed from the beginning of time with God the Father (John 1:1) and the Holy Spirit, He willingly left His throne (John 1:1–14) to become a man. His incarnation was necessary so that He might pay the penalty for our sin, freeing us from paying for it for all eternity in the lake of fire (Revelation 20:11–15). Because our sinless Savior Jesus Christ has paid for mankind's sin, the just and holy God can now forgive our sins when we accept Jesus' payment as our own (Romans 3:21–26). Christ's love is shown in that He left heaven, where He was deservedly worshipped and honored, to come to earth, where He was mocked, betrayed, beaten, and crucified to pay the penalty for our sin (1 John 3:16). Jesus considered our need of salvation as more important than His own comfort and life (Philippians 2:3–8).

People may give their lives willingly for ones they deem worthy—a friend, a relative, or other "good" person—but Christ's love goes beyond that. His love extends to those most unworthy of it. He laid down His life willingly, taking the punishment of those who tortured Him, hated Him, rebelled against Him, and cared nothing for Him—those who were most undeserving of His love (Romans 5:6–8). Sacrifice, then, is the essence of godly love, called *agape* love. This is God-like love, not man-like love (Matthew 5:43–48).

This *agape* love, which Jesus demonstrated toward us on the cross, is just the beginning. When we place our trust in Him as our Savior, He makes us God's children and co-heirs with Him (John 1:12)! He comes to dwell within us through His Holy Spirit, promising that He will never leave us or forsake us (Hebrews 13:5–6). Thus, we have a loving companion for life. No matter what we go through, He is there, and His love is ever available to us (Romans 8:35). Believers now strive to "live a life of love, just as Christ loved us and gave himself up for us" (Ephesians 5:2).

Question: What does it mean that Jesus is the Lamb of God?

Answer: Jesus is called "the Lamb of God" in John 1:29 and John 1:36, and the title refers to Him as the perfect and ultimate sacrifice for sin. To fully understand Christ's role as the Lamb of God, we must begin in the Old Testament's prophecies concerning the coming of Christ as a "guilt offering" (Isaiah 53:10). In fact, the whole sacrificial system established by God in the Mosaic Law set the stage for the coming of Jesus Christ, the perfect sacrifice and atonement for the sins of God's people (Romans 8:3; Hebrews 10:1–18).

The sacrifice of lambs played an important role in the Jewish religious life. The Jews who heard John the Baptist refer to Jesus as the "Lamb of God, who takes away the sin of the world" (John 1:29) might have immediately thought of any one of several important sacrifices. With Passover being near, the first thought might have been the sacrifice of the Passover lamb. The Passover feast was one of the main Jewish holidays, held in remembrance of Israel's deliverance from Egypt. In fact, the slaying of the Passover lamb and the applying of the blood to doorposts of the houses (Exodus 12:11–13) was a beautiful picture of Christ's atoning work on the cross. His blood protects all who trust in Him from spiritual death.

Another important sacrifice involving lambs was the daily sacrifice at the temple in Jerusalem. Every morning and evening, a lamb was sacrificed in the temple for the sins of the people (Exodus 29:38–42). These daily sacrifices, like all others, were simply to point people to the perfect sacrifice of Christ on the cross. In fact, the time of Jesus' death on the cross corresponded to the time of the evening sacrifice in the temple. The Jews at that time would also have been familiar with the prophets Jeremiah and Isaiah, who foretold the coming of One who would be brought

181

"like a lamb led to the slaughter" (Isaiah 53:7; Jeremiah 11:19) and whose sufferings would provide redemption for Israel. Of course, that One was none other than Jesus Christ, "the Lamb of God."

While the idea of sacrificing lambs might seem strange to us today, the concept of payment or restitution is still one we can easily understand. We know that the wages of sin is death (Romans 6:23) and that our sin separates us from God. We also know the Bible teaches we are all sinners and none of us are righteous before God (Romans 3:23). Our only hope is for God to provide a way for us to be reconciled to Himself, and that is what He did in sending His Son to die on the cross. Christ died to make atonement for sin and to pay sin's penalty for all who believe in Him.

Through Jesus' death on the cross as God's perfect sacrifice for sin and His resurrection three days later, we can have eternal life if we believe in Him. Just like God Himself provided a sacrificial ram to spare Isaac's life (Genesis 22:13), God has provided Jesus, the "Lamb of God," to give us life. "It was not with perishable things such as silver or gold that you were redeemed from the empty way of life handed down to you from your forefathers, but with the precious blood of Christ, a lamb without blemish or defect. He was chosen before the creation of the world, but was revealed in these last times for your sake. Through him you believe in God, who raised him from the dead and glorified him, and so your faith and hope are in God" (1 Peter 1:18–21).

Question: What does it mean that Jesus is our high priest?

Answer: "High Priest" is only one of the many titles applied to Jesus (Messiah, Savior, Son of God, Son of Man, etc.). Each one focuses on a particular aspect of who He is and what that means for us. Jesus is called a high priest in the book of Hebrews (Hebrews 2:17; 4:14). The word *priest* carries a couple of primary meanings: 1) one who mediates in religious services, and 2) one who is holy or set apart to perform those services.

The first place we find "priest" used in the Bible is in Genesis 14. The patriarch Abraham (Abram) entered into battle with the

Elamites to rescue his nephew Lot, who had been captured. On Abraham's return, Melchizedek, king of Salem and priest of God, met Abraham. Melchizedek, whose name means "king of righteousness," blessed Abraham and the Most High God who gave victory to Abraham. In return for this blessing, Abraham gave a tithe (10 percent) of all the spoils of war to Melchizedek. By this act, Abraham acknowledged Melchizedek's high position as the priest of God.

Years later, God singled out Abraham's great-grandson Levi to be the father of the priestly tribe. When the Law was given on Mount Sinai, the Levites were identified as the servants of the tabernacle, with the family of Aaron becoming the priests. The priests were responsible for interceding with God on the people's behalf by offering sacrifices. Among the priests, one was selected as the high priest. He entered into the Most Holy Place once a year on the Day of Atonement to place the blood of the sacrifice on the Ark of the Covenant (Hebrews 9:7). These daily and yearly sacrifices temporarily covered the sins of the people until the Messiah came to take away their sins.

When Jesus is called our high priest, it is with reference to both of these previous priesthoods. Like Melchizedek, Jesus is ordained as a priest apart from the Law given on Mount Sinai (Hebrews 5:6). Like the Levitical priests, Jesus offered a sacrifice to satisfy the Law of God when He offered Himself for our sins (Hebrews 7:26–27). Unlike the Levitical priests, who had to continually offer sacrifices, Jesus only had to offer His sacrifice once, gaining eternal redemption for all who come to God through Him (Hebrews 9:12).

One other important point about Jesus' priesthood: every priest is appointed from among men. Jesus, though God from eternity, became a man in order to suffer death and serve as our high priest (Hebrews 2:9). As a man, He was subject to all the weaknesses and temptations that we are so that He could personally relate to us in our struggles (Hebrews 4:15). Because Jesus is greater than any other priest, He is called our "great high priest" in Hebrews 4:14. Through Him, we can "approach the throne of grace with confidence, so that we may receive mercy and find grace to help us in our time of need" (Hebrews 4:16).

Question: What does it mean that Jesus is our mediator?

Answer: A mediator is one who Acts as an intermediary, or go-between, to work with opposing sides in order to bring about a settlement. A mediator attempts to influence a dispute between two parties with the goal of resolving it. There is only one Mediator between mankind and God, and that is Jesus Christ. We'll see below why God has a dispute with us, why Jesus is our mediator, and why we are doomed if we try to "go it alone."

God has a dispute with us because of sin. Sin is described in the Bible as transgression of the law of God (1 John 3:4) and rebellion against God (Deuteronomy 9:7; Joshua 1:18). God hates sin, and sin stands between Him and all of us. "There is no one righteous, not even one" (Romans 3:10). All human beings are sinners by virtue of sin we have inherited from Adam, as well as the sin we ourselves commit on a daily basis. The only just penalty for this sin is death (Romans 6:23), not just physical death but also eternal death (Revelation 20:11–15). The rightful punishment for sin is an eternity in hell.

Nothing we could do on our own would be sufficient to mediate between God and ourselves. No amount of good works or law-keeping makes us righteous enough to stand before a holy God (Isaiah 64:6; Romans 3:20; Galatians 2:16). Without a mediator, we are destined to spend eternity in hell, for by ourselves salvation from our sin is impossible. But there is hope! "For there is one God and one mediator between God and men, the man Christ Jesus" (1 Timothy 2:5). Jesus represents those who have placed their trust in Him before God's throne of grace. He *mediates* for us, much as a defense attorney mediates for his client, telling the judge, "Your honor, my client is innocent of all charges against him." Some day we will face God, but we will do so as totally forgiven sinners because of Jesus' death on our behalf. The ultimate "defense attorney" took the penalty for us!

We see more comforting proof of this truth in Hebrews 9:15: "For this reason Christ is the mediator of a new covenant, that those who are called may receive the promised eternal inheritance—now that he has died as a ransom to set them free from the sins committed under the first covenant." It is because of the great Mediator and His sacrifice on the cross that we are able to stand before God, clothed in the righteousness of Christ Himself. He exchanged our sin for His righteousness (2 Corinthians 5:21). His mediation is the only means of salvation.

Question: What is the purpose of Jesus interceding for us in heaven?

Answer: The writer to the Hebrews says of Jesus, "Therefore he is able to save completely those who come to God through him, because he always lives to intercede for them" (Hebrews 7:25). This verse (and others like it) tells us that, although Christ's work to secure the salvation of the elect was completed on the cross—as evidenced by His cry, "It is finished!" (John 19:30)—His care for His redeemed children will never be finished.

Jesus did not go to heaven after His earthly ministry and take a break from His role as eternal Shepherd to His people. "For if, when we were God's enemies, we were reconciled to him through the death of his Son, how much more, having been reconciled, shall we be saved through *his life!*" (Romans 5:10, emphasis added). If, when humble, despised, dying, and dead, He had the power to accomplish so great a work as reconciling us to God, how much more may we expect that He will be able to keep us now that He is a living, exalted, and triumphant Redeemer, raised to life and interceding on our behalf before the throne (Romans 8:34). Clearly, Jesus is still very active on our behalf in heaven.

After Jesus ascended to heaven and was seated at the right hand of God the Father (Acts 1:9; Colossians 3:1), He returned to the glory He had before His incarnation (John 17:5) to carry on His role of King of kings and Lord of lords—His eternal role as the second Person of the triune God. While this earth continues to be "won" for Christ, Jesus is the advocate for Christians, meaning He is our great defender. This is the intercessory role He currently fulfills for those who are His (1 John 2:1). Jesus is always pleading our case before the Father, like a defense lawyer pleading before a judge on our behalf.

Jesus is interceding for us while Satan (whose name means "accuser") is *accusing* us, pointing out our sins and frailties before God, just as he did with Job (Job 1:6–12). But the accusations fall upon deaf ears in heaven, because Jesus' work on the cross paid our sin debt in full; therefore, God always sees in His children the perfect righteousness of Jesus. When Jesus died on the cross, His righteousness (perfect holiness) was imputed to us, while our sin was imputed to Him at His death (Isaiah 53:5). This is the great exchange Paul talks about in 2 Corinthians 5:21. Jesus' sacrifice took away forever our sinful state before God, so God can accept us as blameless before Him.

Finally, it is important to understand that Jesus is the *only* mediator between God and man. No one else—not Mary, not any previous Christian saint, not an angel—has the power to intercede for us before the throne of the Almighty. Christ alone mediates and intercedes between God and man: "For there is one God and one mediator between God and men, the man Christ Jesus" (1 Timothy 2:5).

Question: How is Jesus our Sabbath rest?

Answer: The key to understanding how Jesus is our Sabbath rest is the Hebrew word *sabat,* which means "to rest or cease from work." The origin of the Sabbath goes back to Creation. After creating the heavens and the earth in six days, on the seventh day God "rested from all His work" (Genesis 2:2). This doesn't mean that God was tired and needed a rest. We know that God is omnipotent, literally "all-powerful." He has all the power in the universe, He never tires, and His most fantastic works do not diminish His power one bit. So, what does it mean that God rested on the seventh day? Simply that He stopped what He was doing.

He ceased from His labors. This is important in understanding the establishment of the Sabbath day and the role of Christ as our Sabbath rest.

God used the example of His resting on the seventh day of Creation to establish the principle of the Sabbath day rest for His people. In Exodus 20:8–11 and Deuteronomy 5:12–15, God laid out the fourth of His Ten Commandments. God's people, the Israelites, were to "remember" the Sabbath day and "keep it holy." One day out of every seven, they were to rest from their labors and give the same day of rest to their servants and animals. This was not only a physical rest, but also a cessation of laboring. Whatever work they were engaged in was to stop for a full day each week.

The various elements of the Sabbath symbolized the coming of the Messiah, who would provide a permanent rest for His people. Once again, the example of resting from our labors comes into play. With the establishment of the Old Testament Law, the Jews were constantly "laboring" to make themselves acceptable to God. Their labors included trying to obey the myriad of dos and don'ts of the ceremonial law, the tabernacle/temple laws, the civil law, etc. Of course, they couldn't possibly keep all those laws, so God provided an array of sin offerings and sacrifices so they could come to Him for forgiveness and restore fellowship with Him—but only temporarily. Just as they resumed their physical labors after a one-day rest, so, too, they had to continue to offer sacrifices. Hebrews 10:1 tells us that the Law "can never, by the same sacrifices repeated endlessly year after year, make perfect those who draw near to worship." But these sacrifices were offered in anticipation of the ultimate sacrifice of Christ on the cross, who, "after He had offered one sacrifice for sins forever, sat down at the right hand of God" (Hebrews 10:12, KJV). Christ "rested" after performing the ultimate sacrifice; He is seated in the heavenlies. He ceased from His labor of atonement because there was nothing more to be done—ever. Because of what He did, we no longer have to "labor" in law-keeping in order to be justified in the sight of God. Jesus was sent so that we might rest in God and in what He has provided. Jesus is our "sabat."

God instituted another element to foreshadow our complete rest in Christ: He blessed the Sabbath, sanctified it, and made it holy. Here again we see the symbol of Christ as our Sabbath rest—the holy, perfect Son of God who sanctifies all who believe in Him. God sanctified Christ—just as He sanctified the Sabbath day—and sent Him into the world (John 10:36) to be our sacrifice for sin. In Him we find complete rest from our labors toward self-sanctification, because He alone is holy and righteous. "God made him who had no sin to be sin for us, so that in him we might become the righteousness of God" (2 Corinthians 5:21). We can now cease from our spiritual labor and rest in Him, not just one day a week, but always.

Jesus can be our Sabbath rest in part because He is "Lord of the Sabbath" (Matthew 12:8). As God incarnate, Jesus decides the true meaning of the Sabbath because He created it, and He is our Sabbath rest in the flesh. When the Pharisees criticized Him for healing on the Sabbath, Jesus reminded them that even they would not hesitate to pull a sheep out of a pit on the Sabbath. Jesus had come to seek and save His sheep who would hear His voice (John 10:3, 27). He told the Pharisees that people are more important than sheep and salvation is more important than their rules. In saying, "The Sabbath was made for man, not man for the Sabbath" (Mark 2:27), Jesus restated the principle that the Sabbath rest was instituted to relieve man of his labors, just as Christ had come to relieve us of our attempts to achieve salvation by our own works. In Christ, we forever cease our labors to attain God's favor. Having obtained righteousness through Christ, we "rest" in Him.

Hebrews 4 is the definitive passage regarding Jesus as our Sabbath rest. The writer to the Hebrews exhorts his readers to "enter in" to the Sabbath rest provided by Christ. The writer pleads with the Hebrews to not harden their hearts against Him, as their forefathers hardened their hearts against Jehovah in the wilderness. Because of their unbelief, God denied that generation access to the Holy Land, saying, "They shall never enter my rest" (Hebrews 3:11). In the same way, the writer to the Hebrews begs them—and us—not to make the same mistake by rejecting God's Sabbath rest in Jesus Christ. "There remains, then, a Sabbath-rest for the people of God; for anyone who enters God's rest also rests from his own work, just as God did from his. Let us, therefore, make every effort to enter that rest, so that no one will fall by following their example of disobedience" (Hebrews 4:9–11).

There is no other Sabbath rest besides Jesus. He alone satisfies the requirements of the Law, and He alone provides the sacrifice that atones for sin. He is God's plan for us to cease from our own works. We joyfully enter the "Sabbath rest" that Jesus provides.

Question: What does it mean that Jesus is the second Adam?

Answer: The apostle Paul tells us, "The first man Adam became a living being; the last Adam, a life-giving spirit. The spiritual did not come first, but the natural, and after that the spiritual. The first man was of the dust of the earth, the second man from heaven. As was the earthly man, so are those who are of the earth; and as is the man from heaven, so also are those who are of heaven. And just as we have borne the likeness of the earthly man, so shall we bear the likeness of the man from heaven" (1 Corinthians 15:45–49).

In this passage, Paul is pointing out the difference between two kinds of bodies—the natural and the spiritual. Genesis 2:7 speaks of the first man, Adam, becoming a living person. God made Adam from the dust of the ground and gave him the breath of life. Every human being since then shares the same characteristics. The last Adam, or the "second Adam," is Christ Jesus, who is one with God. Just as Adam was the first of the human race, so Christ is the first of those who will be raised from the dead to eternal life. Because Christ rose from the dead, He is "a life-giving spirit" who entered into a new form of existence. He is the source of the spiritual life that will result in believers' resurrection. Christ's new glorified human body now suits His renewed glorified, spiritual state—just as Adam's human body was suitable to his natural life. When believers are resurrected, God will give them transformed, eternal bodies suited to eternal life.

Paul says in 1 Corinthians 15:46 that the natural came first and after that the spiritual. People have natural life first; that is, they are born onto this earth and live here. Only from there do they then obtain spiritual life. Paul is saying that the natural man, Adam, came first on this earth and was made from the dust of the earth. While it is true that Christ has existed from eternity past, He is here called the second man or second Adam because He came from heaven to earth many years after Adam. Christ came as a human baby with a body like all other humans, but He did not originate from the dust of the earth, as did Adam. He came from heaven.

The first Adam was tempted and fell; the second Adam (Christ) was tempted and never sinned (Matthew 4:1–11). The first Adam brought separation from God; the second Adam restores peace with God (Romans 5:11). The first Adam brought sin and death into the world; the second Adam brought righteousness and life (1 John 5:11). The first Adam had many physical descendants, all of whom inherited his weakness; the second Adam has many spiritual children, all of whom will inherit His glory (Hebrews 2:10). The first Adam lost the paradise called Eden; the second Adam will restore the earth to its intended beauty and fruitfulness (Isaiah 35).

Paul continues: "As was the earthly man [Adam], so are those who are of the earth; and as is the man from heaven [Christ], so also are those who are of heaven. And just as we have borne the likeness of the earthly man, so shall we bear the likeness of the man from heaven" (1 Corinthians 15:48–49). Because all humanity is bound up with Adam, so every human being has an earthly body like Adam's. Earthly bodies are fit for life on this earth, yet they are limited by death, disease, and weakness because of the sin Adam brought into the world.

The good news is that believers can know with certainty that their heavenly bodies will be just like Christ's—imperishable, eternal, glorious, and filled with power. At this time, all are like Adam; one day, all believers will be like Christ (Philippians 3:21). The apostle John wrote to believers, "Dear friends, now we are children of God, and what we will be has not yet been made known. But we know that when he appears, we shall be like him, for we shall see him as he is" (1 John 3:2).

Question: If His name was Yeshua, why do we call Him Jesus?

Answer: *Yeshua* is a Hebrew name, and its English spelling is "Joshua." *Iesous* is the Greek transliteration of the Hebrew name, and its English spelling is "Jesus." Thus, the names "Joshua" and "Jesus" are essentially the same: both are English pronunciations of the Hebrew and Greek names for the Lord. (For examples of how the two names are interchangeable, see Acts 7:45 and Hebrews 4:8 in the KJV. In both cases, "Jesus" refers to the Old Testament character Joshua.)

In German, our English word "book" is *buch*. In Spanish, it becomes *libro*; in French, *livre*. The language changes, but the object itself does not. In the same way, we can refer to Jesus as "Jesus," "*Yeshua*," or "*YehSou*" (Cantonese), without changing His nature. In any language, His name means "the Lord is salvation."

We refer to Him as "Jesus" because, as English-speaking people, we know of Him through English translations of the Greek New Testament. Scripture does not value one language over another, and it gives no indication that we must resort to Hebrew when addressing the Lord.

The command is to call "on the name of the Lord," with the promise that we shall be saved (Acts 2:21; Joel 2:32). Whether we call on Him in English, Korean, Hindi, or Hebrew, the result is the same: the Lord is salvation.

Question: Is it wrong to have pictures of Jesus?

Answer: When God first gave His Law to mankind, He began with a statement of who He is: "I am the LORD your God, who brought you out of Egypt" (Exodus 20:2) with a warning that Israel was to have no other God but Him. He immediately followed that by forbidding the making of any image of anything "in heaven above or on earth beneath or in the waters below" (Exodus 20:4) for the purpose of worshipping or bowing down to it. The fascinating thing about the history of the Jewish people is that they disobeyed this commandment more than any other. Again and again, they made idols to represent gods and worshipped them; beginning with the creation of the golden calf during the very time God was writing out the Ten Commandments for Moses (Exodus 32)! Idol worship not only drew the Israelites away from the true and living God, it led to all manner of other sins including temple prostitution, orgies, and even the sacrifice of children.

Of course, simply having a picture of Jesus hanging in a home or church does not mean people are practicing idolatry. It is *possible* that a portrait of Jesus or a crucifix can become an object of worship, in which case the worshiper is at fault. But there is nothing in the New Testament that would specifically forbid a Christian from having a picture of Jesus. Such an image could well be a reminder to pray, to refocus on the Lord, or to follow in Christ's footsteps. But believers should know that the Lord cannot be reduced to a two-dimensional image and that prayer or adoration is not to be offered to a picture. A picture will never be a complete image of God or accurately display His glory, and should never be a substitute for how we view God or deepen our knowledge of Him. And, of course, even the most beautiful representation of Jesus Christ is nothing more than one artist's conception of what the Lord looked like.

As it is, we don't know what Jesus looked like. If the details of His physical appearance were important for us to know, Matthew, Peter, and John would certainly have given us an accurate description, as would Jesus' own brothers, James and Jude. Yet these New Testament writers offer no details about Jesus' physical attributes. We are left to our imaginations.

We certainly don't *need* a picture to display the nature of our Lord and Savior. We have only to look at His creation, as we are reminded in Psalm 19:1–2: "The heavens declare the glory of God; the skies proclaim the work of his hands. Day after day they pour forth speech; night after night they display knowledge." In addition, our very existence as the redeemed of the Lord, sanctified and made righteous by His blood shed on the cross, should have Him always before us.

The Bible, the very Word of God, is also filled with non-physical descriptions of Christ that capture our imaginations and thrill our souls. He is the light of the world (John 1:5); the bread of life (John 6:32–33); the living water that quenches the thirst of our souls (John 4:14); the high priest who intercedes for us with the Father (Hebrews 2:17); the good shepherd who lays down His life for His sheep (John 10:11, 14); the spotless Lamb of God (Revelation 13:8); the author and perfecter of our faith (Hebrews 12:2); the way, the truth, the life (John 14:6); and the very image of the invisible God (Colossians 1:15). Such a Savior is more beautiful to us than any piece of paper hanging on the wall.

In her book *Gold Cord*, missionary Amy Carmichael tells of Preena, a young Indian girl who became a Christian and lived in Miss Carmichael's orphanage. Preena had never seen a picture of Jesus; instead, Miss Carmichael prayed for the Holy Spirit to reveal Jesus to each of the girls, "for who but the Divine can show the Divine?" One day, Preena was sent a package from abroad. She opened it eagerly and pulled out a picture of Jesus. Preena innocently asked who it was, and when she was told that it was Jesus, she burst into tears. "What's wrong?" they asked. "Why are you crying?" Little Preena's reply says it all: "I thought He was far more beautiful than that."[25]

APPENDIX—
STATEMENT OF FAITH

Section 1: The Bible

WE BELIEVE THE Bible, comprised of the Old and New Testaments, to be the inspired, infallible, and authoritative Word of God (Matthew 5:18; 2 Timothy 3:16–17). In faith we hold the Bible to be inerrant in the original writings, God-breathed, and the complete and final authority for faith and practice (2 Timothy 3:16–17). While still using the individual writing styles of the human authors, the Holy Spirit perfectly guided them to ensure they wrote precisely what He wanted written, without error or omission (2 Peter 1:21).

Section 2: God

We believe in one God, who is Creator of all (Deuteronomy 6:4; Colossians 1:16), who has revealed Himself in three distinct Persons—Father, Son, and Holy Spirit (2 Corinthians 13:14), yet who is one in being, essence, and glory (John 10:30). God is eternal (Psalm 90:2), infinite (1 Timothy 1:17), and sovereign (Psalm 93:1). God is omniscient (Psalm 139:1–6), omnipresent (Psalm 139:7–13), omnipotent (Revelation 19:6), and unchanging (Malachi 3:6). God is holy (Isaiah 6:3), just (Deuteronomy 32:4), and righteous (Exodus 9:27). God is love (1 John 4:8), gracious (Ephesians 2:8), merciful (1 Peter 1:3), and good (Romans 8:28).

Section 3: Jesus Christ

We believe in the deity of the Lord Jesus Christ. He is God incarnate, God in human form—the expressed image of the Father, who, without ceasing to be God, became man in order that He might demonstrate who God is and provide the means of salvation for humanity (Matthew 1:21; John 1:18; Colossians 1:15).

We believe that Jesus Christ was conceived of the Holy Spirit and was born of the virgin Mary (Matthew 1:23); that He is truly fully God and truly fully man (John 1:1, 14); that He lived a perfect, sinless life (Hebrews 4:15); that all His teachings are true. We believe that the Lord Jesus Christ died on the cross for all humanity (1 John 2:2) as a substitutionary sacrifice (Isaiah 53:5–6). We hold that His death is sufficient to provide salvation for all who receive Him as Savior (John 1:12; Acts 16:31); that our justification is grounded in the shedding of His blood (Romans 5:9); and that it is attested by His literal, physical resurrection from the dead (Matthew 28:6; 1 Peter 1:3).

We believe that the Lord Jesus Christ ascended to heaven in His glorified body (Acts 1:9–11) and is now seated at the right hand of God as our High Priest and Advocate (Romans 8:34; Hebrews 4:14).

Section 4: The Holy Spirit

We believe in the deity and personality of the Holy Spirit (Acts 5:3–4). He regenerates sinners (Titus 3:5) and indwells believers (Romans 8:9). He is the agent by whom Christ baptizes all believers into His body (1 Corinthians 12:12–14). He is the seal by whom the Father guarantees the salvation of believers unto the day of redemption (Ephesians 1:13–14). He is the Divine Teacher who illumines believers' hearts and minds as they study the Word of God (1 Corinthians 2:9–12).

We believe that the Holy Spirit is ultimately sovereign in the distribution of spiritual gifts (1 Corinthians 12:8–11). We believe that the miraculous gifts of the Spirit, while by no means outside of the Spirit's ability to empower, no longer function to the same degree they did in the early development of the church (1 Corinthians 12:4–11; 2 Corinthians 12:12; Ephesians 2:20; 4:7–12).

Section 5: Angels and Demons

We believe in the reality and personality of angels. We believe that God created the angels to be His servants and messengers (Nehemiah 9:6; Psalm 148:2; Hebrews 1:14).

We believe in the existence and personality of Satan and demons. Satan is a fallen angel who led a group of angels in rebellion against God (Isaiah 14:12–17; Ezekiel 28:12–15). He is the great enemy of God and man, and the demons are his servants in evil. He and his demons will be eternally punished in the lake of fire (Matthew 25:41; Revelation 20:10).

Section 6: Humanity

We believe that humanity came into existence by direct creation of God and that humanity is uniquely made in the image and likeness of God (Genesis 1:26–27). We believe that all humanity, because of Adam's fall, has inherited a sinful nature; that all human beings choose to sin (Romans 3:23); and that all sin is exceedingly offensive to God (Romans 6:23). Humanity is utterly unable to remedy this fallen state (Ephesians 2:1–5, 12).

Section 7: Salvation

We believe that salvation is a gift of God's grace through faith in the finished work of Jesus Christ on the cross (Ephesians 2:8–9). Christ's death fully accomplished justification through faith and redemption from sin. Christ died in our place (Romans 5:8–9) and bore our sins in His own body (1 Peter 2:24).

We believe salvation is received by grace alone, through faith alone, in Christ alone. Good works and obedience are results of salvation, not requirements for salvation. Due to the greatness, sufficiency, and perfection of Christ's sacrifice, all those who have truly received Christ as Savior are eternally secure in salvation, kept by God's power, and secured and sealed in Christ forever (John 6:37–40; 10:27–30; Romans 8:1, 38–39; Ephesians 1:13–14; 1 Peter 1:5; Jude 24). Just as salvation cannot be earned by good works, neither does it need good works to be maintained or sustained. Good works and changed lives are the inevitable results of salvation (James 2:14–26).

Section 8: The Church

We believe that the church, the body of Christ, is a spiritual organism made up of all believers of this present age (1 Corinthians 12:12–14; Ephesians 1:22–23; 5:25–27). We believe in the ordinances of believers' water baptism by immersion as a testimony to Christ and identification with Him, and the Lord's Supper as a remembrance of Christ's death and shed blood (Matthew 28:19–20; Acts 2:41–42; 18:8; 1 Corinthians 11:23–26). Through the church, believers are to be taught to obey the Lord and to testify concerning their faith in Christ as Savior and to honor Him by holy living. We believe in the Great Commission as the primary mission of the Church. It is the obligation of all believers to witness, by word and life, to the truths of God's Word. The gospel of the grace of God is to be preached to all the world (Matthew 28:19–20; Acts 1:8; 2 Corinthians 5:19–20).

Section 9: Things to Come

We believe in the blessed hope (Titus 2:13), the personal and imminent coming of the Lord Jesus Christ to rapture His saints (1 Thessalonians 4:13–17). We believe in the visible and bodily return of Christ to the earth with His saints to establish His promised millennial kingdom (Zechariah 14:4–11; 1 Thessalonians 1:10; Revelation 20:1–6). We believe in the physical resurrection of all men—the saints to everlasting joy and bliss on the New Earth, and the wicked to eternal punishment in the lake of fire (Matthew 25:46; John 5:28–29; Revelation 20:5–6, 12–13).

We believe that the souls of believers are, at death, absent from the body and present with the Lord, where they await their resurrection when spirit, soul, and body are reunited to be glorified forever with the Lord (Luke 23:43; 2 Corinthians 5:8; Philippians 1:23; 3:21). We believe that the souls of unbelievers remain, after death, in conscious misery until their resurrection when, with soul and body reunited, they shall appear at the Great White Throne judgment and shall be cast into the lake of fire to suffer everlasting punishment (Matthew 25:41–46; Mark 9:43–48; Luke 16:19–26; 2 Thessalonians 1:7–9; Revelation 20:11–15).

ENDNOTES

1. C.S. Lewis, *Mere Christianity* (New York: Macmillan Publishing Co., Inc., 1952).

2. Cornelius Tacitus, *Annals of Imperial Rome* (New York: Penguin Classics, 1956).

3. Suetonius, *Lives of the 12 Caesars* (Hertfordshire: Wordsworth Editions Ltd, 1997).

4. Flavius Josephus, *Antiquities of the Jews,* trans. by William Whiston (Grand Rapids, Michigan: Kregel Publications, 1981).

5. Julius Africanus, *Extant Writings,* XVIII in the *Ante Nicene Fathers,* ed. by Alexander Roberts and James Donaldson (Grabd Rapids, Michigan: Eerdmans, 1973), vol. VI, p. 130. as cited in Habermas, Gary R., *The Historical Jesus: Ancient Evidence for the Life of Christ,* (Joplin, Missouri: College Press Publishing Company, 1996).

6. Pliny, *Letters,* transl. by William Melmoth, rev. by W.M.L. Hutchinson (Cambridge: Harvard Univ. Press, 1935), vol. II, X:96 as cited in Habermas, Gary R., *The Historical Jesus: Ancient Evidence for the Life of Christ,* (Joplin, Missouri: College Press Publishing Company, 1996).

7. *The Babylonian Talmud,* transl. by I. Epstein (London: Soncino, 1935), vol. III, *Sanhedrin* 43a, p. 281 as cited in Habermas, Gary R., *The Historical Jesus: Ancient Evidence for the Life of Christ,* (Joplin, Missouri: College Press Publishing Company, 1996).

8. Lucian Samosata, *The Works of Lucian Somosata,* trans. by H.W. Fowler and F.G. Fowler (Oxford: The Clarendon Press, 1905).

9. Dan Brown, *The Da Vinci Code* (New York: Doubleday, a division of Random House, Inc., 2003).

10. James Allen Francis, *The Real Jesus and Other Sermons* (Valley Forge, Pennsylvania: Judson Press, 1927).

11. George Buttrick, "The Life of Jesus Christ," *Life*, December 28, 1936, 49.

12. Walter Bauer, *Greek-English Lexicon of the New Testament and Other Early Christian Literature, 3rd edition,* ed. by Fredrick William Danker (Chicago, Illinois: University of Chicago Press, 2001).

13. Louis Berkhof, *Systematic Theology* (Carlisle, Pennsylvania: The Banner of Truth, 1959).

14. Merriam-Webster, *Merriam-Webster's Collegiate Dictionary, 11th Edition* (Springfield, Massachusetts: Merriam-Webster, Inc. 2008).

15. Sir Robert Anderson, *The Coming Prince* (Grand Rapids, Michigan: Kregel Classics, 1957).

16. Holger Kersten, *Jesus Lived in India: His Unknown Life Before and After the Crucifixion,* translated by T.W. Czisch (Rockport, Massachusetts: Element Books, 1987).

17. Nicholas Notovitch, *The Unknown Life of Jesus: The Original Text of Nicolas Notovich's 1887 Discovery,* translated by J.H. Connelly and L. Landsberg (Sanger, California: Quill Driver Books/Word Dancer Press, 2004).

18. Sir Lionel Luckhoo, *The Question Answered: Did Jesus Rise from the Dead?* Luckhoo Booklets, back page. http://www.hawaiichristiansonline.com/sir_lionel.html.

19. Cornelius Tacitus, *Annals of Imperial Rome.*

20. Dr. William Lane Craig, quoted by Lee Strobel, *The Case For Christ* (Grand Rapids, Michigan: Zondervan, 1998).

21. Sir Lionel Luckhoo, *The Question Answered: Did Jesus Rise from the Dead?*

22. *The Babylonian Talmud,* Sanhedrin 98b

23. Rabbi Jonathan ben Uzziel, *Targum Jonathan on Isaiah 53,* ad locum.

24. Rabbi Moshe Kohen Ibn Crispin, from his commentary on Isaiah, quoted in *The Fifty-third Chapter of Isaiah According to the Jewish Interpreters,* (Jersey City, New Jersey: Ktav Publishing House, 1969) vol. II.

25. Amy Carmichael, *Gold Cord* (Fort Washington, Pennsylvania: Christian Literature Crusade, 1992).

Scripture Index

Genesis

1:3	43
1:26–27	197
2:2	186
2:7	189
2:17	86
3:6	86
3:15	84
3:17–18	128
3:21	87
15:16	112
22:13	182

Exodus

3:14	3, 17, 38
9:27	196
12:11–13	181
20:2	191
20:4	191
20:8–11	187
29:38–42	181
34:28	102

Leviticus

14:22	106
16:29–31	125
17:11	56
23:10	161
23:24–32	125
23:34–42	103
23:39	125
24:10	77
24:11–14	39
24:16	35, 38

Numbers

14:41–45	112
15:37–39	78
21:3	112
31:1–7	112
32:20–21	112

Deuteronomy

5:12–15	187
6:4	195
6:13	103
6:16	102
7:1–2	112
7:1–5	77
7:10	112
8:3	102
9:7	184
10:17	25
16:16	78
32:4	196
32:29	147

Joshua

1:18	184
6:20–21	112
8:1–8	112
10:29–32	112
11:7–20	112

Ruth

1:16	77

1 Samuel

2:6	147

2 Samuel

7:16	59
17:12–13	175

1 Kings

19:8	102

2 Kings

9:13	115

Ezra

7:12	25
10:2–3	77

Nehemiah

2:5–8	68
9:6	197

Job

1:6–12	186

Psalms

2:7	13
16:10	14, 17, 159, 176
16:10–11	148
18:46	30
19:1–2	192

22:1	133
22:14–18	127
22:16	176
22:16–18	172
22:17	176
22:18	176
22:19–21	176
22:22–24	176
27:1	30
33:6	57
51:5	86
69:9	106
69:21	134
89:8–9	14
89:27	24
90:2	195
91:11–12	102
93:1	195
107:20	57
110:1	170
118:26	115
119:89	57
130:4	30
130:7	30
136:3	25
139:1–6	61, 195
139:7–13	195
147:15–18	57
148:2	197

Ecclesiastes

1:9	88
3:1	111
3:3	111
3:8	111

Isaiah

6:3	196
7:14	14, 71, 89, 172, 173, 175
9:6	3, 5, 17, 62, 87, 111, 172, 173, 177
9:6–7	14
11:1–2	174
11:4	113
14:12–17	197
28:16–17	22
40:3	98
40:8	111
40:23–24	26
41:4	49
42:8	137
44:6	49
44:24	31
45:22–23	30
48:12	49
50:6	173
52:14	80, 126
53:2	80, 81, 82, 174, 175
53:3	127, 175, 176
53:3–6	137
53:3–7	172
53:5	127, 132, 186
53:5–6	175, 196
53:5–8	176
53:7	175, 176, 182
53:8	176
53:9	175, 176
53:10	142, 176, 181
53:11	177
53:12	175, 176
64:6	184

Jeremiah

11:19	182
23:6	173
31:31–34	79
31:34	30

Ezekiel

26:7	25
28:12–15	197

Daniel

2:37	25
2:44	14
7:13–14	26, 33, 58, 170
9:24–27	67, 173
9:25	67
9:26	111

Hosea

13:14	30

Joel

2:32	191

Micah

5:2	14, 87, 172, 175

Zechariah

9:9	115, 172
11:12–13	14
12:10	30, 173

13:7	14
14:4–11	198

Malachi

3:1	114
3:6	196

Matthew

1:1	78
1:6	68
1:12	68
1:16	68
1:18	71
1:18–25	15
1:20	71
1:20–23	14
1:21	13, 19, 196
1:22–23	173
1:23	18, 30, 71, 196
1:25	74
2:1	70
2:11	34, 35, 113
2:13–15	65, 73
2:20–21	73
3:11	98
3:13–17	89, 102, 116
3:14	98
3:15	98
3:16–17	99
3:17	90, 110
4:1	74
4:1–2	116
4:1–11	190
4:2	65
4:3–4	102

4:5–7	102		14:18–21	36
4:8–10	102		14:25	31
4:10	14		14:29–31	136
4:17	116		14:33	35, 113
5:9	113		14:36	78
5:17	49, 51, 65, 78, 79, 104		15:22	59
5:18	195		15:32	82
5:19–20	78		16:1–4	51
5:28	75		16:15	13
5:39	113		16:18	148
5:43–48	180		16:20	115
6:19–20	88		16:21	31, 124
9:1–7	14		16:21–23	101
9:2	31		16:24	138, 146
9:15	18		16:24–25	113, 131
9:35	31		16:25	146
9:36	82		17:1–8	91
10:9–10	88		17:1–9	104, 170
10:34–36	112		17:5	170
10:38	131, 138		17:24–26	106
11:12	112		18:20	31
11:23	148		19:19	113
11:29	83		19:23	89
12:8	188		20:30	60
12:15–16	115		20:34	82
12:38–40	34, 51		21:1–11	92, 107
12:40	124, 125		21:1–17	114
12:46	73		21:12–13	104
13:10–17	100		21:13	106, 108
13:16	90		21:14–17	92
13:34	99		21:15	60
13:55	73		21:17–23	107
13:56	73		21:18	65
14:3–5	98		21:18–22	107
14:14	82		21:19	107
14:15–21	91		22:37–38	47

24:6–8	111
24:30	170
24:36	61
25:31–46	34
25:41	197
25:41–46	199
25:46	199
26:3–4	141
26:17–29	93
26:26–29	121
26:31–46	62
26:36–56	94
26:37	65
26:39	83
26:41	121
26:57	122
26:57–68	122
26:62	123
26:63	37
26:64	37
26:65–66	37
26:67	80
27:21	141
27:22–23	93
27:22–25	141
27:27–35	141
27:27–37	141
27:29	128
27:30	80
27:32–33	144
27:35	176
27:46	85, 121, 122, 127, 133, 149
27:50–53	146
27:51	122
27:52–53	146

27:57–60	176
27:57–61	165
27:62–66	165, 167
28:1	113, 165
28:1–20	95, 152
28:2–4	165
28:5	152
28:5–7	152, 165
28:6	196
28:8	166
28:9	34, 35, 51, 113, 152, 162
28:9–10	14, 166, 169
28:11–15	166
28:16–17	152
28:16–20	166
28:17	34, 35, 51
28:18	24
28:19	30
28:19–20	198
28:20	31

Mark

1:9–11	89
1:22	83
1:35	62
1:40–42	31
1:41–42	101
1:43–44	101
1:45	101
2:3–12	31, 34, 50
2:27	188
2:28	51
3:5	65, 104, 105
3:31	73

4:19	89	14:61–62	33
4:37–41	14	14:61–64	51
5:35–42	31	14:62	48
5:41	85	15:2	79
6:34–44	91	15:15	144
6:46	62	15:21–22	144
7:34	85	15:27	176
8:31	124, 159	15:34	85
8:34–38	34	15:42	124, 125
9:2–8	91	15:42–45	168
9:2–9	104	15:42–47	165
9:30–32	163	16:1	113, 125, 165
9:31	159	16:1–18	95
9:43–48	199	16:1–20	152
10:16	82	16:2–8	165
10:17–22	47	16:8	166
10:22	47	16:9	152
10:25	89	16:19–20	95
10:32–34	159		
10:45	77, 83	**Luke**	
10:47	60		
11:1–11	92, 107, 114	1:5–6	78
11:12–14	107	1:26–38	15
11:13	107	1:27	71
11:15–17	104	1:30–35	14
11:17	108	1:32	173
11:18	105	1:34	71
11:19–20	108	1:35	13, 17, 36, 37, 71, 173
11:22	108		
12:10	22	1:76	173
12:35–37	60	2:1–2	70
14:12–25	93	2:1–20	89
14:26	121	2:4–7	73
14:32–50	94	2:11	19
14:36	85	2:24	106
14:50	122	2:39	78

2:41–52	72		16:23	148
2:46	84		16:26	148
2:49–50	85		19:10	99
2:51	72, 83		19:29–40	114
2:52	72, 85		19:29–44	92
3:1	116		19:38	114
3:1–2	70		19:39–40	113
3:8	108		19:46	83
3:21–23	89		19:47	60
3:23	68, 69, 70, 116		20:1–8	112
3:23–38	68		21:37	78
3:27	68		22:7–20	93
3:31	68		22:14–15	79
4:2	101		22:20	143
4:13	101		22:24	93
4:15	78		22:34	136
4:16	78, 109		22:39–46	135
4:22–24	109		22:39–54	94
5:1	82		22:42	101, 121
5:3	82		22:43–44	65
7:11–15	31		22:44	121
7:12–15	14		22:47–48	136
7:48–50	50		22:51	121
8:19	73		22:54–62	136
8:23	65		22:66–71	136
8:41–55	14		23:1–25	122
8:43	78		23:7	122, 123
9:12–17	91		23:11	122, 123
9:22	103, 124		23:13–25	137
9:28–36	91, 104		23:20–21	115
9:31	92		23:21	141
9:58	88		23:25	123
10:15	148		23:26	138, 144
12:15	88		23:27–31	139
13:34	176		23:33–38	139
16:19–26	199		23:34	83, 122, 133

23:39–43   139
23:42   134
23:43   133, 148, 199
23:44–46   140
23:46   134, 149
23:47   122
23:50–54   140
23:50–55   165
23:52–54   125
23:56   125
24:1–8   165
24:1–49   95
24:1–53   152
24:9–11   166
24:10   113
24:12   166
24:13   126
24:13–32   166
24:13–35   152, 163
24:20   126
24:21   126
24:32–35   166
24:34   166
24:36–43   34, 51, 166, 169
24:39   13, 59, 159
24:39–40   162
24:44–49   166
24:50–51   169
24:50–53   95, 166
24:52   34, 35, 51

John

1:1   3, 4, 17, 24, 30, 35,
            36, 37, 38, 39, 42,
            49, 57, 58, 59, 76, 87,
            104, 174, 180, 196
1:1–3   13, 14, 50
1:1–14   180
1:2   31
1:3   33, 49, 90
1:5   193
1:9   30
1:10   24
1:11   133
1:11–12   78
1:12   40, 180, 196
1:14   3, 4, 13, 17, 24, 35,
            36, 37, 38, 40, 49,
            57, 59, 65, 66, 71, 76,
            174, 196
1:18   40, 196
1:29   13, 19, 145, 181
1:35–51   116
1:36   181
1:46–50   14
1:49   17
2:1–11   90, 116
2:7–9   31
2:11   90
2:11–12   106
2:12   116
2:13   78, 116
2:13–17   104
2:15–17   112
2:17   104
2:18   107
2:19   13
2:19–21   159
2:23–25   14
3:13   50

3:16	39, 40, 42, 44, 94, 126, 141, 146, 152	7:42	59
3:18	40	8:12	5, 17, 39
3:30	84	8:23	50
3:36	126	8:40	65
4:6	36, 61	8:44	110
4:14	193	8:46	48
4:22	78, 79	8:53	38
4:23	107	8:56–59	38
4:24	114	8:58	2, 13, 17, 31, 35, 36, 50, 84, 87
5:1	79	8:59	2
5:18	39	9:7	31
5:19	46	9:38	34, 35, 51
5:19–27	61	10:3	188
5:21	14	10:7	39
5:22	14, 113	10:9	39
5:23	14	10:11	5, 18, 30, 39, 48, 193
5:27	17	10:14	5, 18, 39, 193
5:28–29	199	10:17–18	13, 51
5:36	43	10:18	134
5:39	177	10:22	78
6:4	116	10:27	188
6:5–13	91	10:27–28	177
6:11	31	10:27–30	198
6:32–33	193	10:29–30	15
6:33	50	10:30	2, 30, 35, 42, 62, 76, 87, 195
6:35	18, 39	10:33	2, 35
6:37–40	198	10:36	188
6:38	50	10:39	65
6:48	18, 39	11:1–44	92
6:51	39	11:5	83
6:62	50	11:14	43
6:71	38	11:25	19, 39, 92
7:1–10	73	11:27	44
7:2	78		
7:10	78		

11:35	83	17:12	38
11:38–44	31	18:1–12	94
11:41–42	62	18:6	121
11:43–44	31, 36	18:11	112
11:47–50	141	18:13	122
11:53	141	18:15	122
11:55–57	116	18:19–24	122
12:1	114	18:28	122, 123
12:12	114	18:36	139
12:12–19	92, 114	19:1	144
12:13	113	19:1–3	137
12:15	93	19:2–3	128
12:41	30	19:3	80
13:1	145	19:7	37
13:1–30	121	19:17	138, 144
13:1–38	93	19:19	132
13:8	93	19:20	132
13:23	83	19:26–27	134, 140
14:2	170	19:28	36, 61, 134, 144
14:3	162	19:30	122, 129, 130, 134,
14:6	3, 13, 19, 23, 39, 83,		143, 149, 185
	193	19:31–33	130
14:9	58	19:31–34	168
14:26	3	19:33	176
14:27	177	19:34	65, 144
15:1	19, 39	19:36	130
15:5	39	19:37	30
15:5–8	109	19:38–42	165
15:10	61	20:1	126, 163
15:11	65	20:1–2	165
16:7	162, 178	20:2–10	166
16:8	99	20:11–18	166
16:13	100, 178	20:13	163
16:28	50	20:15	163
16:33	178	20:17	161
17:5	50, 84, 87, 185	20:19	152

20:19–25	166
20:21	44
20:22	162
20:24–29	152
20:25	162, 176
20:25–27	131
20:26	51
20:26–30	34
20:26–31	166
20:27	161, 168
20:28	3, 30, 34, 35, 51, 114
20:28–29	14
20:30–31	57
20:31	40, 45
21:1–14	34, 51, 152
21:1–25	166
21:4	163
21:25	95

Acts

1:1–11	152
1:3	95, 117, 169
1:3–5	34, 51
1:4–5	166
1:6–8	152
1:6–11	166
1:8	81, 198
1:9	185
1:9–11	95, 169, 196
1:11	169, 170
1:14	73
2:1–4	162
2:21	191
2:22	65
2:22–23	141

2:23	142
2:24	176
2:27	159
2:27–31	148
2:41–42	198
3:14	17
4:1–17	154
4:12	13, 16, 60, 82, 139
4:36	38
5:3–4	196
5:31	30, 31
7:45	191
7:56	33
9:1–6	152
9:2	21
10:25–26	14, 114
10:34–35	81
10:36	18
10:42	17
12:7	132
13:33–35	176
13:38	31
14:14–15	14
16:31	16, 196
17:18–20	12
17:32	160
18:8	198
19:9	21
19:23	21
20:28	35
24:22	21

Romans

1:4	13
1:16	82

3:10	184
3:10–18	127
3:19–20	67
3:20	184
3:21–26	180
3:22	48
3:23	182, 197
3:25	43
4:24–25	147
5:1	177
5:6–8	180
5:8	3, 127, 142, 177
5:8–9	197
5:9	196
5:10	177, 185
5:11	190
5:12	71
5:12–14	86
5:12–21	87
5:17	71
5:19	71
6:2	76
6:4	140
6:16–22	76
6:23	86, 142, 182, 184, 197
8:1	198
8:3	50, 181
8:9	196
8:28	196
8:29	25, 43, 84
8:34	185, 196
8:35	181
8:38–39	198
9:31–33	112
11:26	18
12:1	114

12:9	112
16:17–18	88

1 Corinthians

2:9–12	196
7:15	177
10:4	5, 19, 30, 33
10:13	75, 103
11:23–26	121, 198
12:4–11	197
12:8–11	197
12:12–14	196, 198
15:1	160
15:1–3	13
15:1–5	32
15:1–8	15
15:3–7	34
15:5	166
15:5–7	152
15:6	12, 95, 166, 169
15:7	166
15:11	160
15:12–15	152
15:13	159, 160
15:13–19	15
15:14	147
15:16	159
15:16–19	152
15:17	147
15:20	153
15:20–22	161
15:20–23	153
15:20–28	147
15:24–34	153
15:37–38	161

15:42–44	161
15:45–49	189
15:46	190
15:48–49	190
15:49	161
15:50–58	153
15:58	153

2 Corinthians

5:8	160, 199
5:17	138, 143
5:19–20	198
5:21	3, 13, 36, 48, 56, 74, 86, 89, 98, 127, 142, 149, 174, 176, 185, 186, 188
8:9	87
12:12	197
13:14	30, 195

Galatians

1:3	30
1:19	73
2:16	184
2:20	146
3:13	128
3:22–23	67
3:24	67
3:28	82
4:4	44, 50, 65, 66, 71
4:4–5	56
4:4–6	44
4:5	65
5:22–23	108, 178

Ephesians

1:2	30
1:4–5	99
1:7	81
1:13–14	196, 197
1:20	170
1:20–23	170
1:21–23	27
1:22	16
1:22–23	198
2:1–5	197
2:2	102
2:8	196
2:8–9	18, 49, 139, 197
2:12	197
2:19–21	23
2:20	16, 197
4:1–3	178
4:7–8	170
4:7–12	197
4:8–10	148
4:9–10	170
4:15	16
4:22–24	140
4:26	105
5:2	181
5:23	16
5:25–27	198
6:17	103

Philippians

1:23	199
2:3–8	180
2:5–8	30, 33, 46
2:5–11	26, 37, 62

2:6–8   87, 134
2:7   60
2:7–8   61
2:8   83
2:9   170
2:9–11   26
2:10–11 30
3:21   190, 199
4:7   178
4:21   161

Colossians

1:13–16 44
1:14   81
1:15   16, 25, 52, 193, 196
1:15–18 87
1:15–20 23
1:15–23 52
1:16   16, 43, 53, 195
1:16–17 31, 33, 50
1:17   14
1:17–18 53
1:18   25, 161, 170
1:19   74
1:20   87
1:22   87
2:9   37, 52, 74
2:9–10   87
2:13–14 133
3:1   185

1 Thessalonians

1:10   198
4:13–17 198

4:16   147
5:3   112

2 Thessalonians

1:7–9   199

1 Timothy

1:4   81
1:17   195
2:5   13, 19, 184, 186
3:16   71
6:9–10   88
6:14   25
6:14–16 147
6:15   17, 25
6:15–16 25

2 Timothy

1:8   138
2:22   112
3:7   100
3:16–17 195
4:1   31
4:8   17

Titus

2:13   3, 30, 33, 35, 198
2:14   30
3:5   196
3:9   81

Hebrews

1:2   44, 50, 84

1:2–4	24
1:3	24, 26, 38, 41, 52, 87
1:4	53
1:5	46
1:6	25
1:8	3, 14, 30, 33, 35
1:8–10	14
1:14	102, 197
2:3	139
2:9	129, 183
2:10	190
2:14	59
2:14–17	71
2:15	102
2:17	19, 37, 102, 182, 193
2:18	74
3:11	188
4:8	191
4:9–11	189
4:14	182, 183, 196
4:14–16	170
4:15	48, 56, 74, 86, 102, 183, 196
4:16	184
5:6	183
5:8	62, 83
7:14	78
7:24–25	52
7:25	185
7:26	48, 71
7:26–27	183
7:27	87, 143
8:1	170
8:6	52, 80
8:13	79
9:7	183

9:12	143, 183
9:14	134, 143
9:15	170, 185
9:22	56, 65, 86, 143
10:1	187
10:1–18	181
10:3–4	143
10:4	56, 87
10:5	65
10:10	87
10:11	87
10:12	187
10:19–23	80
10:30–31	112
11:17	40
12:2	18, 49, 193
12:23	25
13:5–6	180
13:8	44

James

1:2	178
1:13	74
1:19–20	106
2:14–26	198
2:26	108

1 Peter

1:3	196
1:5	198
1:18–19	87
1:18–21	182
1:19	66, 143
2:6	23
2:22	74, 86

2:23   176
2:24   13, 130, 132, 197
2:25   30
3:18–20   148
5:4   33

2 Peter

1:1   3, 35
1:3   81
1:21   195
3:9   83
3:10   49

1 John

1:1   17
1:2   50
1:7   149
2:1   186
2:2   3, 15, 36, 127, 130, 196
2:16   76, 102
3:2   191
3:4   184
3:5   86
3:8   44
3:16   180
4:2   59
4:2–3   57
4:8   196
4:9   40
4:9–10   142
4:10   44
4:14   44
5:11   190
5:20   18, 44

Jude

1:24   198

Revelation

1:5   25
1:7   30, 170
1:8   13, 17, 48
1:13   33
1:17–18   15
2:8   33
5:2–7   26
5:9   30
7:17   30
11:15   26
12:9–10   26
13:8   84, 193
14:14   33
17:12–14   26
17:14   25, 133
19:6   196
19:9–10   114
19:10   14, 35
19:11   112
19:11–16   14, 27
19:15   111
19:16   17, 25, 128, 133
20:1–6   198
20:5–6   199
20:6   147
20:10   197
20:11–15   148, 180, 184, 199
20:12–13   199
21:6   48
22:9   14
22:13   17, 48, 49